MOTHERHOOD, ABSENCE AND TRANSITION

For my children, Zoë and Tom, and to welcome Ruaidhrí b. 2009

Motherhood, Absence and Transition

When Adult Children Leave Home

TRISH GREEN
University of Sheffield, UK

ASHGATE

Published by
Ashgate Publishing Limited
Wey Court East
Union Road
Farnham
Surrey, GU9 7PT
England

Ashgate Publishing Company
Suite 420
101 Cherry Street
Burlington
VT 05401-4405
USA

www.ashgate.com

British Library Cataloguing in Publication Data
Green, Trish.
 Motherhood, absence and transition : when adult children
 leave home.
 1. Parent and adult child. 2. Mother and child.
 3. Separation (Psychology)
 I. Title
 306.8'743-dc22

Library of Congress Cataloging-in-Publication Data
Green, Trish.
 Motherhood, absence and transition : when adult children leave home / by Trish Green.
  p. cm.
 Includes bibliographical references and index.
 ISBN 978-0-7546-7733-8 (hbk) -- ISBN 978-0-7546-9451-9 (ebook)
 1. Motherhood--Psychological aspects. 2. Empty nesters--Psychology. 3.
Parent and adult child. 4. Separation (Psychology) 5. Mother and child. I. Title.

 HQ759.G756 2009
 306.874'30844--dc22

2009047203

ISBN 9780754677338 (hbk)
ISBN 9780754694519 (ebk)

Mixed Sources
Product group from well-managed
forests and other controlled sources
www.fsc.org Cert no. SGS-COC-2482
© 1996 Forest Stewardship Council
FSC

Printed and bound in Great Britain by
TJ International Ltd, Padstow, Cornwall

Contents

Acknowledgements

Book completion is not a one-woman achievement and I owe a number of debts of gratitude to a great many people for their help and support. I am of course indebted to the women who participated in my research and thank them for sharing their stories of motherhood with me. I owe enormous thanks to Gabriele Griffin for her inspiring advice, support, guidance and encouragement and for her warmth and generosity during some of the tough times I encountered along the way. My friends Jane, Karin, Maria and Pam sustained me throughout my endeavours with their humour and generosity and with a grace that kept me going throughout; thank you all. More recently friends and colleagues at the University of Sheffield have encouraged and supported me in my writing and research, and I want to give special thanks to Jenny Hockey and Andy Clayden. Finally and most importantly, I want to thank my children Zoë and Tom, who were the inspiration for the work and maintained an unerring faith in me that I would succeed. Without them and their love, care and support, this book would not have been possible.

Introduction:
Motherhood, Absence and Transition

This book is about women's perceptions and experiences of their adult children leaving home. It explores how the absence of the child in the mother's everyday life impacts on her sense of identity as a mother, and investigates her negotiation of the transition in her life course that is precipitated by that absence. It offers a chronological structure to findings from a three-year study of how women sustain relationships with their adult children over time and offers a critical lens to existing formulations of motherhood. In so doing, it yields elements of a new model for motherhood that reaches beyond current representations that foreground the presence rather than the absence of children.

Three decades ago Ann Oakley (1979: 24) commented that 'mothers' lives are incurably affected by their motherhood; in one way or another the child will be a theme for ever', yet to date there remains very little acknowledgement of what mothering means to women once their children achieve the sociocultural status of 'adult' and leave home. In consequence, and although there is no shortage of work that considers women's transition to motherhood, and mothering experiences during the early years of children's lives, some of which is woven throughout this volume as well, our knowledge regarding the later phase of a mother's life course is extremely limited.

Whilst wanting to contribute to the subject of mothering over time and in relation to women's experiences of their children's emerging adulthood and subsequent home-leaving, my initial desire to explore this issue was aroused by my own daughter leaving home for university in 2001, and was further reinforced by my son's leaving for the same reason in 2004. Their absence from the home provoked feelings that indicated I was unprepared for the meaning of their leaving *in my own life*. I began to question why no one had told me earlier about this phase of motherhood, which led me to further ask, if no one had told *me*, what about other mothers? As Shulamit Reinharz (1992: 235) states: 'some feminist researchers [...] start with their experience, are troubled by it, and then collect other data to compare with their experience' and this is indeed what happened to me. There is then much personal investment in the following brief reflection of my story to date and in this volume overall. Lyn Jamieson (1998: 10) comments however that 'when story tellers seek an audience beyond a personal circle, they invariably have an interest in telling a particular version of events' and I shall of course of necessity be selective. I return to this issue when I introduce the women who participated in my research and whose stories unfold in the chapters that follow.

A Personal Story

I qualified as a nursery nurse in the early 1970s and worked briefly in my northern UK hometown before leaving home to work in South Wales. I married in 1977 and returned to my hometown where my husband pursued a university degree. In 1982, my daughter Zoë was born, followed by the birth of Tom in 1984. We later lived in London and then Derbyshire, where we bought our first house. It was there, in 1987, that my husband and I separated. Although a financial struggle I found mothering alone an emotionally rewarding and enjoyable experience and reflect on this aspect of my life as extremely fulfilling. I believe the strength of the relationship the three of us have in the present-day lies in the fact that I brought my children up by myself and that the mutual love and respect we have for each other grew from the close-knit family the three of us became.

In 1989 I fell back on my nursery nurse training and worked full-time in the day nursery of the local university. The contradiction of my life as a mother at this time will never escape me; I was paid to care for the children of others but had I been given the choice, I would have stayed at home to care for my own. However, the lack of welfare support for lone mothers during the 1980s and 1990s (which continues into the present day) meant very little financial support would have been forthcoming. My reason for working during my children's early years is therefore underscored by a commitment to providing us with a home of our own and an attempt to ensure our financial security. I continued working in the nursery for ten years.

During my time at the nursery I befriended mothers who were students and staff at the university. At their encouragement, I enquired about, applied for and was accepted as a full-time student of Gender Studies and Social Policy 1999; I was 46, my children were 17 and 15. In the time that passed between starting my university career and beginning the research for this book, Zoë and Tom left home.

My children were both academically capable and throughout their schooling it was my expectation that they would go to university. Not only knowing my daughter and son would one day leave home in order to pursue their studies, but also wanting them to do so, was then part of the mindset that underpinned my mothering as praxis. My preparation for their leaving home for university focused on it being a positive movement forward for them. I did not think about how I would be affected by their leaving. I was shocked at the depth of emotion I experienced once they left.

The difficulties I encountered at the time of separation from each of my children have over time progressed to my acceptance of them as adults from whom I live apart, of myself as a mother living alone and my acknowledgement of all three of us as separate, yet interconnected and interdependent, people. I value greatly the times we are together and make the most of the times that we are not. My research into women's experiences of their children leaving home has proved an essential component of the management of this transition in my own life. The overall process of this book was then an emotionally challenging and ultimately fulfilling journey.

Experience is part of everyone's life course and the work presented here focuses on a particular episode during the life course of women as mothers. It is underpinned by women's experiences of their adult children's home-leaving and gives space to their accounts of this later life course event. In so doing, it offers an exploration of a relatively neglected aspect of western motherhood. What will be elucidated in the following chapters is that motherhood is about much more than just bringing up children and that there are times during the course of a mother's life that the meanings it holds can emerge both powerfully and unexpectedly.

Chapter 1
Becoming and Being a Mother

Introduction

Although ways into motherhood are increasing in their diversity (Sawicki, 1991; Sistare, 1994; Stanworth, 1987; Teman, 2009) and are no longer predominantly attached to heterosexual coupledom, at the time my research participants gave birth their individual transition was more clearly framed, and between the years 1979–89[1] each participant produced at least one biological child within a heterosexual married relationship.[2] Elly Teman (2009: 50) comments that pregnancy is 'a bodily site upon which identity-work is undertaken', thus the visibility of the pregnant body provided clear outward signs of a changing social status for each of my participants. The delivered baby is the embodied proof of a completed transition to the identity 'mother', dependent as this is on the presence of a 'child'.[3] As Janet Draper (2001: 23) notes, pregnancy and labour provide 'the framework of women's transition to motherhood [whilst] social process[es] structure this transition'.

Transitional experiences are part of everyone's life course and the transition to motherhood and early mothering experiences are a well documented and ongoing foci of research (Bailey, 1999; Brown, Lumley, Small and Astbury, 1994; Gatrell, 2005; Miller, 1998, 2005, 2007; Oakley, 1976, 1979, 1980, 1981a; Richardson, 1993; Rogan, Shmied, Barclay, Everitt and Wyllie, 1997; Wallbank, 2001). My intention in the book is to highlight a particular time during the life course of women whose children are about to embark on independent living away from the family home. I identify leaving home as an event that provides a sociocultural marker of the achievement of an adult identity for the child, but the work presented here hinges on how mothers perceive and then experience this event in *their* lives.

In her research with parents and children, Pat Allatt (1996: 130) adopts a life course approach because 'whilst individual biography is a process of change and becoming, in diverse ways we remain children, held throughout life, willingly or reluctantly, in the web of parent-child relations'. In representations of mothers and children, however, the two are encapsulated within a particular time-frame based upon the categories 'mother' and 'child': the child is perceived as dependent

---

1   The ten-year spectrum was the result of sampling mothers with adult children.

2   The demographics in Chapter 2 provide further information.

3   See Linda Layne (2000) for a discussion of women claiming a motherhood identity in the aftermath of miscarriage and stillbirth. See Elly Teman (2009) for a discussion of pregnancy as a site of collaborative identity work between 'carrying mothers' and 'intended mothers' during and after the surrogacy process.

whereas the mother, as adult, is not. Childhood is, then, related to age so that it becomes difficult to call an adult 'child', although clearly, as Allatt intimates, we are all someone's children. Mothers and their children thus remain opposites in relation to age and social positioning.

Within a western context then, the particular parameters in which the concepts of mother and child are set, and within which women rear their children to adulthood, involve a socially accepted and expected transition in which the child, once deemed able to meet her/his own needs, separates from the mother and the home. What I shall argue here is that the emerging adulthood of the child, which is part of the individual 'process of change and becoming' that Allatt identifies, can have a profound effect on a woman's identity as 'mother'. The chapters that follow highlight how the shifting identity of the mother is intricately connected to the life course trajectory of the child. It is the latter which can cause significant disruption to the former at particular moments in time.

Christina Hughes (2002: 139) argues that the concept of transition suggests 'sporadic and short-term' shifts from one phase of life to another 'bounded by extensive periods of stability'. It is not my intention to apply this to the transition to motherhood, nor to women's experiences of mothering. Indeed, Fisher noted that the mature women 'returners' to education she interviewed 'would conclude that they have been psychologically "in transit" almost all their adult lives' (1989, cited in Hughes, 2002: 140; see also Knowles, Nieuwenhuis and Smit, 2009, for a discussion on women's attempts at combining motherhood with professional workplace identities). My argument is rather that motherhood and mothering have attendant historical and sociocultural scripts that provide the context within which the individual practices of mothering take place and that these contribute to understandings not only of how mothering should be done, but also of what 'mother' and 'child' mean.

Motherhood and mothering are thus 'culturally, socially, historically and politically patterned and shaped' (Miller, 2005: 138). In a western context, representations of motherhood and images of mother and child emanate from a range of sources in political, academic and popular arenas. These images are evident in childcare manuals and magazines aimed at mothers (and fathers, see Sunderland 2006). Thus, once they are mothers, women are able, and I would argue compelled, to shape their motherhood with reference to, and measure their performance of mothering against, these readily available images and representations (Kaplan, 1992; Marshall, 1991; Richardson, 1993; Sunderland, 2006; Woodward, 1997). Moreover, the mother of TV advertising, from 1980s *Katie Oxo*[4] to the modern-

---

4 The *Oxo* advertisements ran for a number of years during the 1980s and 1990s. These portrayed stay-at-home mother Katie cooking and serving the family meal, accompanied by the all-important gravy. During the run of the advertising campaign, her children grew up and one advertisement indicated through the use of an empty chair at the table that a child had left home, but Katie remained in the kitchen, happily providing for her dwindling family.

day *Vodafone* mum, whom I shall introduce in Chapter 5, is a constant presence on our screens. These representations create a tension between the 'real' and the 'ideal' that mothers constantly juggle as they rear their children.

Childhood is also 'shaped by the politics and policies through which the conceptual category and social identity of "child" is given material form in everyday life' (Hockey and James, 2001: 15). During the early years of my interviewees' childrearing, the image of the 'totally child-centred mother' (Urwin, 1985: 166) permeated the ways in which women believed they should respond to childrearing. The mother was held, and as such held herself, responsible for the constant daily care of her offspring in order to ensure their future wellbeing (Jaggar, 1983; Steedman, 1985; Urwin, 1985; Walkderdine and Lucey, 1989). In these circumstances, as Allison Jaggar (1983: 313) observes, a mother might have felt 'that a single word or action, let alone any of her habitual failings, may damage the child for life'. Such uncertainty, the idea that the mother is culpable for the difficulties her child/ren might encounter throughout their lives, continues to prevail (Gattrell, 2005; Lawler, 1999, 2000; Miller, 2005; Silva, 1996; Walkderdine, Lucey and Melody, 2001). This is evident in the following letter from a mother to a UK daily newspaper:

> I am at home with my three-year-old daughter full-time and while we do several activities each week (playgroup, soft play, swimming, etc), I always have a nagging feeling that I'm not up to scratch and could be doing more with her. This guilt strikes me particularly when I'm doing the housework and she has to occupy herself playing in her room or watching TV. She is a happy, healthy and bright little girl, so how can I stop my angst? (The *Guardian*, 17 February, 2007: 6)

In line with advances in time-saving domestic appliances from the 1950s onwards, the advent of what Elizabeth Silva (1999: 61) has termed the 'technological nexus' within the home, the importance not only of children's play but of mothers being actively involved in playing with their children began to take up increasing amounts of a mother's time (Urwin, 1985). As the above reader's letter attests, this constitutes an ongoing theme as women attempt to get their motherhood 'right'.

Mothers' 'time' spent with children was then reconceptualised as an indication of her 'care'. From her empirical research on the women's experiences of mothering their young children, Jane Ribbens (1994: 170) observed that her interviewees' 'belief about time [centred] not just on "spending time" on children, but on "being there", so that mothers are available when their children need them'. Ribbens' concept of 'being there' in this instance implies proximity, being *with*. It is then an element of the mother/child relationship which their separation from one another disrupts.

In drawing on the notion of 'time *in* childhood', Allison James and Alan Prout (1997: 230, original emphasis) illustrate how child- to adult-hood can be plotted sequentially across the western life course: 'childhood follows infancy and is succeeded by adolescence, adulthood, middle age and old age' (231). As they further observe, each of these phases is accorded age-appropriate boundaries. They highlight how 'time is used effectively to produce, control and order the everyday lives of children' (231). In this analysis, time has a structuring force in children's lives. As already noted, mothers' time is equally produced, controlled and ordered to meet the needs, not only of their children, but of the constructions of both mother- and child-hoods. Thus, I suggest that the concept 'time *in* motherhood' is salient for my argument because if, as James and Prout suggest, 'concepts of time play a key role in shaping and contextualising the lives and activities of children' (234), it is logical to assert that mothers' lives are similarly shaped.

Moreover, at the same time that mothers are 'being there' for their children, which I suggest provokes as well notions of immediacy and timelessness, they are also immersed in a developmental process of child*rearing* which focuses upon their children's *becoming* adult. Chris Urwin (1985: 184) argues that the emphasis on ages and stages of developmental psychology of the 1960s and 1970s impacted 'not only on how [mothers] saw their children's development but also on *how* they thought they should spend their time with [them]' (original emphasis). In these terms then, the time mothers spend nurturing their children through the st/ages of development has an underlying purpose; as James and Prout (1997: 239) argue, 'the importance of age during childhood is that it indicates movement towards adulthood, the child's future'.

Mothers are thus situated as pivotal in the process of their children's preparation for the world beyond the family (Jaggar, 1983; Lawler, 2000; Mayall, 1996, 2002; Walkerdine and Lucey, 1989; Walkerdine, Melody and Lucey, 2001). Their responsibility for 'getting motherhood right' was a recurrent theme of the interviews I carried out for my research and was linked to notions of the future; as one of my interviewees said, 'you're raising the next generation'. Ultimately, she expressed a widely-held societal belief that underlies the purpose of mothering – that children are 'adults in the making' (Brannen, 1996: 114). A mother's life course is therefore inextricably linked to that of her child whereby she is placed (and also places herself) as guarantor of the social order (Lawler, 2000; Walkerdine and Lucey, 1989; Walkerdine, Lucey and Melody, 2001).

The characteristics of contemporary western constructions of childhood are identified by Jenny Hockey and Allison James (1993: 69) as rooted in notions of 'innocence, naturalness and vulnerability', which separate children out as different from adults. Indeed as Jane Ribbens McCarthy and Rosalind Edwards (2000: 787) comment, 'the fundamental social categories of "Child" and "Adult" [...] are constructed by reference to one another, so that we know what it is to be a Child because it is to be Other than Adult, and vice versa'. In order for children to acquire the knowledge they need to participate independently in society, they need guidance from 'one or more specific adults, [who give] children the social place and cultural knowledge required to be a participant in the society' (Jamieson, 1998: 8).

As Jaggar (1983: 311) further observes, childrearing is always carried out 'in accordance with prevailing norms of what constitutes acceptable behaviour in children and desired characteristics in adults'. Likewise, in his discussion of postmodern childhood, Chris Jenks (1996a: 79) comments that 'to be socialised is to become one with the normative social structure'. Ultimately then, how adulthood is conceptualised is key to the purpose, and so the practice, of mothering a child. Thus it is that the child awaits instruction on how to become a responsible adult from those who have already achieved that status. As Ribbens McCarthy and Edwards (2002: 201) note, 'the notion of the autonomous, self-contained individual predominates in Western cultures and suffuses the psychological, political, sociological and therapeutic literature'. In consequence, nurturing children's independence and autonomy remains a major goal of motherhood in contemporary UK.

Jamieson's (1998) 'specific adult', particularly during a child's early years, is predominantly the mother, whose 'job' it is to ensure that her child is able to participate in society as an active citizen. Following Nicolas Rose (1991) Steph Lawler (2000: 35) argues that childhood 'has been the focus of scrutiny from governments throughout the post-war period, in order to ensure that families (and especially mothers) fulfil their obligations to produce "good citizens"'. It is therefore the mother's responsibility not only to protect the child's innocence but also to shape the child's future adult life and, as another of my interviewees put it, 'keep them on the straight and narrow'.

Thus being a child is set in the context of being an adult-in-waiting, where the mother is given the task of ensuring that society's desired characteristics of adulthood are achieved by her children. What these desired characteristics are shift over time however and, as Gill Jones, Mary O'Sullivan and Julia Rouse (2006: 381) found in their study of parents' support (or otherwise) of their adult children's partnership formulations, 'there [were] no "traditions" to guide them in this respect, and they [could] not fall back on subjective assessment'.

The child-to-adult continuum continues to be popularly related to age and 'common practice has been to break childhood down into three periods: early (0–4), middle (5–9) and late (10–14), with adolescence accounting for those aged between 14 and 17' (Wyness, 2006: 4). As Sarah Irwin (1995a: 4) comments, 'youth and adulthood are used as terms for describing particular locations with respect to the organisation of social reproduction' and Tim Gill (1999: 67) notes that the 'middle years' of childhood are 'around eight and 14'.

The *Good Childhood Inquiry* launched by the Children's Society in 2006 found that UK parents were reluctant to let their children leave the home unsupervised before the age of 14 years (see www.childrenssociety.org.uk). The Chief Executive of the society stated in a national newspaper report, 'as a society we are in a real quandary: on the one hand we want freedom for our children but on the other we are becoming increasingly frightened to let them out' (*Daily Mail*, 05/06/07: 24). Although, as James and Prout (1997: 236) indicate, there are uncertainties in the position of 'teenagers [as] neither child nor adult', it would seem that the practice of delineating between particular ages and stages of children on their way to adulthood remains fairly intact and that the child's age remains linked to a dual and competing notion of in/dependency (Brannen and O'Brien, 1996).

Understandings of the mother/child dyad have retained some continuity over time as embodiment and age remain major differentials between each member of this coupling. Mother- and childhood are thus encapsulated within a particular time-frame that is reliant upon an unequal pairing and moreover defines the young child through dependency on the mother. As Allatt (1996: 131) observes, 'change is inherent in the physical, psychological and social development of the young' so that, as children get older they become less reliant on their mothers (and fathers), for example, they walk/take the bus to school by themselves or with friends. Many of these 'micro-transitions' (Allatt, 1996: 138) are sited in the home, as the child progresses through the different st/ages of childhood. Thus, the shift to adulthood occurs along a continuum, the consequences of which 'become visible when age distinctions between adults and children are reconstructed, or rather come to assume less salience' (Brannen and O'Brien, 1996: 5).

The characteristics of chronological time include 'shifting circumstances and life experiences, [which] mean[s] that change and transition are major features of every individual's life' (Gillies, Ribbens McCarthy and Holland, 2001: 8). The following chapters show that many of the transitions my interviewees underwent whilst mothering were to a great extent occluded by the parallel transitions of their children. Thus a focus on their children's transitions has enabled me explore how these were experienced by mothers themselves.

As Hockey and James (1993: 5) argue, to participate in western society an individual requires 'an individualistic, knowledgeable, independence'. This therefore contrasts sharply with the social experience of caring for a dependent child, and also with non-western collective practices and parenting goals (Brannen and O'Brien, 1996; Ghuman, 1999). As Paul Ghuman (1999: 24) notes in his comparative analysis of western and non-western childrearing practices, '[western] children from the early years are encouraged to develop autonomy, independent thinking, self-expression and achievement for themselves. The overall aim is to develop into inner-directed persons'.

A chronology of developmental ages and stages in which western childrearing is enmeshed, and that James and Prout (1997: 246) identify as 'a series of small transition points', creates and perpetuates an environment in which the child is in effect 'becoming' adult. Thus a sequence of st/aged accomplishments leads to the time of the child's acquisition of independence both within, and later from, the home. A timed logic is thus accorded the home leaving of adult children into which mothers (and others) are acculturated from their children's birth onwards.

Separation is then a seemingly inevitable part of the mother/adult child relationship. Indeed, as Kate Figes (2002: 357) indicates, childrearing incorporates multiple separations between mothers and their children, such as starting school and so forth, which 'accumulate over the spectrum of a child's life'. This being so, at the time they leave home, children are supposedly 'ready' and their mothers supposedly 'prepared' for this 'final' separation. Thus, for the majority of young people in the UK, leaving home is a culturally sanctioned and expected experience of the life course, for both the child and the mother.

However, the phase of a mother's life course during which children leave home has also been identified as a 'crisis period' (Bart, 1972; Lurie, 1974) and loss of maternal identity expounded as underlying the 'symptoms' of women's depression at this time. Diane Richardson (1993: 6), for example, has suggested that the centrality of motherhood in women's lives limits their opportunities to 'maintain a sense of independent identity' so that, at the time of her children's home-leaving a mother 'may experience a crisis of identity'. Relinquishing an identity that formerly structured their everyday practices was thus perceived to have implications for women's ability to cope. As Allison Jaggar argues:

> The dependence that the mother develops on the child often is not obvious until the child leaves home. At this point, the mothers who have been most devoted to their children suffer most intensely from the 'empty nest' syndrome. They often become extremely depressed because they feel unloved, unwanted and as if there were no meaning left in their lives. (Jaggar, 1983: 314)

In her study of mothers' depression during the 'empty nest' period, Dolores Borland (1982) provides a comparative analysis of white, black and Mexican-American women's experiences. Each of the white women Borland interviewed was a full-time homemaker/mother living within a nuclear family. Her black and Mexican-American counterparts worked outside the home and most lived in extended family situations. Borland concluded that the white women were more prone to symptoms of depression and loss of identity due to their domestic circumstances. Her conclusions indicate similarities with those of Richardson and Jaggar above, as she found that in the case of the white women who participated in her study: 'empty nest syndrome might be closely tied to the absence of alternative roles in which to continue building an identity after the children leave home' (1982: 127).

Much of the 'empty nest' literature, as the term implies, places the mother within the domestic arena and, although focused on the mother's experiences of the child's home-leaving, is reliant upon particular models of motherhood. As such, the changing context of mothering is not accommodated but rather fixes motherhood, and so women as mothers, into a particular time/less frame that does not equate with continually transforming practices and lived experiences. During the time my interviewees reared their children, for example, the numbers of women working outside the home increased dramatically (Brannen and O'Brien, 1996; Silva and Smart, 1999; Silva, 1999). The concern of my own study is not however the 'empty nest' as several of the women I interviewed still had one or more children living in the family home. My focus is the mother's experience of separation from her adult child, her negotiation of the absence of the child in her everyday life and the transition of the mother/adult child relationship in the aftermath of the child's leaving.

The application of terms such as 'nesting' and other metaphors, for example, 'fledglings' (Raup and Myers, 1992) are not of course without their problems, not least because of the conflation of nature with human life course experiences (Hockey and James, 2003). However, I was surprised at the number of times my interviewees called on this terminology and indeed at the references to it I encountered in newspapers and elsewhere during the course of my research. For instance, in her discussion of domestic technology, Silva (1999: 61) cites an advertisement for a dishwasher in a 1997 *Good Housekeeping* magazine: 'when the children have flown the nest, you'll be glad of the Top Solo option, a programme that washes a half load'. Similarly, a letter to the *Guardian Weekend* in April 2007 asking for advice on how to cope once children leave home receives the following response: 'the risk of empty nest syndrome (depression and loss of purpose) has been rather exaggerated [...] so start spending your children's inheritance now ... before they move back in!'. One year later the magazine *Woman and Home* (November, 2008: 163–5) ran a two-page article entitled 'Empty nest or new beginning?', which focused on couples' experiences of their last child leaving home. These examples do then indicate some currency within non-academic public sites of this phase of a mother's/parents' life course.

However, and seemingly in parallel with changes on the domestic front, the 'empty nest' has lost its research impetus, (although see Wadsworth and Green, 2003: 213–7, who include a discussion of the 'empty nest' phase in their research into women's experiences of the menopause). There has, however, been a surge of interest in family and youth transitions. Indeed, as Elizabeth Silva and Carol Smart (1999: 5) comment: 'families remain a crucial relational entity playing a fundamental part in the intimate life of and connections between individuals'. Thus, mothers are not overlooked in work that focuses on family transformation and relationality. In contrast to many of the studies on early childrearing (and also those on the 'empty nest'), fathers are also present as a focus of empirical enquiry in several studies (Allatt, 1996; Brannen, 1996; Gillies, Ribbens McCarthy and Holland, 2001; Holdsworth and Morgan, 2005; Eggebeen, Dew and Knoester, 2009; Kenyon, D. and Koerner, 2009). Changes in the individual life course of each parent, for example, are linked 'with the changes in their children's lives' (Gillies et al., 2001: 8).

Research explorations of parent/adolescent child relationships are based upon the premise that there is little empirical knowledge regarding how these relationships are experienced by family members themselves. In order to address this gap, Val Gillies and her colleagues' study was conducted with 32 16- to 18-year-olds, 30 mothers and 31 fathers about their views on being/parenting a teenager. The authors state it was important for their study to identify families/family members 'not labelled and identified as problematic [that were] just getting on with their lives' (7).

Gillies et al. report that independence 'was a key feature of their interviewees' discussions of their relationships and their lives together' (14). Increasing agency and autonomy for parents and teenaged children emerged as salient themes in their data. The tentative divide between dependence and independence that continues into parent/adolescent child relationships was also evident:

> Accounts from teenagers, mothers and fathers were of constantly modifying relationships and situations. Yet, running across the individual, evolving experiences of being or parenting a teenager was also a more general appreciation of the continuities associated with this particular family relationship. For most of the individuals taking part in this study, parent-teenager relationships were experienced in terms of enduring responsibility, love and interdependence. (Gillies et al., 2001: 8)

As these authors identify, in*ter*dependency was a core component of the parent/ teenager relationship that evolved as a lived experience of home-life. The home environment thus gave shape and structure to the relationships within it. In my research, interviewees articulated that their relationships with their children had evolved in very similar ways to those identified by Gillies et al.: 'freer, more companionship-based interactions' (7). I build on their work but also diverge from it in my singular focus on mothers' experiences and perceptions of their evolving relationships with their children. My aim is, in effect, to bring the mother back into the debate as a centralised focus of enquiry, as I believe she still has something to tell us about motherhood from her experiences of mothering during this phase of her life course during the current period of late modernity.

Much of the literature on youth transitions highlights how it continues to be structured by the gendered, classed and raced locations of young people (Benson and Johnson, 2009; Bynner, et al., 2002; Furlong and Cartmel, 1997; Henderson, Holland, McGrellis, Sharpe, Thomson and Grigoriou, 2007; Jones, 1995, 2000; 2002, 2005; Kenyon, D. and Silverberg, 2009; Patiniotis and Holdsworth, 2005; Walkerdine, Lucey and Melody, 2001). Indeed, as Sheila Henderson et al. (2007: 8) argue, 'the UK is a diverse and unequal society [...] it is not possible to talk of standard "youth transitions" in a society in which young people's lives are shaped by such uneven material, social, cultural and symbolic resources'.

Jackie Patiniotis and Carol Holdsworth (2005: 82) observe that 'the term "working class" encompasses a complex web of differences in economic status, educational and career aspirations and cultural and material capital'. Women I interviewed who identified as working-class (either upbringing, present-day, or both) and whose daughters and sons left home for university, encouraged their children to study outside their hometown and as such were adhering to a traditional, and thus, middle-class, expectation that leaving home was part of the higher education package (Patiniotis and Holdsworth, 2005). Similarly, participants' children who did not leave home for university were encouraged to buy property and/or to travel/work abroad, all of which I suggest were previously middle-class aspirations for young people.

In their turn, my interviewees provided examples of their agency in pushing children towards a form of independence that adhered to notions of bourgeois individualism. As Zygmunt Bauman (2002: xiv) observes: 'casting members as individuals is the trademark of modern society'. Moreover, there were links between interviewees' experiences of mothering their children to adulthood and contemporary debates regarding the effect of the individualization process on western family life, which emphasises the impact of structural and social change on individual biographies (Beck, 1992; Beck and Beck Gernsheim, 1995). Ulrich Beck (2002: 202) for example, comments that 'individualization consists in transforming human "identity" from a "given" into a "task" – and charging the actors with the responsibility for performing that task and for the consequences'. There has been contemporary shift from individualism in a philosophical sense toward that of the individual's immersion in a process of individualization, defined by David Morgan (1999: 23) as 'a social product [where] the stress would seem to be increasingly on the individual as the key unit and with this individual comes an emphasis upon the self, fulfilment, choice, rights and freedom'. Each of the elements Morgan identifies as part of the present-day individual was present in the data I gathered.

Janel Benson and Monica Johnson (2009: 1266) note that the transition to adulthood now takes place over 'an extended period of time'. It is also the case that the transition from the parental home into a home of one's own (whether accommodation during the years of higher education and beyond, partnerships, or shared living) is not a linear and seamless experience for growing numbers of young people (Furlong and Cartmel, 1997; Jones, 2002). As Allatt (1996: 132) observes, there are varied experiences such as 'leaving and returning [to the parental home] due to entry into higher education, periods of employment away from home, experimental independence, or trial partnerships or marriages which break down'. However, I use the adult child's first move out of the family home as an indicator to mothers of their children's adulthood.

In empirical work on young people's experiences of leaving home, the concept of home is often articulated as holding ongoing relevance in terms of emotional, practical and financial support (Henderson et al., 2007; Holdsworth, 2004; Holdsworth and Morgan, 2005; Kenyon, 1999; 2003, Thomson and Holland, 2004). In her studies of students' transient experiences of home (1999) and young people's divergent household formations (2003), Liz Kenyon, for example, explored the meanings her research participants accorded the concept of home. The majority of the students who participated in Kenyon's earlier research perceived the parental home as a safe place to which they could retreat between university semesters, or in other times of need, whereas their term-time homes were viewed as temporary and transient and their imagined post-graduation homes of the future were envisaged as signifying that the leaving home process was completed. Thus, the young people Kenyon interviewed perceived the severing of the ties of home as a process that occurred over the three years (plus) that they studied, and during which the parental home was in effect held in place until they formulated their own permanent future (adult) homes.

Underpinning Kenyon's analysis is the implication that her participants' experience of the transition to adulthood was a gradual process of 'how conceptions and meanings of home adapt and evolve for young people on the verge of adult life' (1999: 95), thus implying change over a period of time. Her findings resonate with Julia Brannen and Margaret O'Brien's (1996: 5) formulation of home as 'providing young people with a sense of attachment reaching back into the past and holding the potential for extension into the future'. What can be gleaned from these authors' analyses is that the concept of home for the majority of young people in the UK 'concerns feelings of belonging, of moral claims to be there, as well as material and emotional support and physical place' (Allatt, 1996: 132). It thus contains, as Carol Holdsworth and David Morgan (2005: 79) also observe, all the elements of Lasch's much earlier discussion of home as a 'haven in a heartless world' (1977). I need to state however that in focusing on the positive images and experiences of home and home life I am not negating the fact that the parental home can be a site of unhappiness and sometimes violence for young people (see Coles, 1995; Furlong and Cartmel, 1997; Jones, 1995 for discussions).

In their study of parent/adolescent child relationships, Brannen et al. (1994) argue that mothers constructed relationships of disclosure with their children in order to maintain contact with young people in the future. As the above discussion highlights, Brannen and her colleagues' findings complement other studies. In discussing the reliance that mothers (and fathers) are said to be placing upon their children, it might thus be important to consider not only, as Holdsworth and Morgan (2005: 99) do in their study of youth transitions, 'who is becoming independent from whom', but also to further problematise the concept of independence that underlies much of the rhetoric on motherhood and childrearing. Indeed in their research with parents and teenage children, Jones et al. (2006: 389) identified a 'complex blend of autonomy and dependence' in formulations of young adulthood. I suggest, however, that this mix has always been the case. This problematic is an ongoing theme throughout the rest of the book.

The analyses of the transformations occurring in families and young people's lives that I have discussed so far suggest relationships of increased equality between mothers (and fathers) and their growing children (Giddens, 1992). Indeed, in her discussion of 'disclosing intimacy', Kath Woodward (2002: 190) talks of 'a material shift in the exercise of power in the practice and experience of different relationships', including those of parents and their children. Following Brannen et al. (1994) and Jamieson (1998, 1999), Jones et al. (2006: 387) note that disclosure is 'associated with increasing democracy in families'. Moreover, Beck and his co-author Elizabeth Beck Gernsheim (1995) argue that in a climate of increased divorce and relationship uncertainty, the stability and security of the mother/child relationship has replaced the trust that was once an expected part of coupledom. Sasha Roseneil and Kurt Mann (1996: 209) also talk of the increased intimacy and the 'permanence' and 'stability' of mothers' relationships with their children. Indeed, as Beck (1992: 118) previously observed, 'partners come and go. The child stays'.

The increased fragility of heterosexual couple relationships is an area of interest for Brannen and O'Brien (1996) who argue that transformations in these relationships must be considered in any discussion of childhood, and similarly in his account, Jenks observes how wider social change is experienced as 'disorienting' which, he argues, has ramifications for how children are currently perceived by their parents:

> Children are seen as dependable and permanent, in a manner to which no other person or persons can possibly aspire. The vortex created by the quickening of social change and the alteration of our perceptions of such change means that whereas children used to cling to us, through modernity, for guidance in their/our 'futures', now we, through late-modernity, cling to them for 'nostalgic' groundings. (Jenks, 1996b: 20)

I agree with Jenks that nostalgia plays a part in family life histories, and this was certainly present in my interviewees' reflections on their mothering, not least the yearning to return to the days of early childrearing and for the younger, pre-childbirth self in some instances. However, there was also the uncertainty of the unknown space outside the home that many of my participants envisaged as part of their children's lives as adults. As John Bynner et al. (2002: xii) state: 'the situation of young people today is substantially different from that which prevailed 25 years ago'. I therefore suggest that there is a need to consider what mothering children to adulthood constitutes in a contemporary UK context. The chapters that follow highlight that my interviewees' mothering was not only focused upon their adult children's achievement of an independent lifestyle, but also that a mobile and flexible adult citizen was clearly the outcome they desired for their daughters and sons. I propose this signals a shift in the performance of mothering when discussed in the context of late modernity.

In turn, I also suggest that mothers' nurturing of a relationship of disclosing intimacy with their children might well prove an essential component of the mother/child relationship once these children leave home. In consequence, my focus on mothers' descriptions of their children's home-leaving and accompanying transition to adulthood will offer an opportunity to investigate how changes to the sociocultural landscape are impacting at the micro-level of experience, in particular on women's mothering as praxis and the reconfiguration of the mother/adult child relationship.

However, if, as Brannen and O'Brien (1996: 3) state, 'the child of these theoretical accounts is vital in constructing adult identities' (although I would argue that the 'child' has always been vital in constructing the identity 'mother'), then the mother/adult child relationship is in need of further scrutiny in light of the push for independence and autonomy that underpins models of mothering in a contemporary western context. If as well, mothers are becoming increasingly dependent upon their children, inasmuch as the latter provide them with security and, I suggest, anchor mothers' identities when all around is perceived/experienced as fragmentary and unstable, I further propose that children's home-leaving disrupts and thus destabilises this identity because, and in contrast to Beck's (1992) postulation, the child *does not* stay.

Whilst I agree with Ribbens McCarthy and Edwards (2001: 768) when they state that 'parent-child relationships are about a great deal more than (disclosing) intimacy, encompassing a much greater range of activities and experiences', it clearly emerged from my data that the loss of the child's physical presence was felt most strongly once children left home and face-to-face interaction with them was no longer part of mothers' everyday experiences. Part of my focus then is to examine whether there was indeed a shift towards 'disclosing intimacy' between them and if so, how this aspect of their relationship was maintained when the majority of children resided some distance from their hometown, both within and outside of the UK. The following chapter provides information on the post home-leaving destinations of my participants' daughters and sons.

Experiences of transition through the life course incorporate change and in the case of young people leaving home the shift from dependent to independent living underscores the transformation of child- to adulthood. However, the focus on the young person's movement out of the family home, with the concomitant privileging of the transition from child to adult that I suggest home-leaving affirms for the mother, occludes the latter's parallel shift. The non-discussion of the mother's individual experience of this time in her life course is evident in much of the present-day literature on youth transition. Rosamund Billington, Jenny Hockey and Sheelagh Strawbridge describe the following passage from Laurie Lee's autobiographical text as 'a description of how the author's social identity underwent a transition at the age of nineteen':

> The stooping figure of my mother, waist-deep in the grass and caught there like a piece of sheep's wool, was the last I saw of my country home as I left to discover the world. She stood old and bent at the top of the bank, silently watching me go, one gnarled red hand raised in farewell and blessing, not questioning why I went. At the bend of the road I looked back again and saw the gold light die behind her: then I turned the corner, passed the village school, and closed that part of my life forever. (Lee 1969, cited in Billington et al., 1998: 63)

Billington et al. use this extract to underpin a discussion of western life course transitions that centre on the protagonist's trajectory from his family home. The authors later draw on traditional cultures, for example the Bemba ritual of *chisungu*,[5] as having 'relational implications that endured across generations' (75), so implying the youth's life course transition is not experienced in isolation but resonates across the kin network. The Lee autobiography of course privileges the transition of boy to man and this brief narrative creates a still-life image of the author's mother; she is 'caught there', literally frozen in time, whilst the sun sets in

---

5   *Chisungu* is a marriage ritual of the Bemba people of north-eastern Zambia (Billington, Hockey and Strawbridge, 1998).

the background. A particular representation of the mother as a static figure nearing the end of her life is thus captured, by both author and reader. Although it can be presumed that Lee's mother is most likely to have returned indoors to carry on with her everyday life after her son's 'big moment' (Turner, 1976) and thus crucial turning point in his life, we cannot be certain what she did afterwards, nor how she was affected by her son's leaving. Embedded within this extract from Lee's novel is the experience of separation between a mother and her child, enacted by the son's physical move out of the home. I take this as my starting point. But it is the unexplored territory of what a mother experiences when her child leaves home that provides the core of this text.

Structure of the Book

In the following chapter I discuss the methodological underpinnings of my research and the methods of data production I chose to use. I am aware that throughout the book I have relied on my research participants' partial stories and 'moral tales' (Ribbens McCarthy, Edwards and Gillies, 2000: 786) to provide the grounding for the production of the work I present. However, the interpretation of their narratives is my own.

The cultural representations and discursive constructions of mother and child, which emanate from a range of sources in both academic and popular arenas, are the focus of Chapter 3. I draw on these to argue that becoming and being a mother is predicated upon the presence of a dependent child. Interviewees' reflections on the early years of mothering were narrated in terms of loving and caring for their dependent children, in which closeness to the mother translated as safety and security for the child. Alongside this, the development of their children's independence and autonomy was the ultimate goal of each of my interviewees' mothering practices. The chapter explores how adult children's home-leaving enforced the reconfiguration of the concept of 'being there' (Ribbens, 1994) for my participants which, in its turn, provides an ongoing theme of the book. The chapter also discusses interviewees' relationships to time's passing and 'sudden' realisations of their positioning further along the life course. Ultimately, the chapter exposes a gap in our knowledge of what it means to mother over time and in particular at the time of the child's emerging adulthood their home-leaving signifies.

Women's management of the process of separation from the adult child is the focus of Chapter 4. Whilst my interviewees were acculturated into the discourse of western childrearing, discussed above, this chapter illustrates how children's shifting status and ultimate achievement of 'inner direction' (Ghuman, 1999: 24) was not clear-cut for their mothers but instead raised multiple dilemmas. Not least of these was the conflicting mix of emotions women experienced at the time of separation from their adult daughters and sons. The chapter argues that the privileging of the child's transition to adulthood, exemplified by their exit from the home, masked women's simultaneous transition. Thus the shift in the mother's status, a by-product of the child's home-leaving, is an unacknowledged and for the most part silent experience. The chapter also explores the aftermath of children's home-leaving, when the 'safe haven' of the family home underwent an immediate transformation that rendered it an unsettled space for my interviewees. In contrast to the studies on youth transitions cited above, my focus is on mothers' perceptions of the home in the absence of the child and when, from this vantage point, their children's adult lives began.

Exploring notions of gender and class in their study *Growing Up Girl*, Valerie Walkerdine, Helen Lucey and June Melody (2001: 81) observe that 'everything is presented as possible today'. My interviewees had aspirations for their children as adults that equated with the perceived transformation of opportunity Walkerdine and her colleagues identify. Expectations of what their daughters and sons would/could achieve were often articulated with reference to interviewees' own life chances as younger women, prior to motherhood. In many ways their own histories, alongside their knowledge of sociocultural change, impacted on the aspirations they held for their children as adults. Advances in technologically-mediated communication have run in parallel with changes in young people's education and employment patterns and expectations of mobility. Chapter 5 discusses how living apart from their children affected the mother/adult child relationship. Women's use of communication technologies, such as land line and mobile phones and the internet, to maintain contact with their daughters and sons across geographical distances is a major focus of the chapter. The mother figure in mobile phone advertising directs its focus.

Women's experiences once they had adjusted to living apart from their children forms the basis of Chapter 6. All of my interviewees' children were engaged in higher education, secure employment or travel/work abroad. This is not to suggest, however, that they did not 'struggle to establish adult identities and maintain coherent biographies' (Furlong and Cartmel: 1997: 108). The chapter discusses how adult children's short- and long-term returns to the family home affected interviewees' perceptions, both of their children and of their mothering selves. Also problematised is the notion of the mothers' autonomy. The chapter asks how shifting perceptions of self and child impacted on my interviewees' desires to make individual lifestyle choices that at times ran counter to their 'promise' of constant availability to their children. All of the women I interviewed were employed for some years prior to their children's home-leaving. Chapter 6 also offers a discussion the impact of paid work in their lives. Interviewees were also a mix of partnered and unpartnered women and a discussion of their perceptions of relationships with male partners provides a further avenue of enquiry.

The focus of my research is the experience of separation between mother and adult child. In the concluding chapter I discuss the contribution the work has made to understandings of mothers' experiences of this phase of the life course and the implications for further study the research might stimulate. A brief overview of an event I held for participants is an additional feature of the final chapter.

Although routes out of the family home for young people have become increasingly varied and complex, for the majority of the UK adult population leaving home remains a culturally sanctioned, expected and thus planned-for event. So far I have argued that when women successfully manage the mothering of their children to adulthood, by which I mean their children are considered 'ready' to leave home, there is scant acknowledgement of the mother's experiences that are embedded in the process of separation from her child. I propose that her individual experience is silenced firstly by the sociocultural constructions of motherhood *per se*, secondly by the privileging of the child's transition to adulthood, underscored by her/his movement out of the home, and thirdly by a masking of the transformation of the mother/adult child relationship with its ensuing transition in women's mothering as praxis. Leaving home is an ordinary, everyday occurrence that most of the adult population of the UK experience, and one that mothers expect to be part of their children's life course yet, and as Jenks (1995: 6) asserts, 'in the familiar we find the most strange and the least known'. It is my intention in the chapters that follow to confront a 'familiar' occurrence in order to explore what I consider to be one of the 'least known' stories of motherhood.

Chapter 2
Researching Mothers' Experiences

Introduction

> In research-specific contexts the demand to be explicit regarding the research
> process has become increasingly pronounced, prompted by the recognition that
> the process itself exerts influence on the research outcome and therefore needs
> to form an articulated aspect of the research. (Griffin, 2005: 178)

As Gabriele Griffin observes, it is necessary to make the practices of research and
its processes transparent. In this chapter, the methodological basis of my empirical
research and the impact of this on the methods I chose with which to explore
women's experiences of their adult children leaving home are discussed. Caroline
Ramazanoğlu and Janet Holland highlight the need to distinguish between the two
terms method and methodology:

> Methodology links a particular ontology (for example, a belief that gender is
> social rather than natural) and a particular epistemology (a set of procedures
> for establishing what counts as knowledge) in providing the rules that specify
> how to produce valid knowledge of social reality. (Ramazanoğlu with Holland,
> 2002: 11)

Thus, the reasons why particular methods are chosen and how they are applied
in social science research is indicative of the researcher's ontological and
epistemological standpoint. As Mary Maynard (1994: 23) succinctly states: 'all
feminist work is theoretically grounded'. To further clarify my own research
practices, I add here that my background in gender studies, with its inherent
interdisciplinarity, heavily informed the decisions I made in the design of the
research and the data analysis.

Making women's experiences visible is a foundational goal of much feminist
research on motherhood (Reinharz and Chase, 2003). As already discussed, the
transition to motherhood and mothers' childrearing practices have been and
continue to be areas which draw a great deal of academic interest (Gatrell, 2005;
Oakley, 1976, 1979, 1980, 1981a; Miller, 1998, 2005; Ribbens, 1994; 1998; Rich,
1977; Richardson, 1993).[1] These issues also attract considerable attention from
many diverse areas within formal settings, such as the medical profession and the
political arena, as well as more informally, from women's partners, families and

---

1   I provide only a few examples here.

friends. However, as Reinharz and her colleague Susan Chase observe: 'despite the explosion of feminist interview research over the past three decades, many groups of women continue to be unrecognized as competent social actors' (2003: 74). I count my interviewees in this category.

The women who participated in my research are 'successful' mothers, and I use the term successful to draw attention to the fact that the majority of mothers in contemporary UK raise their children to 'fit' the accepted role of independent adult in western society. In those terms, my interviewees could be perceived to fit a typology of mothering that has not been labelled as 'problematic' (unlike teenage mothers, single mothers, mothers of disruptive teenagers or overweight children, for example). Jane Ribbens argues for a close examination of such stereotypes because 'if we do not listen to women living in these circumstances, we fail to look behind the ideology to explore how women themselves experience and understand "conventional" family life' (1994: 40). Indeed, Ribbens' argument follows that of Valerie Walkerdine and Helen Lucey (1989) who assert:

> By examining the most boring details of domestic and childrearing practices, we are not simply engaging in a debate about education and development, but uncovering the most fundamental political questions about the production of democracy, about freedom and about women's oppression. (Walkerdine and Lucey, 1989: 33)

As such, by exploring the mundane occurrence of adult children's home-leaving the following chapters uncover many of the themes identified by these authors, not least mothers' compliance with an understanding of motherhood based on notions of childrearing that nurtures the child's autonomy and independence which they simultaneously enact alongside their caring practices. This contradictory matrix is discussed more fully in the next chapter.

Although as the demographic information later shows, interviewees raised their children under a diverse set of circumstances, autonomy for the adult child was the perceived and achieved goal of their mothering. Therefore, a successfully reared adult child leaving home is an ordinary and everyday event that may generally be expected amongst parents and other family members and friends, especially with planned-for and structured leavings such as going to university. However, there are very few if any sites where mothers can talk formally or informally about what happens *in their lives* when their adult children leave.

Women's emotional experiences of separation from their children are discussed fully in Chapter 4 where it will be revealed that there was often no support network available for women to draw upon once their children left home. In consequence, some of my interviewees were faced with an unemotional man (Lupton, 1998a) whilst others felt unable to talk about their feelings with those who did not share the same life experience. Taking part in my study thus offered a legitimate space in which to talk about how their children's leaving impacted on their own lives, including understandings and renegotiations of the mother/adult child relationship and consequently, their mothering as praxis. Women's stories therefore contribute to contemporary understandings of motherhood identities because, as Steph Lawler (2002) recommends, it attends to the stories they told of their mothering experiences. The interviews thus offer insight into what Ribbens (1994: 37) argues is often missed in academic writing on motherhood: 'the emotional content of mothers' experiences'.

In their discussion of notions of the public and the private, Edwards and Ribbens proffer the concept of 'bringing in the personal' as a way of

> Drawing attention to experiences that are constituted around a sense of self or identity, to do with emotions, intimacy or the body [because the personal] concerns the social as ontologically experienced by the individual; that is, in relation to a person's own sense of being or existence. (Edwards and Ribbens, 1998: 12)

The personal in these authors' definition is then a part of the self that, although carried across the tentative divide of private/public, often remains hidden. In addition, I suggest that emotional experiences are at time at variance with the face we show the world. As already established, women's experiences of the transition to motherhood provides an example of the contradictions that might be experienced between personal/hidden emotions and lived reality. My interviewees' transition from hands-on to hands-off mothering reflects yet another paradox in women's internal/external lives, as their inner feelings about their adult children leaving home often remained unarticulated. This was largely because the former ran counter to the culturally perceived goal of their mothering: the production of an independent adult. Asking women how they felt and thereby incorporating the personal enabled an exploration of how each child's emerging adulthood and subsequent home-leaving impacted on interviewees' sense of self with regard to their understandings of motherhood and their mothering identities.

My motivation for researching this aspect of motherhood stemmed from my own experiences as a mother of two children who have left home. Oakley comments that 'academic research projects bear an intimate relationship to the researcher's life [and] personal dramas provoke ideas' (Oakley, 1979: 4). Her observation is echoed by Reinharz (1992). Thus the notion that the topic of research can often be grounded in questions raised by issues pertaining to a researcher's life experiences is a prominent adjunct to feminist research.

There is also increasing recognition of the place of the researcher within the research design and its ensuing process, and an acknowledgement of this positioned self as an instrument of research inquiry (Coffey, 1999; Dey, 1993; Edwards and Ribbens, 1998; Mauthner and Doucet, 1998, 2003; Maynard and Purvis, 1994; Morse and Field, 1996; Ribbens, 1989; 1998; Stanley and Wise, 1993). As such, by explicitly stating my place within my own research study I acknowledge my position as 'a data creating social being' (Ribbens, 1989: 590) whose experiences and consciousness are integral to the research as process. As such I am the interpreter of the data created, as argued by Stanley and Wise: 'the researcher is an active presence, an agent, in research, and she constructs what is actually a viewpoint, a point of view that is both a *construction* or version and is consequently and necessarily *partial* in its understandings' (1993: 6–7, original emphases).

The positioning of the self of the researcher as an integral part of the research process lies in tension with the history of traditional social science research, which seeks to eject the researcher's own experience and value judgments from the enquiry, in effect mirroring research procedures of the natural sciences (Hughes, 2002). The design of such research assumes that in order to generate objective knowledge the researcher should remain detached from the research process. Catherine Parr explains this:

> The starting point is a theory, a hypothesis is formulated and data collected to test it. Data have to be objectively observed and classified (which makes the assumption of course that there is a single, tangible 'reality' which everyone defines in the same way). [...] There is considerable stress on the researcher's own values being kept out of the research arena. (Parr, 1998: 89)

As Parr also observes, in the design and execution of the type of research she critiques there is an implicit assumption that 'internal meanings, motives, feelings and emotions cannot be truly observed and so they cannot be measured in any objective way' (89). In this scenario therefore, and in contradistinction to my previous discussion, the 'personal' aspects of the researcher's life and the lives of those whom she studies are not a valid area of enquiry. However, as Parr (1998) concludes, it is not possible for research decisions to be made without reference to one's own values and beliefs about the social world and these are explicitly stated in feminist research regarding the decision-making behind its design and subsequent data production and analysis.

The work I present in the chapters that follow uses 'both "insider" and "outsider" perspectives on women's lives with their children, while prioritising the importance of listening to what mothers have to say' (Ribbens, 1994: 27). As such I view myself as a feminist involved in a research study that seeks an understanding of mothers' lives from their own perspective. Oakley has more recently observed that 'self-labelling as a feminist means only that one declares one's values, whereas the dominant [research] tradition is not to do so' (2000: 21). My decision to 'self-label' and declare from the outset my values both as a feminist and as a mother have underpinned the methodological decisions I made. They also construct me as an integral part of the research as process. In consequence, because I wanted to know how mothers were affected by their adult children's home-leaving and because I believe that these experiences have previously been silenced, the decisions regarding the research methods I used to generate the data were firmly embedded in my desire to produce knowledge that is rich in women's own feelings, perceptions and experiences of this event in their own lives.

Designing the Research

> Research design, methods of data collection, theoretical and analytic approaches and writing strategies are all part of an overall methodological approach and imply one another. (Edward and Ribbens, 1998: 19)

As Edwards and Ribbens indicate, and my earlier discussion highlights, the epistemological standpoint of the researcher, the design of the research and the methods utilised are intertwined. The catalyst for my study was my experience, and therefore embedded within the research design was an urge to answer a personal question built upon the knowledge that my own experience of this 'everyday' occurrence was not unique. As Gayle Letherby (2003: 53) states: 'feminism does aim to deconstruct the taken for granted'. In consequence, I made the decision to ask other mothers about their experiences of a 'taken for granted' experience. To do so, I needed a research method that would encourage women to talk about an everyday issue, hence my decision to use a semi-structured interview format. In order to elicit narrative responses from interviewees I followed the lead of Wendy Hollway and Tony Jefferson (2000) who suggest using open-ended questions beginning with the words 'can you tell me about ...?' In so doing I hoped to create a research environment which would, as Roseneil (2006: 6) puts it, 'give the interviewees time and space to construct their own stories in which meaning and values gradually unfold'.

A brief questionnaire was also used gather information from interviewees prior to our meeting so that demographic questions could be eliminated from the interviews. This meant I could focus on eliciting data from our meetings that would provide me with an in-depth picture of their experiences. Moreover, prior knowledge of women's circumstances was useful as I was able to some extent to individualise each of the interviews, although in some instances changes had occurred in their lives rendering some of the questionnaire data 'out of date' and which was updated when we met. This is a condition I suggest can be attributed to empirical research enquiries more generally because, unless longitudinal, they elicit only snapshots of participants' lived realities.

An issue that emerged from the majority of the interviews was that adult children leaving home engendered feelings of isolation, an aspect of participants' narratives more fully discussed in Chapter 4. With regard to the research design, this issue shifted my thinking towards the idea of presenting my work to them as a group, creating an opportunity for their discussion and feedback in an informal arena where they could meet and talk with one another. The event is discussed in the concluding chapter, but I refer to it here to illustrate how the research evolved as it progressed; empirical data were integral to the research process. As Jennifer Mason has argued:

> Qualitative research designs invariably need to allow for flexibility, and for decision making to take place as the research process proceeds. Especially if

you are working with an ontological and epistemological model where theory is generated from empirical data. (Mason, 1996: 33)

Mothers in Context

In order to find women willing to take part in the study I initially placed a brief call in a monthly newsletter circulated to all academic and non-academic departments on the university campus where I worked. Through this medium, eleven women responded. One of them contacted a further three women, and through friends and work colleagues, eight more participants were recruited. Links with ex-work colleagues resulted in three more women agreeing to participate. Overall twenty-five women showed interest in the research in a fairly short space of time. Snowballing was very effective in reaching participants, although this meant of course that they were drawn from particular social circles, in turn resulting in certain commonalities within the group. I did not specifically sample for class, race or sexuality issues, all of which merit specific attention. Rather, respondents were self-selecting within the reach of the immediate environment. The group might well have looked quite different had I sampled elsewhere.

I agree with Benson and Johnson's (2009: 1267) suggestion that 'social identities are constructed through interaction with significant others and are largely influenced by the social structures or contexts within which people are embedded'. It is important therefore to contextualise my participants' lived circumstances in order to shed some light on the influences they encountered throughout their lives that shaped their identities as women and as mothers, both before they participated in my research and at the time that I met them.

As aforementioned, my study participants were self-selecting and contacted by snowballing, which set certain parameters on the research in that the majority (22) were drawn from the same town, a further two participants lived on the east coast and one lived in the south of the UK and I am aware that they could be described as from a particularly homogenised geographical base. They self-identified as follows regarding their ethnicity: twenty-two White British/English; one British origin/New Zealand birthplace; one White/Asian and one British/Anglo-Indian parentage. All of my participants were able-bodied; financially secure; in academic or professional employment; similarly aged (44 to 58) and all were homeowners. The average age at which participants gave birth to their first child was 26, with the youngest aged 22 (n: 3) and the oldest aged 34 (n: 1).

The only criterion for women's participation in my research was that they were waiting for, or had experienced, a daughter or son leaving home. Although all who participated had experienced at least one adult child leaving, the timing of this ranged from one year to eleven years prior to our meeting. Sixteen participants still had a child or children living in the family home. The women recruited were therefore at different stages of this event in their adult children's and thus their own lives.

Collectively my research participants had thirty-nine children who had taken various routes out of their family homes so that in some instances women had experienced more than one child leave. Children's destinations were as follows: sixteen women experienced a child leave for university, none of whom attended their hometown university; seven women in the study had children who had moved out of the family home into homes of their own in the same town; two women had children who had moved out to live in different towns within the UK for reasons other than higher education and a further two had children living abroad; four participants' children were travelling during their gap years. Of the twenty-five women, six experienced the long-term return home of their adult children, and two were awaiting the return of their daughters following graduation.

During the early years of their children's lives, ten of my participants worked part-time and four worked full-time. Eleven were at home full-time during their children's early years, although Denise[2] and Rachel both worked from home during that time. Denise undertook 'a few hours' as an ICT consultant and Rachel ran a farm with her husband. Lois, a lone mother, worked part-time in bars during her first son's early years and was studying for her degree when her second child was born. Linda worked full-time both before and after her children were born. She was financially responsible for the welfare of her family whilst supporting her husband's undergraduate and postgraduate degrees. During their children's later school years, all of my participants took up paid work outside the home.

All twenty-five participants were employed at the time of the interviews; twenty-three in full- and two in part-time paid work outside the home. The majority of women worked in administrative posts. Three taught in further education, Angela and Gina lectured on childcare courses and Maggie taught psychology. Dawn and Helen worked as teachers' aids in a special needs school, Lois was a nursery assistant in a local school and Heather and Nancy were both primary teachers. Sandra and Serena were in care-related employment. These data are indicative of the increase in women's employment outside the home over the last three decades (Brannen and O'Brien, 1996).

Regarding their class status, seventeen participants self-identified as having a working-class upbringing and of these, thirteen identified as working-class at the time of the study. Lois described her upbringing as working/middle class, with her current status as middle-class. None of the participants who identified as having a middle-class upbringing noted downward class mobility so at the time of the study, eleven participants identified as middle-class. Angela did not answer this question.

Although all of my participants had begun their mothering from within a heterosexual (married) relationship, at the time of my research the partnership status of several women had changed. Eleven women were in their original relationships/marriages (that is, they were with the partner with whom they had their children) and seven had re-partnered/married. Three women had re-partnered

---

2 All participants' names are pseudonyms.

but were not cohabiting and four were single. Nine participants experienced a period of mothering alone, with two of this number experiencing two periods of lone mothering. I return to these data in chapter 4, where I discuss women's relationships and support networks in the immediate aftermath of their adult children's home-leaving and in chapter 6 I analyse how their children's leaving impacted on partnerships.

The demographic information presented above was collected from the brief questionnaire participants completed prior to the interviews. They indicate the context-specific characteristics of women's interview narratives, which are illustrative of a given experience rather than representative of wider society. (Appendix 1 provides a further brief biography of each participant).

Generating and Producing Data

In describing how I carried out the semi-structured interviews[3] I prefer to use the terminology of data generation and production rather than collection, as the latter implies that the data is out there waiting to be collected 'like rubbish bags on the pavement' (Dey, 1993: 15), whereas generation and production imply a more interpretive and reflexive approach to the process and subsequent analysis. Jennifer Mason also eschews the term collection in favour of generation because this 'encapsulate[s] the much wider range of relationships between researcher, social world, and data' (1996: 36). As such, these terms are more in keeping with my own epistemological standpoint regarding how knowledge of the social world can be co-constructed within the research interview environment. The rest of the discussion focuses on the practicalities of creating the 'right' environment for semi-structured interviews in order for them to be successful generators of rich data.

Fourteen interviews took place in my workplace, ten at participants' homes and one at a participant's workplace. The interviews lasted between sixty and ninety minutes. Bridget Byrne (2003: 33) observes that 'the context of the interview may be very important in determining what kind of response is produced' and I anticipated some differences to emerge in women's narratives dependent upon where the interviews took place. Although I cannot be sure of course, the resulting data did not indicate that this was necessarily the case as overall women were equally keen and responsive at each interview site. There were however some practical differences that are perhaps noteworthy. When the interviews were taking place on my 'home-ground', for example, I set up and tested the recording equipment prior to their arrival, whereas in the case of those that took place in participants' homes I had to set up when I arrived, so each time I needed to ensure that I had all the necessary equipment with me: an extension lead, enough tape-time, batteries and so on. For the last two interviews I had access to a digital recorder, which was easier to 'forget about' and proved much less 'intrusive'. Prior to meeting with

---

3   See Appendix 2 for the interview guide.

participants on their 'territory' I tested the recording equipment, feeling this could not/should not be done on site and in the presence of my interviewees. This led me to consider why it was important to obscure this, and other actions, from my participants. The face-to-face interview situation takes place between two people in close proximity and I suggest that the equipment the researcher uses might act as a reminder that the research interview is not a 'natural' event. It is as well, of course, about professional competence – wearing the researcher's mask and being prepared before entry into the research field.

When interviews took place in my own office space, I ensured there were minimum interruptions, I unplugged the telephone and placed a 'do not disturb' notice on my door, for example. In participants' own homes these 'precautions' could not be taken. Ultimately there were more disruptions during these interviews; telephones rang for example, or a visitor might call at the house, so that the interview process was interrupted. These small incidents were a source of (hidden) irritation to me because they hindered the flow of 'conversation'. In turn, they provide an important reminder that, however much I describe the interactions with my participants as relaxed and friendly, I was nevertheless encouraging them to talk to me for a purpose. Thus interview equipment alongside pre-interview preparations and reactions to the everyday interruptions of women's lives at home served to consolidate my place as first and foremost a researcher embedded in a process of research and women as the 'subjects' of that research.

In her discussion of women interviewing women, Janet Finch (1984: 78) suggests that: 'being "placed" as a woman has the additional dimension of shared structural position and personal identification'. I would add to this that in the interviews I conducted my age and motherhood status also impacted on the relationship and thus on the data produced. Participants were not aware of my age or that I was a mother until we met and I explained how I came to my decision to research this aspect of women's lives. I did not disclose any further information regarding my own experience as I was cognisant of the questions posed by Reinharz and Chase:

> If the research arises in part from the researcher's personal experiences or needs, to what extent – and why – should that personal connection play a role in the research relationship itself? Under what conditions might self-disclosure put the interviewee at ease or pressure her to adopt a particular point of view? When does self-disclosure indicate openness to the other's experience or a sharing of power within the interview relationship, and when does it indicate that the researcher prefers to speak rather than listen? (Reinharz and Chase, 2003: 80)

Although I was cautious about telling too much of my own story I nevertheless found that my brief 'unmasking' (Finch, 1984: 79) had a positive effect on the interaction between myself and interviewee. This in turn was conducive to the interview situation in that a good rapport was created and, in consequence, rich and useful data were produced. Indeed, as Maynard (1994: 16) points out: 'the personal involvement of the interviewer is an important element in establishing trust and thus obtaining good quality information'.

When women asked me personal questions I answered them, but this did not occur very often as they were more involved in telling their own stories, rather than in listening to mine. Unlike Oakley's interviewees (1979; 1981b), my participants did not ask me for any advice, nor did they treat me as an 'expert' on motherhood during this phase of the life course. Rather, I believe I was perceived as a kindred spirit who, to some extent, understood what they were talking about. This assumed 'likeness' was evident when participants would look to me for confirmation of their experiences, using tag-lines such as 'you know what I mean' and 'you know what it's like'.

Although there were differences between women's reactions to the interview situation I did not encounter any 'reluctant respondents' (Adler and Adler, 2003). I distributed a brief outline of the research prior to interview so participants were aware of its main focus. I started each of our encounters with 'can you tell me what being a mother has been like for you?', and this opening question sparked women's narratives; they 'just talked'. In a few instances women needed/expected more prompting and on one occasion an interviewee asked if I would like her to stop talking so that I could ask my next question. I suggest this was partly due to it being arranged as 'an interview': 'a conversation between two people in which one asks questions and the other answers' (Reinharz and Chase, 2003: 77).

Reinharz (1992: 19) comments that 'interviewing offers researchers access to people's ideas, thoughts, and memories in their own words, rather than in the words of the researcher'. My decision not to stick rigidly to an interview schedule but to use a prompt guide meant that women were able in effect to direct the interviews themselves as they recalled experiences they felt were significant, a more empowering position for participants to inhabit, although I was conscious of the times when the interview veered too far away from the topic I was pursuing and I then guided the conversation back. Again, this provides another indicator of my place as a researcher looking for a particular narrative response. Interviewees did not discount the significance for themselves of their adult children leaving home and it was obvious in a great number of instances that their own feelings were previously subsumed by the privileging of the young person's movement out of the family home. In each of the interviews my participants had plenty to say about the impact of this event on their own lives.

In order to maintain my position as an active listener I did not make notes during the interviews so that there were times that I missed salient points; listening to the interviews afterwards revealed where I sometimes failed to ask participants for further clarification. Although this inevitably occurs in all research situations, it nevertheless revealed an occasionally frustrating shortcoming of the interview as a research technique more generally. It also exposed a dilemma between the need to allow participants time to 'chat on' against the need to generate the sought after information. However, by not pursuing some areas, others might have been focused upon by the women that further allowed for good rapport between the two of us and in turn benefited the participant.

Whilst I agree with Finch (1984) when, following Oakley (1981b), she states that feminist research should 'articulate women's experiences of their lives – rather than merely creating data for oneself as researcher' (Finch, 1984: 86), it would be dishonest for me to state on a personal level that the former overrode the latter. The reason for undertaking the research was to expose a particular set of experiences appertaining to motherhood and my decision to interview mothers about these produced the data I wanted. Did I then engage in a 'pseudo-conversation' (Oakley, 1981b: 32) with them? I do not believe that I did, and agree with Griffin (2005: 184) when she argues that 'in most interview situations both the interviewer and the interviewee stand to gain and want something that the interview provides: data, a listening ear, or an opportunity to exchange views on a specific topic'.

Ethical Considerations

In order for a researcher to gain the trust of her study participants she must openly provide them with the reasons for her research and be clear when explaining what will be expected of the participants during the research process. Interviewees are more likely to talk openly once this kind of trust is established. I now go on to describe how I addressed the matter of trust and some of the dilemmas the interviews at times provoked.

My research participants were provided with an outline of the research design that clearly stated the interviews would be recorded, that only I would have access to these, and that the transcripts produced from the recordings would be anonymised, thus making their identities 'less obvious' (Summerfield, 2005: 61). Knowing from personal experience that we might touch on sensitive or upsetting issues during the interviews, I made assurances that recording could stop at their request and they were not obliged to pursue any issues they felt uncomfortable with. Refreshments were offered and tissues were to hand, and needed on several occasions. The issues of ownership and dissemination also need to be acknowledged however.

As Penny Summerfield (2005: 61) notes, the words spoken in an interview belong to those who said them and it is therefore 'common to secure the interviewee's written consent to the release of the material on the tape of the interview'; this I did once interviews ended. Further dilemmas surrounding this issue are however the questions Beverley Skeggs (1994: 86–7) asks of feminist research more generally when she describes the difficulties encountered in writing about young, working-class women's lives for an academic audience: 'who do we do research for?' and 'who speaks for whom?'. A conflation of feminist research with feminist politics is implicit here. As Glucksmann (1994: 150) noted, when discussing the production of feminist knowledge 'the researcher's self-awareness and reflection on her research should include a realistic appraisal of the limits of research as a locus for authentic political activity'. I am aware therefore that the work I have produced will probably not engender political change, I am however hopeful that it will activate some discussion around a previously under-researched experience in women's lives as mothers. As well, and although an element of the study was my desire to offer my participants the opportunity to talk about a previously silenced experience, the overarching reason for conducting the research, and as such its overall outcome, was not only restricted to answering a personal question, but was rather aimed at producing knowledge for an academic audience.

Linked to the above issue is the question of researching sensitive issues. As indicated, I informed participants that the interviews could be terminated at their request, and I did on occasion turn off the tape-recorder. Once an interview had started however, it is possible that women might have felt a sense of obligation to continue and this does raise questions of how far one should proceed with an enquiry that has the potential to cause distress. As Maynard argues:

> It may be possible for participants in the study to have their consciousnesses raised without the corresponding channels for action being available. Feminists have raised issues about the ethics of research which, having generated all sorts of issues in respondents' minds, then abandons them to come to terms with these on their own. (1994: 17)

Maynard's comments resonate with some of my experiences of the interview situation. Although prepared for the topic of my research to touch on sensitive issues, I was not prepared for some of the revelations within the women's accounts. Searching into women's mothering histories at times uncovered previously hidden experiences and, although a relative stranger to the majority of the women I interviewed, several of them nevertheless shared some very intimate details of their lives. In several cases they had not talked about these experiences with others and I was at times given information that women explicitly stated they did not want to appear in my work. Of course, I have respected these requests.

Furthermore, women's off-tape comments made me aware of the ethical implications of the type of disclosure that the research interview can evoke. Summerfield (2005: 58) comments on the 'proximity of the research interview to a therapeutic session' and Reinharz and Chase (2003: 81) suggest: 'it may be the very fact that the researcher is not involved in the participant's life that allows the participant the freedom to express herself in ways she might not otherwise'. Whilst these authors do offer some explanation, they do not fully address the question of what a feminist researcher should do when she is given unsettling information that does not fit neatly into her research design. Although I have referred to some of the issues women spoke about (not of course those I was requested to omit), in order to protect their anonymity, I have not attributed them directly.

In considering the ethical implications of my research, and feminist research more generally, I feel I raise more questions than can be answered. In the immediate context of this particular study I am aware of these problems but do not offer any solutions save those of ensuring the transparency of the process of my research, the acknowledgement of my place as researcher within it and a commitment to the women who gave their time to the production of feminist knowledge. Thus, I have acknowledged the limitations and inherent problems for feminist research more generally, whilst also negotiating a research practice that is best able to work within a feminist framework on a political, practical and ethical level. To strengthen my argument, I now offer an interpretation of my participants' expectations and experiences of the interview situation.

Experiencing the Research Interview

> I decided there was one thing that I decided I wasn't going to talk about and I haven't talked about it. I've skirted round and over the top of it but I haven't talked about it in any depth so I feel, you know, ok about it all. And it's been nice talking to you. (Dawn)

In pursuing my 'line of enquiry' I do not feel I coerced information out of my participants by presenting myself as a willing listener. At the end of each interview I asked my participants if there was anything else they would like to add or any questions they would like to ask me, and Dawn's final comments above indicate that researchers are given only a partial glimpse of their participants' life stories with which they later build a 'bigger picture'. Inspired by what Dawn said, and in recognition of Mary Maynard and June Purvis' (1994: 4) observation that little attention has been paid 'to the direct impact and meaning participation in a research project can have', I provide here a discussion of other comments made by interviewees. I believe this adds a valuable dimension to the research and its outcomes and offers some insight into participants' reasons for participating in an academic study.

Helen and Gina highlight two different expectations of what 'an interview' might entail:

> I didn't know what to expect when I came. Until I'd spoken to you when we arranged it, I didn't know the length of time and I didn't know whether it was a question and answer type of thing, you know? I hadn't really thought how, I mean, it's nicer this way, just to be able to talk. (Helen)

> I knew what we'd be talking about, you know, your sort of feelings about yourself and your children, yeah. (Gina)

My participants here provide two ways of conceptualising the interview situation from the perspective of the interviewee. Helen indicates the tentative expectation of a 'question and answer' interaction, which I suggest is process-focused and linked to the interpretation of the term 'interview' given earlier. In contrast, Gina's quote is content-focused; seemingly she was more attuned to the fact that the interview would be a forum in which we would talk about her feelings about motherhood and childrearing. Her background as a teacher of sociology might have impacted on Gina's understanding of the workings of some social science research. The interviews were thus experienced as a talking forum by participants which, alongside their placing of me as a mother talking to them as other mothers, meant the interviews worked very well in that they were relaxed and friendly interactions that in turn produced rich data.

The interview situation served as a cathartic experience for several women who had previously not been given space to voice their concerns and anxieties regarding what their adult children leaving home meant in their own lives. The purpose of conducting the interviews was to 'elicit and listen closely to the interviewee's life experiences' (Reinharz and Chase, 2003: 82) and the fact that I disclosed the catalyst for my research, that is, my own experience, meant that women responded to me in particular ways. Fiona for example said: 'it's nice to talk to somebody about it who understands'. This comment, alongside Helen's above and others like it, made me confident that the research met a previously unvoiced need for these women.

In their turn, of course, such comments resonate with Finch (1984) who discusses the development of trust between women in the interview situation and questions the moral implications arising from this. Finch is concerned with 'the extreme ease with which [...] a woman researcher can elicit material from other women' (Finch, 1984: 71) and the potentially exploitative nature of this interaction. She concludes by suggesting that interviewees may need protection from feminist interviewers. I would argue however that my interviews with the women were a reciprocal arrangement. They gained something valuable from our interaction inasmuch as they were able to talk openly about an issue they had until then, for the most part, suppressed. I suggest they were keenly aware that our interactions would be 'transformed' once I began my analysis. As such they were concerned I was able to work with what they gave me: 'I just hope it's been useful' (Janice); 'You'll pick out the bits you want anyway, won't you?' (Linda); 'I hope I've been able to cover fully enough the points that'll help you' (Nancy). Often women had been prepared for particular issues arising in the interview prior to our meeting: 'I've been thinking about this' (Angela); 'I was talking to somebody about this' (Lois). In the broad sense of the term then, women were aware that their participation in the research potentially rendered them 'statistics-to-be' (Oakley, 1981b: 33).

My participants also indicated a variety of reasons for their involvement in the research. All were keen to talk about their feelings regarding adult children leaving home, for example Rita said, 'when I saw your advert ... I thought, that's me, I want to talk about that!' Alongside this, some women wanted to know others responses: 'how do I compare with other mothers?' (Barbara). There was also the indication that their own experiences engendered concern for others: 'I just feel for other women now really, to be honest' (Paula); 'it's useful for mothers who are coming up to this type of thing to know the experiences of others' (Alma). Ingrid's participation instigated a desire to find out about her husband's feelings: 'I'll go home and I'll ask him how he feels now because I hadn't considered asking him how he felt. I just made an assumption about how he felt'. Still others were keen to know the outcomes of the research: 'I'd be interested to see the end results' (Rachel).

I have included this discussion here to indicate that my interviewees were actively engaged in the research process and interested in its outcomes. Moreover, although I was willing, following Oakley's (1981b) lead, to talk about my own experiences if asked, my participants were not interested in me *per se*. Instead they wanted to talk about their own experiences in order to give something to the research and to get something from it, which is precisely what I wanted them to do. The reasons for our interactions were obviously different: the aim for me, although initially instigated by a desire to answer a personal question, was because in exploring the issue I might gain academic recognition; for interviewees, it was the opportunity to talk about a lived experience. However, and as their narratives attest, during and after the interviews our interest in the subject matter converged in several ways.

Handling Data and Making Connections

> In narrating a story, social actors organize events into "episodes" which make up the plot. (Lawler, 2002: 250)

Once produced, the interview transcripts alerted me to the fact that my participants accounts of their mothering experiences did not always follow a linear pattern, for example, the beginnings of an interviewee's thoughts about a particular issue might appear on one page and be finished a few pages later, with much important meandering along the way. For this reason I chose not to use a software package to 'order' my data. Although electronic packages are proving useful in the management of larger data sets (Barry, 1998), I was not convinced that the software would retain the plot of my participants' narratives. Instead I coded the transcripts by hand and felt more secure that I was not missing some of the important threads women had woven through their narratives. I am not alone in this thinking. In their study of young people's experiences of leaving home in Norway, Spain and UK, Holdsworth and Morgan (2005: 45) generated huge data sets. They comment however that they 'decided not to make use of any of the available computer packages, preferring to familiarize ourselves with the transcripts through repeated reading'. Indeed, it was important for me to handle the interview transcripts in the way described and, like Holdsworth and Morgan, familiarise myself with the data through re-reading and making theoretical connections with women's words, as Mason describes:

> Interview methodology begins from the assumption that it is possible to investigate elements of the social by asking people to talk, and to gather or

> construct knowledge by listening to and interpreting what they say and how they say it. (Mason, 2002: 225)

Mason's observation regarding the interpretation of interview data as the basis for the construction of knowledge is in keeping with my decision to use semi-structured interviews. The research I undertook explored not only the changes to participants' relationships with their children (and others) once adult children left home, but also the continuities inherent in that leaving. It examined how each woman negotiated the shift from a proximal relationship with her child/ren towards one experienced across geographical distances, how this absence altered women's perceptions of their mothering selves in relation to the child as adult and, in consequence how motherhood was reshaped.

These issues emerged from the interviews in which the women talked about their experiences and by my listening to and then later interpreting what they told me. Although committed to representing women's experiences I was also aware of my 'obligation [as a feminist] to go beyond citing experience in order to make connections which may not be visible from the purely experiential level alone' (Maynard, 1994: 24). In the chapters that follow I will:

> Explain the grounds on which selective interpretations have been made by making explicit the process of decision making which produces the interpretation, and the logic of the method on which these decisions are based. (Holland and Ramazanoğlu, 1994: 133)

The production of thick description (Geertz, 1973) poses the quandary identified by Edwards and Ribbens (1998: 20): 'theoretical and practical dilemmas and challenges are involved when we are concerned with hearing, retaining and representing research participants' "voices"'. To make decisions regarding what to include from women's accounts and so in turn, what to disregard was a struggle. I was keenly aware that my history and personal investment would impact on the analysis. The management of this became a real balancing-act during the initial stages. Although vigilant in my attempt to engage in an empathic interpretation of women's words (Riessman, 1990) I remained alert to my own position within the research puzzle (Mason, 1996).

A number of broad categories were identified from the close reading of the transcripts and in so doing I began to control what I can only describe as the data's unruliness. As Natasha Mauthner and Andrea Doucet (1998: 121) have stated, initial findings felt 'more intuitive than anything else'. However, these early 'intuitions' did in turn formulate a structure with regard to the number of chapters, chapter headings and chapter content. This allowed space to slot relevant themes from the data under four loose chapter headings: 'Modelling Motherhood'; 'Managing the Process of Separation'; 'Post-Separation Dis/Continuities'; and 'Mothers' Futures'.

As the transcripts were revisited and I was able to immerse myself more fully in the data new understandings and meanings emerged. In consequence, I did not adhere fully to my initial structure, although three out of the four main chapter headings remained the same whilst their contents shifted. One major change was the decision to devote a chapter to issues of contact and communication between mothers and their adult children. This resulted in the replacement of 'Post-Separation Dis/Continuities' with 'Post-Separation Communication'. This change in direction provides an example of how 'qualitative research interviews are more open to pursue new themes and ideas that appear during the interview' (Christensen, 2009: 437).

As Lucy Bailey (1999: 338) found in her study of women's transition to first-time motherhood: 'a single section of a transcript might deal with a number of themes' so it was for my data so that over time, as Mauthner and Doucet (1998: 121) note the process of data analysis became 'structured, methodical, rigorous and systematic'. Continued close reading of transcripts and scrutiny of identified themes, alongside links between existing literature and women's experiences, meant the data became more manageable and the vital connections between data and theory evolved. Throughout the analysis I remained alert to Ribbens' (1994: 33) crucial question: 'how are we to conceptualise women's lives in ways that both value women's perspectives [...] yet also allow for critical insights from outside?' and I consciously strove to ensure 'outsider misinterpretations' she discusses were not imported into the analysis. I am aware, of course, that the interpretations of the interview data are my own.

As so far indicated, the themes that structured the writing emerged from the rich data generated in and produced from the semi-structured research interviews. The outcome was dependent on the narratives produced within the interview situation and are thus at the heart of my interpretation. Maynard and Purvis (1994: 6) have however argued that 'a focus on experience alone is not sufficient when conducting feminist research. [...]. Analysis of women's experiences must therefore be complemented by material sourced from other arenas'.

With the comments of the above authors in mind, my participants' experiences formulate the bedrock of the work presented here, but are only one, albeit key, aspect of its analysis. As Lawler states:

> Narratives [...] are related to the experience that people have of their lives, but *they are not transparent carriers of that experience*. Rather they are interpretive devices, through which people represent themselves, both to themselves and to others. Further, narratives do not originate with the individual: rather, they circulate culturally to provide a repertoire (though not an infinite one) from which people can produce their own stories. (Lawler, 2002: 242, my emphasis)

As Lawler indicates, narratives are produced in particular cultural and historical contexts and as such cannot be analysed without reference to wider sociocultural understandings and beliefs. Maynard (1994: 23) argues that the accounts people give of their lives 'are a construction of the events that occurred, together with an interpretation of them'. The experiences of my interviewees were embedded in a western construction of motherhood. Thus their stories of mothering and the meanings they attributed to their experiences were interpreted within, and told from, this location. This is an issue I discussed in the previous chapter and one that is developed further throughout the book. Of course, these constructions are partial and might not fully be understood by participants themselves, nor by social science researchers.

Existing theories informed interpretations made of the data, and in turn were enriched by the addition of participants' insights and experiences. As such, a dialectical engagement between the data and existing literature was created. For example, in Chapter 3, 'Modelling Motherhood', so named because of my identification of women's lack of a cultural model on which to draw at the time of their adult children's home-leaving, I searched for women's accounts of their experiences of being mothered themselves, their relationship to wider sociocultural representations of motherhood, and their experiences of mothering as praxis. Within the broad categories identified, further themes developed that ultimately shaped the chapter.

As Ribbens (1998: 28) observes in her study of mothering: 'it was striking how all these mothers seemed to hold images of what motherhood, and childhood, should be like'. She further notes how these 'were very significant in providing a framework for the ways in which mothers talked about their childrearing'. Similarly my participants' mothering was narrated from within a conceptual framework of motherhood based on theories of child development that define the goals of successful childrearing as nurturing autonomy so that the child will become a responsible and independent adult citizen. In Chapter 4, this is contrasted with my participants' experiences of separation from their adult children in order to highlight the fit and also the disjuncture between their expectations of this separation set against its lived reality. Thus the concept of hegemonic motherhood that shapes the realities of mothers' experiences until particular moments in time is exposed to highlight the rift between the concepts of autonomy and independence that adulthood is based upon and the relational aspects of mother and adult child post-separation.

At times, the data drew me towards academic literature I had not previously encountered, nor had I, at the outset of the study, considered I would drawn upon. This was so for Chapter 5, 'Post-Separation Communication'. My interviewees mothered over a period of rapid political and social change (Walkerdine et al., 2001; Harris, Charles and Davies, 2006), during which advances in technology ran alongside changes in employment and social mobility. It emerged within women's interviews that preparations and expectations of their children as adults were based upon this transformed sociocultural landscape. On leaving home, the majority of participants' children moved away from their hometown, which in its turn highlighted the importance for their mothers of contact across geographical distances. Although participants' references to technology formed only a small part of the interviews *per se*, they nevertheless emerged as key to women's ability to cope with the experience of separation from their adult children and this issue is the overarching focus of Chapter 5.

In making connections between data and existing literature, interview extracts were thus located within different theoretical frameworks. In this I follow Ribbens (1994: 45) who comments that 'what is said should always be understood in relation to the social context and cultural understandings of the individual who is speaking'. Although women's narratives were enriched by the theoretical perspectives drawn on, they remain the resource that underpins the core of the work rather than merely a starting-point for analysis. Similarities with the practices of some elements of grounded theory (Glaser and Strauss, 1967) are evident here. Ian Dey (2004: 80) comments that 'grounded theory was conceived as a way of generating theory *through* research data rather than testing ideas formulated *in advance of* data collection and analysis' (original emphases). As I have discussed, this to some extent is what occurred during my analysis, as readings of the data certainly evolved and broadened my areas of enquiry.

As Maynard (1994: 23) argues however, 'no feminist study can be politically neutral, completely inductive or solely based on grounded theory'. As I have revealed, I entered the research arena with a particular set of personal, academic and political beliefs regarding the topic of interest for my research and notions of how I should proceed. In turn, these directed the research process and ultimately impacted on how I analysed, interpreted and presented the data. Edwards and Ribbens (1998: 17) stress the importance to feminist researchers of 'claiming and asserting our interpretation'. I hope in this chapter to have made clear how I managed the balancing act these authors identify of representing my participants' 'voices' as well as my own.

Re/presenting Women's 'Voices'

Throughout the process of my study there was a continuous and reciprocal dialogue between the data and existing theoretical debates. Each enriched the other so that women's narratives and my interpretations are presented together as the final phase of analysis. I briefly discuss here the choices I made regarding how to re/present the words of the women I interviewed.

Fundamentally, extracts from my research participants' narratives are presented verbatim. The pauses in their dialogue are indicated by three dots, and I include participants' 'ums'. Significant non-verbal communications appear in square brackets, for example: [laughs] and edited extracts from quotes appear as three dots in square brackets: [...]. However, although I was vigilant in not straying from the meanings women conveyed by altering the underlying structure of their narratives (Glucksmann, 1994) I nevertheless decided to 'clean up' some of the language of the transcripts in order to present women's words 'equally'. In so doing I 'corrected' some of the language, for example, I replaced participants' 'dropped aitches'.

The underlying reason for my decision to make these changes follows Summerfield (2005: 61), who notes that 'textualised conversation offends literary rules of phrasing, grammatical construction and so on'. This is reiterated by Griffin (2005: 192), who further comments: 'we are acculturated into assuming that we speak in well formed sentences'. It was not my intention to give my participants a copy of their interview transcripts prior to my analysis in order to confirm their legitimacy (Skeggs, 1994; Summerfield, 2005). I did however present them with an outline of some of my findings, and this included extracts from their interviews.

My decision therefore to make these changes was done in order to offer a consistent approach to the presentation of the data (to both an academic and non-academic audience) and provide a 'vicarious experience for the reader' (Sandelowski, 1994: 480) and, I would add, the listener. In so doing however, my participants' voices have not been silenced although the interpretations of their narratives are of course my own. As such, at this stage of the research process I remain aware that I stand as 'the personalized interface between the expression of private meanings and their ultimate reception by the powerful audience of public knowledge production' (Ribbens, 1998: 37).

Concluding Remarks

> Reflexivity means reflecting upon and understanding our own personal, political and intellectual autobiographies as researchers and making explicit where we are located in relation to our research respondents. Reflexivity also means acknowledging the critical role we play in creating, interpreting and theorizing research data. (Mauthner and Doucet, 1998: 121)

This chapter has discussed the methodological decisions that structured my research design and influenced my choice of research methods. In explicitly stating my own location within the study, I have highlighted my ongoing connection between the methodology and the process of data production and its analysis, providing a reflexive account of the research process that, as Mauthner and Doucet imply above and further state, 'lies at the heart of feminist research' (121). In the chapters that follow, I turn to give space to my research participants' words and in so doing present my analysis and interpretation of their experiences of their adult children leaving home.

Chapter 3
Modelling Motherhood

Du Palais Tempi à Florence.

Figure 3.1 *Madonna and Child*, drawing and engraving based on the original tableau by Raphael, by Aug. Boucher Desnoyers, © British Museum

Figure 3.2   *La Pietà* © British Museum

Introduction

The juxtaposition here of Figure 3.1 and Figure 3.2 is symbolic of the main focus of this chapter. The characters in each image are the same, but they are identified in different ways. *La Pietà*[1] is an iconic image which importantly is never referred to as 'Mother and Child'; instead the mother is locked into a timeless state and is

---

1   *La Pietà*: A picture or sculpture of the Virgin Mary holding the dead body of Christ. (*Oxford English Dictionary*, 2006).

represented as in the first image, as a young woman, whilst her son is depicted as a baby in the former and an adult male in the latter image.

Marina Warner (1976: 336) observes that, in 'Marian iconography [...] the interlocking of myth and ideology is camouflaged' and later she argues that 'a Myth is a kind of story told in public, which people pass on to one another' (1994: 13). As Roland Barthes (1973: 109) also observes 'myth is a system of communication [...] a message'. In their critique of mother and child images used in advertising, Hockey and James (1993: 59) suggest that 'at the level of myth ... [the] cradling arms connote the child in its dependent relationship: as belonging to someone, as dependent'. Images of *Madonna and Child* and *La Pietà* thus convey particular meanings of what 'mother' and 'child' are, and in turn how they are understood. In these terms then, they are mythologized.

In order to unpack the mythology of the two images I suggest that whilst the mother figure of *La Pietà* might see her 'child', the onlooker perceives the figure of Christ as a dying or dead adult male figure. The child has thus undergone change – from babyhood in the first image to adulthood in the second – whilst the mother seemingly has not. The child of the first image is cradled by his mother; both her arms support him. In the second, the mother's arms are outspread; she is unable to hold/contain her child. More complexly, the adult held in a child's pose is a dead or dying rather than a living adult, raising the unimaginable thought of a living adult as 'child'; potentially the child as adult is 'dead' to the mother (and others). A paradox is thus created between the mother's perceptions of her offspring and, I would argue that of herself, as opposed to that of potential onlookers. I do not intend to discuss these two images further but introduce them into the chapter because they are iconic images of mother and child in western, Christian cultures, and are indicative of the problematic of thinking of 'mother and child' beyond the period of the child as baby, infant or pre-pubescent. They also form a link with the mother figure in Laurie Lee's novel, which I problematised in Chapter 1 and adds a further dimension to the argument I present in Chapter 5, in which the mother figure of television advertising for mobile phones makes her appearance.

Although it is possible to offer a critique of some of the myth making that underpins religious imagery, myth-breaking becomes more difficult when representations of motherhood and of mother and child proliferate in everyday settings inasmuch as the stories they tell are conveyed across wider social spaces. Woodward comments on the number of different media in which such images are to be found: 'television, soap operas and advertisements, films, magazines and novels' and observes:

> Any woman who has a baby is likely to be inundated with advice from relatives, friends and, most especially in the late twentieth century, from 'experts' – medical experts, health personnel and the promoters of products related to pregnancy and childcare. (1997: 241)

Sociocultural parameters thus dictate the practices of motherhood, placing mothers and their children within a particular time-frame; a continuum along which women's mothering is performed. The mother's life course is therefore entwined with that of the child from the latter's conception and birth. In its turn, motherhood itself is linked to notions of women's youthfulness and fertility. My interviewees often reflected that children's leaving home was a clear reminder of their own ebbing youth, particularly when accompanied by bodily changes such as the menopause (for discussions of the menopause and other bodily changes, see Goldsworthy, 1993; Greer, 1992; Hunter and O'Dea, 1997; Wadsworth and Green, 2003). It was so that nostalgia, and in some instances a longing for times past, played their part in my participants' reminiscences of their mothering experiences.

My use of the phrase 'Modelling Motherhood' is therefore deliberately ambiguous. It denotes both representations of motherhood on the one hand and doing motherhood, motherhood as activity and process, on the other. In order to fully explore the relationship between models of motherhood and mothering as praxis my participants' perceptions of mothering over time is discussed. In so doing, I shall illustrate that as my participants progressed through motherhood, only limited models existed for them to draw on, none of which took them beyond pregnancy, childbirth, the early years and the young adolescence of their children. The empirical data is threaded throughout in order to convey women's experiences of modelling motherhood over time.

Learning to Mother

As established, sociocultural representations of mother and child portray the pair in an age-bracketed state of being that figures the mother as adult and the child as her dependent. This chapter reveals how my interviewees' narratives revealed to me how they were acculturated into the dual-discourse of child*caring* and child*rearing*. This effectively engendered a paradoxical situation; on the one hand, my participants perceived themselves as providers of love, care and support for their dependent children, where closeness to the mother was translated as safety for the child, whilst on the other, they were immersed in a discourse of child development which encouraged them to nurture their children's autonomy in the push towards adult independence. The discursive structuring of motherhood and my participants' experiences of mothering were frequently experienced as contradictory.

> But you see, all these baby books and magazines and shows like Trisha, you know, they all say, 'you're having a baby'. They don't say, 'you're having a teenager'. But you are! Because it goes so quickly. They think they're getting a cute little bundle and it doesn't stay like that for more than three months ... you just don't realise when you're having this baby, what it entails. It's years and years. People don't think about the future and I'm sure I didn't either. (Linda)

In a shift away from iconic representations towards those of everyday contemporary images with which women grapple, Linda clearly outlines above how media representations and literature on motherhood are limited in their portrayal of the realities of mothering over time and in fact offer only a partial glimpse of what motherhood actually entails. Linda's observation indicates how portrayals of mothers and babies discourage mothers' (and others) thoughts beyond children's dependent state. Collectively these images impact on women's perceptions of motherhood and on themselves as mothers. Linda's brief critique references a broad sweep of cultural models of mother- and child- hoods which are exposed as limiting in the extreme. Her narrative illustrates how these images continue to mask the realities of motherhood and obscure the 'years and years' mothering involves, the transformation of the 'cute little bundle' and the mother's negation of thoughts of the future.

Images and representations thus have the power to suffuse our culture and so ourselves, they become a part of us. Following Louis Althusser (1971) Woodward (2003: 21) comments that: 'the concept of interpellation [explains] the ways in which people are recruited into the subject position by recognizing themselves – "yes that's me". Motherhood carries considerable weight as an identity, especially the image of the "good" mother'. Commenting on the 'idealism' of marriage and motherhood Gina said 'those images stay with you'. She also stated that when a woman becomes a mother, she becomes the focus of society's gaze:

> You're very aware of how judgmental people are as to what you're doing with your life and whether you're making the right choices and dealing with things properly. [...] I think our society is very judgmental and you do feel those pressures, mothers especially, about what you should and shouldn't be doing with your children. (Gina)

There is little wonder, then, that feeling judged by society and being members of that same society, women as mothers should attempt to live up to the cultural representations of motherhood they encounter. In her research into women's experiences of the transition to first-time motherhood, for example, Tina Miller (2005) found that the new mothers she interviewed felt unable to voice the difficulties they encountered because they were expected, and expected themselves, to 'naturally' embrace their new status.

In consequence, and as Miller observes, women's assumed natural capacities for love and care placed them in a precarious position if/when they did not immediately feel 'naturally loving' towards their infants. As Miller argues, 'this self-silencing only serves to further perpetuate the old myths of motherhood' (138). Miller's argument lends itself to my own, as my participants' feelings regarding their children's emerging adulthood were effectively silenced by the discourse of independence and 'letting go', in which the purpose of their mothering practices was embedded. I discuss the purpose of mothering later in the chapter and return to women's self-silencing in Chapter 4, where it formulates an important strand within women's experiences of separation from their adult children.

Limited models of mother and child act on the understandings and expectations of women contemplating motherhood. Indeed, from interviewees' narratives it was not difficult to ascertain how their aspirations for motherhood were linked to a specific set of accepted practices as the norm for them as younger women. The majority of the women (18) left home to marry. As Gina reflected, 'there's an idealism that's built into you, that you get a partner and you get married and you spend the rest of your life together'. Indeed, all twenty-five women said that when younger they expected to become wives and mothers. Their narratives resonate with the findings of Jones et al. (2006: 378) whose participants 'follow[ed] a "traditional" ordering of life events, on a trajectory over which they had little control'.

Although Jones and her colleagues attribute their findings to working-class life course trajectories, this was a common experience of my participants regardless of their class positioning: 'it was my ambition to be a mother ... marriage was a way of having children' (Bridget); 'I always wanted to be a mother. I didn't want a career and I couldn't see myself as anything but being married and having children' (Serena). Similar expectations were common when participants reflected on their younger selves. As such participants' future aspirations as young women cut across their class and ethnic differences. As Judith and Lois quoted below confirm, the destiny for my participants as daughters was to become wives and mothers, and this was often nurtured during their early childhood:

> I was always brought up with it. I did the baking every week from being about
> 9 years old, I did the baking every week, um. I always helped with the ironing. I
> was a perfect housewife even before I left home at 21, you know? (Judith)

> When I was a little girl, my whole life revolved around dolls and then, when
> my little brothers and sisters were born, I was like their mum. So it was always
> something I really, really wanted to do. (Lois)

Interviewees' reflections on their lives as younger women reveal 'a deep-rooted desire to take time out to have children, to stay at home to rear them and to be "looked after" [by a husband]' (Walkerdine et al., 2001: 81). As young women growing up in post-World War II nuclear families in the North East of England in the 1950s and 1960s my participants' thoughts about the future were entangled within a prevailing discourse that 'powerfully formed feminine subjectivities' (Walkerdine et al., 2001: 81), that is, the ideal of a heterosexual relationship, marriage and children. These aspirations are linked to issues of time and place and the limitations of opportunity women were presented with. During the time that my interviewees became mothers, for example, it was widely expected that 'women [would] experience a period of full-time work within the home and financial dependence after the birth of a child' (Richardson, 1993: 24).

In their discussion of the proliferation of self-help manuals for all areas of life, Stevi Jackson and Sue Scott (1997: 561) comment that 'being told how to do what supposedly comes naturally is a feature of much advice for women'. This in turn points to the socioculturally constructed dimension of women's 'natural' ability to mother their children. As Woodward (1997: 242) observes, 'motherhood is taken for granted as an identity for women, and as such is constructed within naturalistic discourse as a biological role where motherhood is seen as the distinguishing female characteristic'. Some interviewees drew on a similarly naturalised/ essentialist discourse when they talked about their entry into motherhood. Serena, for example, said, 'I just think you're complete then, really. [...] everything sort of seemed to come naturally, like the giving birth and the breastfeeding' and Denise commented, 'it's what you're here for as a woman, isn't it, to have children'.

In discussing the concept of the 'ideal mother' Woodward (1997: 243) comments that 'motherhood is not only about having children, it is about having a mother; that is, about being mothered too'. Several interviewees deferred to their own mothers' practices inasmuch as their own experiences of being mothered informed their own mothering during their children's early years. As Jones et al. (2006: 383) observe: 'some parents hang on to fixed beliefs derived from their own upbringing'. In my study, Ingrid identified her own experience of being mothered as the model she adhered once she became a mother:

> You expect at that early age, in your twenties, that your parents are the perfect parents and that, if you do things the way they did, because you've turned out alright, your kids'll turn out alright. I guess that's a little bit of what's happened to me. Rather than thinking, well no, times are moving on and things have changed and children want different things and I have to move along with that, I guess I haven't. But I think that's what makes me feel as though I haven't been the best mother, you know? Because I haven't moved on. (Ingrid)

Ingrid perceived that her own resistance to make changes alongside the changing times she articulates had a negative impact on her mothering; she felt she had not fulfilled the role of mother as well as she might. She expressed regret at having steadfastly adhered to a particular model of mothering which she told me had impacted negatively on her relationship with her daughter: 'there was an issue when she was a teenager when she went and talked to one of her brother's female friends and I was aggrieved at that. I thought, oh yes, I am like my mother, you know?' The circumstances of Ingrid's entry into motherhood throw some light onto the choices she was able to make; she became the step-mother of two young children at the age of 22, at which time she also gave birth to her son. One can assume therefore that her ability to create an individual model of motherhood seemingly more appropriate to changing times was limited by her lived circumstances.

Maggie described her own mother as 'all-consuming' and told me their relationship was based on her mother's 'emotional blackmail'. She thus vehemently opposed the model of motherhood she experienced as a daughter: 'my role as a mother has been completely defined by what my mother was like. [...] everything that I thought she was wrong in, I have changed' (Maggie). Other women also consciously mothered differently from their own mothers, particularly in their approach to their children's teenage years. Both Judith and Janice, for example, indicated how they drew on experiences from their own youth to inform the way they would respond to the same period in their children's lives:

> I think being a mother has made me look at things in a different way, because I don't want my sons to feel like I felt. I always felt like I had to do everything the right way, because if I didn't do it the right way I would upset my mum. (Judith)

> I've tried to think, um, don't do as what my mother did, you know, in things like, well, what happened when I was a child. So I've always given them their freedom, their privacy and got them to sort of speak openly about most of the things. (Janice)

Denise also revealed her reluctance to draw on her own experience of being mothered when a teenager to assist her in the mothering of her daughter's turbulent teenage years: 'your mother would just say "lock her up and don't let her out again until she's 20", you know? …It doesn't work like that anymore.' So being without advice or reluctant to follow that of their mothers, women called on their own experiences as teenagers to inform their mothering practices during children's teenage years:

> You never know whether you're doing the right thing … Well, nobody puts a training manual out for it, do they? You just have to go by your own best instincts and, you know, think, what did I feel like when I was that age? (Judith)

The cultural models of be(com)ing a mother for the women I interviewed were further shaped by women's actual experiences of mothering their children. Effectively, they learned how to be mothers from 'doing' their mothering. All of my participants had more than one child and as such, provided examples in the interviews of learning to mother subsequent children from the hands-on experience of first-time mothering:

> I've learnt much more through being a mum of my second child than I did through my first son. But I always say I think your first children are guinea pigs a little bit. […] Because I had to learn how to be a mum with him, but I kind of knew how to be a mum when the second one came along and I could kind of look back … So I did learn that from the two different experiences of being … two different motherhoods, really, in lots of ways they were. (Lois)

> I think the experience you've had with one affects your experience with, you know … You think you might've got it right by the time you've had about six [laughs]. (Denise)

Exposure to representations of motherhood and their own experiences of being mothered informed this group of women's decision-making and the vision they adopted for themselves as mothers. Although five influences on women's mothering practices can be identified from the discussion so far: mother and child images; expert advice; societal expectations; interviewees' own history of being mothered; and the 'doing' of mothering, it was evident from my interviews with them that as my participants moved through their mothering years, many of them were without appropriate reference points from which to draw advice and support. This became particularly acute when their children left home.

What has been illustrated so far is that when women embarked upon motherhood in the 1970s and 1980s they were exposed to and had experienced particular models of mothering. At the same time, they responded to varying degrees both to the social and political climate in which they lived, and the dependent children they produced. What they took with them to inform their motherhoods and also what they left behind highlights how models of motherhood emerged from different arenas and how, in consequence motherhood was at times a contradictory and perplexing experience. As young mothers, they were immersed within the rhetoric of childcare 'experts' of all persuasions, whilst simultaneously living within their own realities of motherhood and ultimately making, or attempting to make, their own choices on how to mother. What is clear is that as this group of women progressed through their childrearing years, there was an increasing absence of models on which they could build that shifted them forward in time alongside their children.

Mothers, Children and Time

> Parents are unified in their sense that children 'grow up so quickly' and are no
> sooner walking than they are asking to borrow the car! (Jenks, 1996a: 38)

When interviewees reflected on their experiences of mothering many responded in the way Jenks describes. Children's childhoods were perceived to have passed very quickly, in some instances enforcing a realisation of their own ageing and transformation of self-perception.

> Seems like it's gone really fast, yeah. I was saying the other day, um, it doesn't
> seem two minutes ago since I was twenty and I was having the children. Now
> I'm 45 and I've got, er, three. One of which is married, one of which is pregnant,
> different one. It just seems to change my whole outlook really. I'm my mum all
> of a sudden, know what I mean? (Dawn)

When tackling the question 'how do we know that we are ageing?' Hockey and James (2003: 34) suggest that 'ageing is a process which is imperceptible to the self. It takes place behind our backs, creeps up on us and is not therefore easily amenable to self-articulation'. On an individual basis this might well be so, and it is possible that the subtlety of what ageing means to those of us who are mothers might 'creep up' over the time of our children's growing years and culminate in their becoming adults and our becoming the mothers of adult children and thus, as Dawn asserts in her quote, older women. The transformation of the child to adult therefore acts as a marker of age/ing for the mother.

What emerged from the interview data was that for much of their children's childhoods, participants seemed to have existed outside of time, in a state that foreclosed considerations of ageing. A feeling commonly evoked in my participants' reflections was that mothering and childhood for them seemed never-ending. When asked if they thought about their children growing up and leaving home during their children's early years, or if they considered what their children might do as adults, they revealed a lack of thought. The issue of children getting older and going to school and beyond, for example, held an unreal quality. Living in the 'here-and-now' as seemingly demanded by mothering a small child occluded thoughts of the future, in relation to child and mother alike:

I can remember funny things from when they were really little, like not being able to imagine that they, one day, would be going to school, um, they were so little and that day seemed so far off that, well, it can't be real! (Bridget)

You were just coping at the time with what you had to cope with and you didn't really look to them being in their twenties and what they would do. (Janice)

I'm sure I did think about them growing up when they were little. Um, it seemed such a long way ahead. (Nancy)

It never occurred to me. You just think it's going to go on forever. (Frances)

These extracts from women's interviews are indicative of the feelings of timelessness generated by women's time *in* motherhood, discussed in conjunction with the concept of 'time *in* childhood' (James and Prout, 1997) in the introductory chapter. The model of motherhood to which participants adhered when children were in their early years did not encourage mothers to look towards the future. As such, mothering was experienced as a state of *being* rather than as a process of *becoming*. This anchored the women in a particular concept of time, or timelessness, which was then disrupted when their children grew up and left home.

As children 'got older' many of my interviewees experienced a rift in their life course, which enforced changed perceptions of themselves and of their children. Vanessa described this period as 'the beginnings of not being needed. That beginning feeling that actually gets more and more as you get older'. Changes in the life course can then have a dramatic effect on an individual's perception of self and, as Hockey and James (2003: 39) argue, these might be 'experienced as profound, having not only a deep emotional and personal significance but also radically altering the course and direction of their lives'. Clearly, as women's narratives highlight, such transitions do not have to be 'your own', nor anything extraordinary. Sally's commentary below provides an example of how this might happen, with the ordinariness of a familiar and expected event in the life course of her children running alongside the unexpected feelings it created for her:

> What I did find strange was when they actually left school. When the youngest left school it made me realise that they'd both grown up and that's when you realise that they're going to be doing other things and leaving home.
> [...]
> You don't really think that far in advance. It's only when they get to secondary school, um. I never really did with my eldest son. It was just when the youngest one was going to be leaving and then you lose all your ties with the school and, you know, things change completely. Your involvement with the school is just cut off, you know? (Sally)

Sally says she did not think ahead whilst mothering her young sons. She comments on two radical changes experienced herself because of changes in her children's daily lives. Firstly the realisation that her sons were growing up and approaching the time when they would be leaving home, and secondly that she would no longer be involved in the day-to-day routines of school-life, which had until then structured her sons' lives and so in consequence, her own. The child's transition out of compulsory schooling is therefore another point where the occlusion of mothers' life course experience becomes apparent. Catherine Hughes (2002: 150) argues that linear time 'shapes our material realities and our understanding of selfhood and development'. As established so far, child*rearing* is couched in terms of development and becoming adult (Brannen et al., 1996; James and Prout, 1997; Mayall, 2002).

However, although Sally's life as a mother of two sons was conducted along a linear path, she seemingly lived outside of this conceptual framework; she experienced her re-entry into the linear time of her children's lives as 'strange'. Many interviewees provided similar vignettes concerning an apparent surprise at their children's grown-up status that effectively confirmed their children as potential adults who would be leaving home. As Hughes further notes, 'child and adult development is charted predominantly in terms of chronological age' (140) and although this developmental model of the life course was expected of their children, and indeed nurtured by them, children's seemingly 'sudden' achievement of adulthood evoked feelings of uncertainty in each woman's sense of self-as-mother.

These data reveal a complex nexus of women's experiences of time: being immersed in the everydayness of motherhood and so seemingly existing outside of linear time; the experience of living life in 'slow motion', so that time passes without one being aware; and a sudden acceleration of time experienced at the point of the child's emerging adulthood and home-leaving. Furthermore, interview narratives incorporate women's looking forward from and back to their children's childhoods that indicate they occupied/experienced different concepts of time simultaneously. In her discussion of Julia Kristeva's (1981) concept of 'women's time', Moi comments:

> According to Kristeva female subjectivity would seem to be linked both to *cyclical* time (repetition) and to *monumental* time (eternity), at least in so far as both are ways of conceptualizing time from the perspective of motherhood and reproduction. The time of history, however, can be characterized as *linear* time: time as project, teleology, departure, progression and arrival. (Moi, 1989: 187, original emphases)

Kristeva's concept of time thus illuminates how mothers' time and linear time might conflict with one another during particular phases of the mother's life course. It adds to my proposal that women's time *in* motherhood is performed within a conflicting and contradictory set of models of child *caring* (cyclical time) and child *rearing* (linear time), and that these are further confused by representations of mother and child (monumental time). McNay (2000: 113) talks of 'multiple levels of temporality [...] that are simultaneously lived but not reconcilable'. Very often my interviewees talked of experiences which shifted them 'back in time' as they identified practices they performed for their children as fitting the model of mothering they had 'lost' when children left home. Sandra's daughter, for example, had a period of illness and returned to Sandra's home to recover: 'she came round here and, you know, I was doing all the comfort things and I was thinking, this is wonderful, *I'm back to where I was*'. Effectively, Sandra 'returned' to a time that fitted her concept of motherhood through mothering a child who was dependent upon her care. This leads me to elaborate on my participants' perceptions of the purpose of their mothering.

The Purpose of Mothering

Women's aspirations for their children as adults were often shaped by reflections on the restrictions they perceived had governed their own lives as daughters. For many, their experiences of growing up resulted in them working towards ensuring their children were given wider opportunities and different life chances from those they experienced themselves:

> I left home to get married, yes. I think that's why I've tried to be a bit more, um, involve the boys in other things, because my parents brought me up in a very sheltered environment. We didn't really mix with anyone else apart from just family which, to me you know, once you go out in the big wide world, you're terrified of everything around you because you don't know how to cope with anything. (Sally)

Wanting 'something different' for children recurred throughout the interviews with my research participants. As Bridget said, 'I would hate for my children to feel in any way tied, or that they've got to live their lives around my aspirations, um, in that way. I do want them to be free to do their own thing'. The notion of 'freedom' and adult children 'doing their own thing' was often stated by interviewees and this invariably involved their daughters and sons leaving the family home and, in the majority of cases, hometown, to pursue their life goals and interests. The aspirations of some of the women for their children were built on feelings of having 'missed out' themselves as younger women. As Dawn said of her daughters, 'the only thing I ever wanted was for them to do all that I didn't'. Similarly Rita said:

> I wanted my daughter to do all the things I hadn't done and I wish, in a way, I had done. I mean, it was different in the seventies, the fact that you went to school, got your O-levels and got a job and went to work.
> [...]
> We were a very poor family and they didn't encourage me at all to go to university. It wasn't their thing, you know? They're just working-class people and, um, so I went straight from school to work, met my husband after two years, then married at 20. (Rita)

Issues from women's own lives thus fuelled their resolve to work towards something else for their children. For some women this involved an aversion to making their children 'feel' like they did themselves towards their own mothers, who were regarded as having placed unrealistic demands upon them as daughters. Judith for example said, 'I've been dictated to all my life by my mother'. In rejecting the model of motherhood their own mothers performed, many women worked towards ensuring children did not feel in any way responsible for meeting their mothers' needs even though this involved the paradox that wanting children to have different experiences also constitutes a maternal aspiration:

> I've never wanted my kids to feel as though they've got to do anything, if you know what I mean. You know, my mum looked after my grandma and my grandma looked after her mother, so. Like, my mother thinks, right, well it's my turn now to be looked after. Whereas I don't have that attitude. I think that'll stop anyway, because I think society's changed. (Denise)

Although the quality of the relationship between mothers and daughters of earlier generations was often a pre-requisite for elder care (Finch, 1989; Finch and Groves, 1983; Finch and Mason, 1993) there was a pronounced shift in the perception of care and family obligation amongst my interviewees; as Denise said, 'society's changed'.

Each of my participants was aware they had mothered over a period of rapid political and social change (Walkerdine et al., 2001). As previously indicated there were profound differences in their situations at the time of the interviews from when they started out as mothers. Alma's comparison between her own and her daughters' experiences confirmed her perception of the shift in opportunities for women in present day UK: 'my girls are having a completely different experience to my own. They're not waiting until they get too old to do something about it! [laughs]'. As Ingrid observed:

> Motherhood's changing though, it's bound to change. Children are changing, we're changing. I mean, children become mothers and each time there's a movement on, something changes. (Ingrid)

Ingrid's comments acknowledge the impact of social and historical shifts on mothering as praxis. As Woodward (2003: 26) observes, 'there is no fixity in maternal identity, and changing times and changing social, economic, political and cultural circumstances can produce new figures'. Indeed, the teenage and young-adult years of participants' children were experienced in very different ways from their mothers'. Thus women's child*rearing* was shaped both by their response to wider changes in society and so in turn by consciously mothering differently from their own experiences of being mothered:

> My sister and I didn't go to university, we stayed … we did all sorts of stuff but we didn't go to university because my mum didn't want us to go, um. I had a place at a training college and my mum said, it was only in Huddersfield, and she said, 'oh, what will I do without you?' I was very much the sensible, practical, older daughter who looked after her emotional needs, you see. (Angela)

Angela's experience of her mother's wish for her to remain at home (until she married and left home to live around the corner from her parental home) was implicit in the narratives of other interviewees; their experiences as daughters impacted on their desires for their own daughters', and sons', lives to be different:

> I'd always thought that they would leave home. I'd always planned that they would. I just think they're only lent, you know, for a certain time. I didn't want them to be at home forever. I just wanted to bring them up as good as I could, to be independent really, and stand on their own two feet, really. (Serena)

Serena's idea of children 'being on loan', indicates her view of the child as a separate individual and potential adult in a tenuous relation to the mother. Judith also spoke of her sons as 'on loan' and the notion of 'standing on their own two feet' was drawn on several times during my interviews with the women. They often perceived there to be a cut-off point for childhood and a time when children would leave the family home as independent adults. Seemingly for my interviewees then, children's journey towards adulthood was narrated as a 'natural' progression, as Maggie said, 'children are looked after by other people, children go to school, children go, you know?'

Children's leaving was often linked to age and women called on culturally recognised age-transitions as signposts for their own children's adult status. As established, our contemporary notions of childhood are immersed in issues of reaching the next st/age of development (Brannen, 1996; Jaggar, 1983; James and Prout, 1997; Lawler, 2000; Mayall, 1996, 2002) and women highlighted their immersion in this discourse; their children's independence was a remarkably resilient theme within my research participants' narratives. In consequence it is safe to suggest that within a contemporary UK context nurturing children's independence remains a major purpose of motherhood.

Preparing children for adult life was considered, as Alma said, to be 'part of being, um, a good parent. You're supposed to be able to prepare your children for life away from you'. Rita's daughter had left for university and although Rita told me she missed her daughter desperately, she perceived her achievement of adulthood would more easily occur away from the family home. This impacted on her thoughts regarding her younger child's future: 'I still want him to go away and have that experience of living away from home and actually, um, I think it would make him grow up a bit'. Similarly, Heather said of her four sons: 'the experience of going away to university is something that you can't give them if they stay at home'.

That their children were now perceived to be autonomous individuals with responsibility for themselves, thus meeting the ideal of western citizenship, was evident in a number of my participants' narratives:

> You know, I really believe that once they get to eighteen, they're classed by the world as an adult so therefore it's up to them, isn't it? It's up to them what they do. (Sandra)

> My husband says, 'he's twenty-one now, so we've done what we needed to do, really. We've got him to adulthood and he's safe and sound and well. He's set up, he's got a car'. So I think in that way, he sort of thinks, job done! Well, not quite job done but I think, in a way, we've succeeded at least, you know, and in a sense there is a relief we're not responsible for him anymore. (Barbara)

Sandra objectively describes the sociocultural transition from child- to adulthood, and both she and Barbara attach a linear trajectory to the life course of their children. Thus emerging adulthood is articulated as an age-transition; the end of dependent childhood and a beginning of their independence as adults. All of my interviewees felt responsible for ensuring their children would be able to cope in the outside world. As Sandra said: 'you know you've done a good job if they do go, don't you?'

Nevertheless, for many of my participants, the anticipation of children's pending home-leaving was coupled with feelings of anxiety. Bridget for example said: 'I've been dreading it for ages … even though I knew it was going to happen'. Fiona was equally alarmed by thoughts of her son's leaving and yet clearly perceived his future involved leaving home to go to university and that her responsibility as a mother was to ensure that this was achieved:

> My whole aim, I mean, all the way through him being at school and everything, I knew he was going to go away to university, you know? That was the whole … the whole purpose of … You raise your children to leave home, don't you? Um, bring them up to be considerate with other people and to live with other people and be happy and successful. (Fiona)

Even though women's childrearing was couched in a discourse of independence, and this was perceived to be achieved when children left home, many of my interviewees' experiences of this time were suffused with mixed emotions and confused meanings regarding their children's status. As Janice said, 'it was like your little boy is now this individual, but you want them to be that, it's not like you don't want them [to be]'. Similarly, although she earlier drew on an age-transition as an indicator of adulthood *per se*, Sandra also articulated the confusion she experienced when she left her son at university for the first time:

> I think it's just the fact that, yes, they are an adult now, aren't they? Because, even when they turn eighteen, they're still your child and it's difficult to class them as an adult, yeah, it's hard to … view them in that way, I think. […] And I was crying for myself, because I didn't have him anymore. (Sandra)

Sandra said she was crying for herself and what she felt she had lost. She found it difficult to perceive her son as adult although he had reached the age of eighteen, the culturally recognised age of transition she earlier articulated; by her previous reckoning, he would now be viewed by the rest of society as 'adult' not 'child'.

The move from the home to a new environment sometimes enforced a shift in women's perceptions of their offspring from child to adult:

> We dropped all his stuff off and we went out for lunch and he just morphed from a boy to a young man within the space of about thirty seconds. […] He stood up straight and he changed from the boy to the young man. It was almost as if something in his head was saying, 'you're away, you're growing up, you've got everything you want now'. (Maggie)

> She was so … vulnerable, you know? You saw her in a different light to how you'd seen her ever before. She always had this barrier, you know, this bitch-like, teenage, awful thing. But then you saw her as … as sort of a person … That sounds awful, but as a person rather than a daughter, you know? Rather than someone who was trying to make your life hell, you saw her as someone who was upset about it. (Denise)

For Maggie and Denise, the transition from child- to adult-hood was voiced in seemingly gendered terms; autonomy and freedom for Maggie's son, and the vulnerability and being 'upset about' the separation for Denise's daughter. Even so, each woman responded to her child as 'adult' differently from her child as 'child', perceiving them in different terms which seemingly happened in an instant. The child's move out of the home and into another place thus signalled a change in mothers' perceptions of their children.

Clearly however, and although occupying the role of mother and performing practices from within that role was understood and undertaken as nurturing their children's independence, many of my participants had not envisaged what their children's transition to adulthood might mean *in their own lives*. I explore women's experiences of separation from their children in more detail in the next chapter. My purpose here is to highlight how several of my participants did not connect the mothering of their children to adulthood with what this might mean for them as mothers. In some instances, for example, the child's leaving was a signal that motherhood itself had ended:

> You know that's the way it should be, um, but that's it, your job's over, isn't it?
> Your job as a mum is just … finished. You know that you're there whenever
> they need you, um, and if they've got any problems or anything, you know,
> they phone you up and whatever but … basically, you know, your job's finished
> because they're looking after themselves now and *you stop feeling like a mum*.
> (Sandra)

Clearly, and as her previous statements also attest, the model of motherhood Sandra practised was built upon the concept of caring for a dependent child; this made her 'feel like' a mother. Even though she expressed her availability to him after he left she experienced a shift in her identity from mother to not-mother. Changes in children's lives therefore acted as a catalyst for potential change in women's own. In Sandra's case, this transition limited her input into her son's life once she perceived he had become adult, signalling for her the end of motherhood as she understood it. Gina highlighted her realisation that in attending to her children's needs throughout her childrearing years she had occluded consideration of her own:

> I think as a mum, you spend so many years doing things for everybody else
> and sacrificing maybe things that you would like to do or should've done for
> yourself. (Gina)

This in turn points to the suppression of women's needs by the all-consuming nature of the mothering practices women are encouraged to adopt. On reflection, Gina felt she sacrificed her own desires in favour of those of her daughters. The circumstances in which she reared her children had some impact here as Gina mothered alone for the ten years preceding her eldest daughter's home-leaving. She infers that she should have spent some time meeting her own needs and pursuing her own interests and this was partially due to her awareness that her children would, eventually, both leave home. As she later commented:

> You always know that your children are going to grow up and leave home but you never really ... Well I've never really given it a tremendous amount of thought as to how it's going to impact on my life. (Gina)

Stating that they always knew children would grow up and leave home was common across the interview data. Clearly, my participants perceived that their purpose as mothers was to nurture their children to a particular point in their lives and ensure they were able to cope in the world beyond the home. As Gina shows, this was undertaken to the exclusion of thoughts about *their own* futures. For many women the seemingly ordinary and everyday occurrence of young people leaving home had a significant and unanticipated impact on their own lives.

Established so far in this chapter is that women's lived experiences of mothering are often in tension with sociocultural representations and models of motherhood. Alongside this, women's compliance with and resistance to the mothering experienced during their own upbringings, meant that in the case of my interviewees at least, individual models of motherhood were constructed by drawing on a mixture of the contradictory elements provided by cultural representations of motherhood, their own experiences of being mothered, and the 'doing' of mothering itself. Julia Brannen and her colleagues comment on the perceived role of parents as follows:

> To guide and to be seen to guide rather than to control children; they should regard it as 'good' to let go of their teenage children, and to give them space in which to create adult identities and take up their individual rights of citizenship. By contrast, there are no exit rituals for parents as they leave behind their more onerous responsibilities as parents. (Brannen, Dodd, Oakley and Storey, 1994: 136)

The transition from child-to-adult is interpreted by Brannen et al. as symbolic of the parents' exit from the ties of responsibility for their dependent children. Later chapters discuss further whether/how my own research participants were able to let go of the responsibilities they identified as part of their mothering. For now, I want to highlight how the lack of ritual for parents that these authors comment upon has the potential to fix them, and more specifically for my argument, mothers, within a particular model of parent/motherhood so that when change occurs in their children's lives, for example leaving home, change in the mother's life is not acknowledged. As my interviewee Vanessa said, 'nobody tells you about that bit'.

Several women talked to me about children's changed behaviour and a mis-match of opinions between themselves and their teenage children that had preceded their home-leaving. As Allatt (1996: 133) observes, 'threats to the parental ... meanings of home appear most forcibly at those transitional points of the life course when the older adolescent hovers between dependence and independence'. Vanessa indicated that her sense of home was threatened as she found it difficult to come to terms with her daughters' decision-making when it differed from her own; perhaps finding it hard to accept their emerging independence, even though she strongly articulated this as the goal of her mothering. During her daughters' pre-school and early years, for example, she adopted the Montessori educational approach, which advocates children making discoveries for themselves: 'you let the child become the man [*sic*] sort of thing' (Vanessa) (see www.montessori.co.uk for a discussion of this educational philosophy). Nevertheless, as her growing daughters more firmly asserted their choices of lifestyle and opinion, Vanessa experienced uncertainty in her sense of self-as-mother (Miller, 2005):

> There's, you know, a chipping away when they're growing up, of a lot of things that you've done for years, and thought they liked for years. Suddenly they're changing their minds and making decisions on things, um, that they've actually tried from new and they liked and replaced. It made me think, god, what have I wasted my time doing this for? You know? Was I doing this and they really didn't like it at the time? That sort of thing [laughs]. (Vanessa)

Similarly, children leaving to live in their own homes created mixed emotions and an element of unrest for some of the women I spoke to:

> She said, 'no, I do my own washing at home', you know? And that was 'at home' ... And I felt a little bit, I don't know, sad really. Sad but glad, you know, mixed with ... Glad that she was responsible but sad that you felt that that was the end. That she's no longer my responsibility in a way, really, you know? (Denise)

Although mothers' nurturing of children's independence was highlighted by my participants as the purpose of their mothering, and independent living the desired outcome for their children, many of their narratives revealed how they continued to cling to the notion of motherhood in terms of caring for and meeting their children's needs. Thus women grappled with two conflicting views. They perceived their children to be adults taking their place in society, whilst simultaneously they lived with an image of their children as continually dependent upon them, highlighting the contradictory discourse of child- *rearing* and *caring* in which the western concept of motherhood is immersed. Participants' dependency on the model of the child-as-dependent acted as an affirmation of their own motherhood identities. In turn their narratives reinforce my argument regarding the inadequacy of the models of mother and child currently promoted and endorsed in contemporary images and child development discourse.

Children's assertions of independence were translated by my participants as a rejection of, or less dependency upon, maternal activities and in some instances, women were excluded from key phases of their children's lives and western family celebrations that mark child to adult transitions, the 'exit rituals' Brannen et al. (1994) allude to. For example, Dawn did not attend her daughter's wedding because she was married in America and Dawn was unable to travel there. This profoundly affected they way she was able to perceive her daughter's new status: 'I don't feel that she's married … It's strange, she's still my little girl'. Rachel too was denied the celebration of her daughter's culturally recognised age-transition to adulthood:

> Um, it was quite difficult. I wanted to have a birthday party for her eighteenth and she didn't. She decided she didn't want to have one and I was really very hurt, very disappointed. I thought, oh, I want to celebrate that I was there too! You know? I was there too and I had you! (Rachel)

Secondary, or default, transitions such as becoming the mother of a married woman (and a mother-in-law) or the mother of an adult, not child, are here unmarked by formal ritual, rendering Dawn and Rachel unable to publicly embrace their own transformed status. Possibly in consequence for Dawn, her daughter remained locked in a state of childhood. Granting children freedom might then effectively exclude mothers (and others) from aspects of children's lives as adults. As such, the loss at these times and the ability to cope with such exclusions might prove both difficult and perplexing. It was clear from the interviews that for a significant number of my participants, children's independent and now-adult status cultivated an element of uncertainty in the otherwise 'secure' identity of 'mother' they had, until that time, inhabited.

Meeting their children's needs was undoubtedly how my interviewees perceived their motherhood role. Being caught up in this discourse therefore subsumed their own interests should they differ from those of their children. As Anne Woollett and Ann Phoenix have commented:

> The invisibility of mothers in much psychological work is probably linked with the lack of a conceptual framework for analysing mothers' feelings and experiences as distinct from those of their children. It is not surprising, then, that conceptualizations of motherhood and of good mothering merely reflect ideas about children. What children are considered to need for development is generalized to define good mothering. (Woollett and Phoenix, 1991: 40)

Similarly, as Lawler (2000: 133) argues, mothers are responsible for developing the 'good self' of the child. As she states: 'in nurturing the child's "self", the mother's self threatens to disappear'. In these accounts, then, the good mother nurtures the good child, yet remains invisible in this process. Once their 'good children' became adults however, meeting their needs was an aspect of mothering that women had to re-negotiate. This was particularly so when their daughters and sons left home.

This chapter has pursued familial interactions inherent in the practices of mothering over time. In so doing, it has attempted to make mothers more visible in children's lives as adults. I suggest that if, as Allatt (1996: 135) concludes, 'parents are the archivists of identity' for their children, then child-caring and - rearing practices are key to the identities of their parents, and more importantly here, to that of mother. I suggest that these practices continue to lock women into particular models of mother and child, a point from which the mother might have difficulty in articulating her own desires (Lawler, 1999, 2000; Woollett and Phoenix, 1991). Vanessa interpreted a mother's commitment to her children's needs as follows:

> If you're going to be a good mum, you have to consider someone else's wants, needs, desires before your own. You're not suppressing it, you're just putting someone else first and later, if you've got time, you can sort yourself out, after you've done everything for everyone else. Often you don't have time to do that so that puts it on hold. I think it's an automatic response. That a mother thinks that this is the priority, that's the most important thing, to sort out somebody else's needs and desires. What you want is not important. (Vanessa)

Evident in my interviewees' narratives was a strong feeling that giving things up for their children was the right thing for mothers to do. They either forfeited their claim on having their own needs met via an 'automatic response' to meeting the needs of others, as Vanessa clearly indicates, or perceived that their own needs changed in line with their children's: 'you've got to give up things for your children, haven't you? You must, it's the way of the world. You don't give it up really, the children become more important, don't they?' (Frances). Both women adhere to 'expert' childcare advice literature that was available during their early mothering years (Jolly, 1986; Leach, 1977, 1994; Spock, 1968; Stoppard, 1983. See Marshall, 1991; Richardson, 1993; Sunderland, 2006 for critiques of childcare 'expert' texts).

Although now the mothers of adult children and so perceived by others if not by themselves, as less responsible for their children and more able to make their own choices, my participants nevertheless continued to feel accountable for meeting their children's needs. In considering how meeting children's needs might impact on women's lives over the time they mothered, Lawler has argued:

> If the (age category) 'child' has needs which it is the mother's responsibility to meet, the relationship between mother and child can be structured by these needs and this responsibility, so that even relationships between mothers and adult children are constituted in terms of what the child needs and what the mother should provide. (Lawler, 2000: 4)

Lawler found that a discourse of children's needs permeated her participants' practices; as children grew up the relationships between mothers and their children were shaped through the formers' continued meeting of the needs of the latter. The same was true for my research participants; each one made it clear that she would always be there for her child in times of need although these were not assumed to have remained static in some instances. Maggie, for example, reflected on how her children's needs transformed over time, changing the way she responded:

> I'm not saying that the children don't need me, that need's changed. They needed me when they were younger, physically, for their survival. As they got older ... their need has, I suppose, um, their need for me has been, yeah, different, um, and what I hope to have achieved eventually is that they've always got me in the background, that they're not being overwhelmed by my presence, by my interference, but no matter what they do, or what they want to do, there's always somebody supporting them, in that role. (Maggie)

I discussed earlier the concept of 'being there' in relation to women's early mothering practices and commented that it was dependent upon the proximity of mother and child, which is an element of the mother/child relationship that is disrupted when children leave home. Ribbens McCarthy and Edwards (2002: 210) further suggest that the notion of being there 'may define a key aspect of caring'. In Maggie's case, the concept of 'being there' clearly emerged as a metaphorical bridge between her and her children. This maintained the mother/child relationship across time and space once children left home. Sandra also stated she was 'always there' for her son and Judith similarly said, 'I want them to know that I'm always here to help them. I'm always here for them'. In utilising this concept these women effectively fixed themselves in time and space – as available.

I return to the issue of the mother's availability later. For now, I suggest that the concept of 'being there' was my participants' attempts to reconfigure the discourse of needs in relation to children who were adults and from whom they lived apart. This signals both transformation and continuity in mothering practices and, in turn, the identity 'mother'. Children were not set adrift on reaching adult status because their mothers' 'being there' performed a vital function; it formed a connection between mother and child and its enactment confirmed the enduring bonds between the pair and in turn, reinforced women's identities as mothers:

> They are the centre and have been for so long that everything revolves around them [...] You've just done it all their lives and, even though they're in adulthood, you still want to help, you know? But I don't think you ever stop, my mother says that. And I don't think that, until you become a parent, you can understand that, you know? (Janice)

> I think you always have that bond if, if anybody upsets them, you know? It's not a case of, um, blaming anybody but you think, oh, I just want to go wrap my arms round him, say 'it's going to be alright', you know? Um, so I think you've always got that bond. (Judith)

Judith's desire to cradle her son during times of his distress and offer him comfort and protection is evident here and effectively returns her to the role she performed as the mother of a dependent child. Janice's intimation, 'I don't think you ever stop' highlights the placing of herself, like her mother before her, as responsible for meeting her adult child's needs. Lois McNay (2000: 19) discusses 'the investments individuals may have in certain self-conceptions that render them resistant to transformation'. Evidently, interviewees' children occupied a central space in their lives that they did not wish to lose, rendering them resistant to change. This resistance served two purposes, as the adult child continued to need the mother for practical as well as emotional labour and the mother meets her own need to feel needed by fulfilling her perceived mothering role. As Linda reflected, 'it makes me feel better, doing those things for him'.

Women's narratives illustrate that the model of motherhood my research participants performed was integral to their identities as mothers and in turn to their sense of a mothering self. In reconfiguring the needs discourse they actively attempted to adapt motherhood to fit the changed circumstances of their mothering as praxis. I suggest they reinterpreted the rhetoric of 'being there' to ensure the continuity of their relationships with their children at the time of the latter's home-leaving thus supplying them with an affirmation of the motherhood identity as they understood it. Recognising the 'child' as 'adult' was, to varying degrees, a difficult task each of my interviewees had worked towards during the process of their children leaving home. In some instances women were unable to accept the changed/changing status of their children:

> He's still a child, I can't think of him as a man. He's still a child to me and, I don't know, you look at pictures of them don't you, you know, when they're little and they'll, um, they'll always be little to me. In my old house I had the living room full of pictures of them from babies, you know, but we had a lot bigger living room then, there's not enough room here, but I love photographs. (Paula)

Paula illuminates here how the meanings of 'child' and 'mother' might be disrupted at particular moments of a mother's life course, and one way in which the mother might respond. Although Paula later said her son's transition to adulthood enforced a realisation of her self as 'getting old', I suggest that she was longing for a period in the past that 'made sense' to her. The interview took place in Paula's living-room where photographs of her sons as younger children that she refers to above were displayed on her walls. I suggest that these photographs represented a period during her mothering years that Paula was comfortable with. Her focus on historical moments thus locked her into a time that held meaning; she identified each son as 'child' and herself, in turn, as youthful. This is a further reminder of the absence of a model of motherhood that creates an acknowledged space for mothers in the lives of their children as adults from whom they live separately. Moreover, it reveals the lack of recognition of mothers' lives as dynamic and processual rather than as static and unchanging. Paula's narrative is further testament that, for a mother caught up in such a model, it might prove difficult to accept and/or engender change.

Concluding Remarks

My research participants maintained, at varying levels, a dual notion of their daughters and sons as both dependent 'children' and independent 'adults'. I suggest that this is due to the lack of a model of motherhood that takes women beyond their children's early years and into their adult lives so that when children leave home, the mother/child relationship is disrupted and the identity 'mother' becomes unstable. Women thus retain an image of themselves as nurturers of their children's needs, set up in their own earliest childhood and I have argued they do this in order to sustain their mothering identities.

This way of thinking about our children is reinforced by the images and representations we have access to as well as 'expert' advice on childcare and childrearing within the public domain. Having no cultural script that carries mothers forward from the point of leaving home created the hiatus many of my participants experienced. Ultimately they were faced with a dilemma regarding their feelings about themselves as older mothers and of their children as adults. Just as there are silences surrounding the realities of early motherhood (Boulton, 1983; Brown et al., 1997; Miller, 2005; Oakley, 1979, 1980, 1998la) similar lack of knowledge about mothers' later life experiences exists. This goes some way towards explaining the sense of timelessness that many of my participants attached to their mothering years, why some experienced an element of surprise at 'suddenly' being the mothers of adults, and why so many of the women I interviewed were faced with a sense of bewilderment when their children's adult status was achieved. Although articulating an expectation that children would one day grow up and leave home, available models of motherhood did not promote thoughts about themselves regarding the time beyond their children's dependency.

When faced with having to recognise the emerging adulthood of the child, a rift occurred in the life course of each participant in which, to varying degrees, she found herself ill-prepared. The naturalising and normalizing of independent adulthood in discursive constructions of western childrearing explains to some extent why we do not think about the relational aspects that are attached to this time of transition and why women's feelings remain muted, but it is also, and more importantly, to do with the models of motherhood we have access to and our relationship to the cultural representations of what mother and child are.

Chapter 4
Managing the Process of Separation

Introduction

> Now that she is a woman, and full of the stirrings of independence to separate
> from me, she likes to hold herself at a certain distance.
> [...]
> So we dance together, often awkwardly, and fumbling, and missing each other,
> and sometimes with a rhythm of understanding.
> [...]
> The invisible cord between us is still there.
> [...]
> Sooner or later my daughter will cut it. (Roberts, 1984: 178)

In her novel *The Wild Girl,* Michèle Roberts' portrays the dynamic relationship
between mother and child. I use an extract from her novel here to symbolise
the situation in which my interviewees found themselves at the time of their
children's pending home-leaving; I have argued that at this point, the mother/child
relationship was in a state of flux. Roberts' brief extract conveys that the mother is
an active participant in, but also a passive witness to, the actions of the daughter,
who she perceives is preparing to separate from her.

In anticipating the consequences of her daughter's transition to womanhood
the mother is awaiting separation between herself and her child. She senses that
change emanates from the daughter and is waiting for her to cut the links that
previously held mother and child together. As such, Roberts highlights the mother's
anticipation and expectation of severed ties. Her passivity in front of an event
that is not directly engineered by her effectively means that the mother constructs
herself as the object of the daughter's actions, not as an initiator/subject. In a
similar way to the mother in Roberts' novel, my research participants were waiting
for their children to break the ties that previously bound them together. Although
children leaving home was an anticipated and planned for time, many women were
not adequately prepared for the reality of separation from their children, for what
this would mean in their lives and for them as mothers. Nurturing independence
as the goal of childrearing in contemporary western discursive constructions of
motherhood has been revealed as underpinning the purpose of my participants'
mothering. Women's aspirations for their children and children's own ambitions
for the future clearly ran alongside each other, so that mothers seemingly worked
towards the time of separation from their children during their childrearing years.
They were then immersed in this powerful discourse and yet clearly experienced

contradictory feelings regarding themselves as mothers and their children as adults when their children left home. I have linked the emotional turmoil experienced at this time to the limitations of available models of motherhood.

Stevi Jackson and Sue Scott state that the emotions 'continue to be subject to rational management while always threatening to exceed the bounds of manageability' (1997: 551). This chapter investigates what was 'managed' by my interviewees and what was not at the time their adult children left home. By using the concept of 'manageability' as a backdrop the intertwining of women's emotional experiences before, during and after the time of separation from their children guides the chapter. Also pursued is the notion that children's transition to adulthood and subsequent home-leaving created a rupture in the life course of each of the women I interviewed, precipitating their own transformation towards that of accepting themselves as the mothers of children who were adults. As Ian Craib comments:

> We can think through all sorts of situations with which most people must be familiar: experiencing feelings we cannot express to our satisfaction, having feelings that we can express but that others find difficult to understand, and most important, perhaps, the regular experiencing of contradictions between our thoughts and our feelings. (Craib, 1995: 153)

It was clear from the interview data that my research participants had experienced each of the emotional states Craib identifies. Although they expected to be affected when separated from their children, their experiences of this event were fraught with mixed emotions. This chapter provides an exploration of these experiences and reveals the internal contradictions women often encountered that raged against the imposed external norms in which adult children's home-leaving is embedded.

The themes of preparation, separation and acceptance emerged from the interview data and although each woman travelled through these three phases, it was seldom straightforward. Instead their journeys were ragged, often difficult and for some not fully completed. As Thompson (2002: 1) comments, 'life is characterized by movement, change and development – and therefore by transitions, losses and grief' (2002: 1). In their interviews, my participants often likened the experience of their children leaving home to that of bereavement. Thompson continues:

> We have sets of rituals that come into play at the time of death and these rituals give a very clear signal that we are dealing with loss and grief. Other losses, however, tend not to have such rituals associated with them, and so awareness of the grief being experienced by the person or persons concerned tends to be at a much lower level. (2002: 2)

As will become clear in what follows, women's experiences of loss at the time of separation from their daughters and sons was acknowledged at a 'much lower level' and at times not acknowledged at all. This means it is possible that women will go through the emotionally charged process of separating from their adult children in isolation.

Preparing for Home-Leaving

The women I interviewed were aware that their children would one day grow up and leave the family home, as Ingrid said, 'you know your children are going to leave you, naturally. You bring your children up to be independent and to go away'. My explication of women's experiences begins with an exploration of the anticipation and planning involved prior to actual separation. Preparation is deliberately loosely stated here as it is used to mean both the practicalities of home-leaving, with all that this entails, and the emotional preparation that is part of a mother's life course.

As established, leaving home is an anticipated and to some extent planned-for life event. Within the British tradition of higher education, for example, 'students were expected to leave home' (Patiniotis and Holdsworth, 2005: 82). The majority of my participants' children left home to attend universities away from their hometown. As such, several women shared with their children the vision that school-leaving was to be followed by university in another place, even where this had not been their own experience. Janice for instance said of her son:

> He knew what he wanted to do, knew what he had to work at, um, and he was more than ready, you know, once he got his grades through in the August time. You know, you forget now, but it's all set out, isn't it? Then that was it. He wanted to be off. He was really ready to go. (Janice)

As Janice said, 'it's all set out' gesturing towards a sociocultural structure that appears given and to which one submits. This pattern generates a linear trajectory in the child's life course which in turn 'makes sense' of their home-leaving. As previously illustrated, age was often called on as an indicator of the child's now-adult status and readiness to leave home for university. Rita for example said:

> Oh yes, certainly she was ready to go. In the last year of being in the Upper Sixth, or whatever it's called now, um, she was, you know, tending ... not to stay out but to be out longer, to be away, to be on holiday with her friends, that type of thing. When she was seventeen, that's when she started to feel ... she was definitely ready to go away to university.

Higher education was thus a signpost to independent living for their children that my participants had gradually moved towards; an age-transition and a sociocultural expectation which enabled this group of mothers to consider that their children were ready to leave home. Clearly there are parallels here to my earlier discussion of age transitions in child development literature that act as markers in the child's progression towards independent adulthood. Where the traditional route into higher education is the goal, the child's age becomes a particularly salient indicator of their readiness to leave home, and the peer pressure of pre-university school-life acts as yet another; leaving home becomes essentially a collective expectation.

The child as 'ready to go' was a phrase women often used and for some it was mixed with the mother's equal readiness for the child to leave. For example, Linda described her son's going to university as equally desired by them both:

> I was ready for him to go, and he was ready. I don't know what he would've done if he'd stayed at home. I mean, university was a get-out. I don't think he particularly wants to study, but it was a way of getting away from home and not having a job, for him.

That mothers were ready themselves for their children to move out, was often coupled with notions of their children needing to free themselves from parental constraints. Janice said her son was 'ready for a bit of freedom as well, probably, you know, from living at home and his dad was quite strict with him.' Ingrid also said: 'my daughter was ready to leave home because she didn't like the regimented feeling of home, you know? She was ready to get away from all that'. Ultimately then children were assumed to need to free themselves from the restrictions of home in order to achieve adult independence. This resonates with Liz Kenyon's study of students' transitions out of the family home and into university accommodation:

> Very often an independent dwelling away from the childhood home is seen to be both a physical manifestation of independence and citizenship, as well as the arena in which other adult emotional and social developments are most likely to occur. Leaving home is therefore viewed as one factor associated with the complex movement from childhood towards full adulthood. (Kenyon, 1999: 84)

Comments from the students participating in Kenyon's study and her subsequent analysis complement the data from my study; women acknowledged that the independence deemed so necessary for full adult citizenship was only possible with the child's move away from the family home and thus the mother. Indeed, in their study of young people's transition to higher education, Den Kenyon and Susan Koerner (2009: 293) state that 'a key developmental task [...] is for adolescents to gain autonomy from their parents and become independent adults'.

Leaving home was envisaged by some of my interviewees as a way of enforcing a 'growing-up' in their children. In these instances, leaving home was perceived to engender changed behaviour, as in the case of Ingrid, or the fulfilling of career aspirations, as Alma indicates. Although their children were considered 'not ready', they nevertheless left home for university:

> My daughter needed to go. She wasn't ready and it frightened the life out of her to have to go and fend for herself. She'd never really done anything for herself.

As I say, she was lazy and mum being mum, was silly and did it all for her. So in the weeks leading up to university, she had the most dreadful panic attacks about going and at one point decided that she wasn't going to go. (Ingrid)

My daughter wouldn't have got the career she's got if she'd stayed at home, she realises that. She wasn't ready but ... she needed to find things out for herself. It wouldn't have done any good somebody telling her. She's the sort of person who has to find out some things for herself. (Alma)

Whether the child was 'ready' or 'not ready', both views nevertheless articulate the 'best interests' of the child. Children were perceived to have 'outgrown' the time for living at home and this was considered one of the main reasons for them to leave. In these scenarios, the structure of higher education lent weight to mothers' assumptions of children's development, and their expectations and preparations for children's adult futures.

Being included in children's preparations for leaving also met the practical and emotional needs of both mothers and their children:

I was putting the bond up for the flat [laughs] so they needed me really! And also I drove. I drove them up and down and took their luggage in the back, you know. Hired a van and took them to university. So yes, I was involved. I thought I was doing them a favour but, actually, it was probably very good for both of us that I was involved, you know? (Rachel)

Clearly being involved was part and parcel of Rachel's transition as well as those of her three daughters'. As she also recognised, being involved was 'very good' for all four of them. The reciprocal nature of the process of leaving home thus means the practical and emotional needs of both mother and child might be met through joint involvement in the process. Again, going to university provided a forum for long-term planning for several of my participants as mothers and children were aware in advance of the child's destination and the timing of their leaving structured around the academic year.

When children left home for reasons other than higher education there was a less predictable lead-up and thus a different experience regarding mothers' expectations and preparations. Planning to move in with friends, for example, was a topic of discussion between Frances and her son for quite some time before he moved out of the family home: 'he'd been talking about it, but nothing had happened' (Frances). However, his decision to move out was experienced as sudden and consequently upsetting. Frances explained that her son told her he was leaving whilst the family were on holiday: 'he said "oh, I've got a house. I'm moving out". So I was in floods of tears! Awful! I thought, oh no, he's leaving home! He won't be able to manage!' indicating her immediate perception of her son's inability to cope alone; his non-readiness. Her son took a more gradual approach to his actual departure:

> They were there painting for about a week before so what he did was, he just took so much stuff every night. So it wasn't like he just packed everything up in a case and went. It was quite gradual, really. Now, whether he did that for my benefit, or whether he did it for his own benefit, I don't know. (Frances)

Although her son's plan to move out of the family home initially 'shocked' Frances, there was a period of adjustment prior to his leaving. Having time to acclimatise to the idea of the child's move out of the family home was then an important element in the process of separation for several participants, as Helen explained of her daughter's decision to move in with her partner:

> They'd decided in their minds that they were going to move in together for two or three months before she sort of said to me that she was planning on doing it. Even when she told me, I can't remember how she phrased it, but it didn't sound as if she was going to do it straightaway. So I had time to get used to the idea before she actually did move out. (Helen)

Children's surprising or sudden departures were unusual in my research and breaches in the mother/child relationship were even less common (only two participants talked about a child's unexpected leaving, in each case a subsequent child left under more gradual circumstances). When unexpected leaving occurred it was difficult, the pain of abrupt separations provoked feelings of being instantly 'redundant':

> I came home from work on the Monday and she said, 'I'm going to London tomorrow, I've got an interview'. It was that quick. And she packed her bags, took all her bags with her, rang me up and said, 'I've got the job'. It was that quick … She just went. And that was hard. (Dawn)

Unlike Rachel, my research participant Dawn was denied an opportunity to help with her daughter's move out of the home so in consequence had no time to prepare herself. However, even when women had plenty of 'warning' that children would leave, for example through their going to university, and where the child's future was meeting mothers' aspirations, preparing themselves for children's leaving was different from the actual event:

> I knew it was going to happen and I knew they'd go and I knew, I suppose my brain knew, that that's what I wanted for my children and, um, if they were of the adventurous type, and two of them certainly are, um, I thought it was fantastic, but there's your heart, which is, um, a different thing [laughs]. (Bridget)

Although an expected and anticipated transition, the reality of children leaving home was difficult for several of the women I interviewed. Bridget highlights the gap between intellect and emotion. Her juxtaposition of 'head and heart' reveals a clash between the two concepts; the reasoning of her 'head', when she considered the 'fantastic' opportunities that lay ahead for her children, was accompanied by the undertow of her emotional 'heart' and the feelings she experienced when anticipating her children leaving. Ramazanoğlu and Holland (2002: 28) list 'passion, prejudice, madness, subjectivity, superstition, magic, tradition' as standing in opposition to rational thought and action. Jaggar notes how rationality has historically been contrasted with emotionality:

> This contrasted pair has often been linked with other dichotomies. Not only has reason contrasted with emotion, but it has also been associated with the mental, the cultural, the universal, the public and the male, whereas emotion has been associated with the irrational, the physical, the natural, the particular, the private, and, of course, the female. (Jaggar, 1989: 145)

The persistence of such binary oppositions, and the tensions created by women's attempts at rational control of their emotional expressions, was evident when interviewees talked about their experiences of separation from their children. As Bridget later explained, 'there's a real double-edged thing' attached to this time in a mother's life. For many women, the knowledge of the child's leaving created a confusing dilemma for them as they attempted to rationalise the powerful emotions they experienced. Paula for example told me that during the year before her son's departure for university, she tried to prepare herself by thinking positively about his future rather than her own:

> All last year I just felt ... I could just see it coming and I knew it was coming and I tried to prepare myself for it ... but I didn't ... In my head I tried to think, well, it's good for him to go. (Paula)

The anticipation of children's leaving for Bridget and Paula was immersed in a conflicting set of emotions; on the one hand going away to university was perceived as a good experience for their children and something they both worked towards during the years of their childrearing, yet the situation they envisaged for themselves once their children left was anticipated, as Bridget said, as something to 'dread'. Many women talked about a similar emotional confusion. Heather explained how she felt about her children leaving home and reiterated the fact that, in leaving, her sons were meeting her aspirations for them:

> Because they're doing what they want to do and they're doing, really, what you want them to do, so you shouldn't be feeling miserable about it. It's a very mixed feeling'.

Believing that children's home-leaving is 'right' for the child, especially in terms of their achievement of adult independence, did not then coincide with several women's feelings about their own readiness, their own emotional preparedness for that leaving:

> I did feel that he was ready to go. I did feel it was time to leave home for him, for him. What bothered me and … I had not understood the impact of that, what that would mean when he did, I have to say [cries], ok? But for him, he had to be independent. He needed to have his own front door, that kind of thing. (Angela)

As Angela and other women's narratives indicate, helping children get ready to leave meant that preparing *themselves* for children's leaving was neither prioritised nor often considered. Again women's rationalising of their children's leaving: 'he needed to have his own front door', overwrote their emotional selves (Lupton, 1998a). Often the realisation that tasks which structured women's everyday lives would no longer be necessary catapulted women into a realisation of what their children's impending departure from the home meant in real terms:

> It wasn't until I was actually packing him up for work and I said, 'oh, I won't be doing this next week' and I burst into tears. And I hadn't realised how it was affecting me. But I kept thinking, oh, he'll be alright, he'll be alright, you know? He knows where we are if he wants us, kind of thing, but it was … it was really strange. (Judith)

Judith helped her son to decorate his new home so that the rituals of him setting up home elsewhere superseded Judith's thoughts of herself until a particular moment in time, when she was engaged in a daily ritual that would terminate on her son's departure. It is clear that my interviewees practised what Lupton calls 'internalized policing' (1998a: 52). They attempted to regulate their own feelings (and behaviour) with thoughts of their children; as Judith said, 'I kept thinking, he'll be alright'. Thinking of their children's well-being managed the emotions women experienced and in turn suppressed feelings about themselves prior to separation:

> You've brought this tiny little bundle into the world and you've nurtured it and loved it and cared for it and everything else and you can't imagine life when they're not there at your side and it's hard, very hard indeed. I don't think there's anything you can do to prepare yourself for that except be aware that you've done your job properly if they can leave home and, um, um, have a nice life. (Alma)

Thus it is that in a contemporary UK context, successful mothers are those whose children leave home and 'have a nice life'. Women's feelings are imagined as mitigated by children's success and happiness away from the home. However, a mother's experience of separation from her adult-child is not something that can be fully planned or prepared for and interviewees' expectations of separation from their children were in reality experienced quite differently.

Experiencing Separation

The planning and preparation my participants were involved in leading up to their children leaving home was for the most part constructed along practical lines. It was during this period that several women experienced a set of contradictory and conflicting emotions. Sally, for example, said, 'you're doing all these things to help them to leave but really, you don't want them to go!' My participants were actively engaged in the kind of emotional labour that Craib (1995: 155) describes as 'the "internal" work of coping with contradiction … and the "external" work of reconciling what goes on inside with what one is supposed or allowed to feel'. The following discussion delves more deeply into the actual experience of separation between mothers and their children.

As indicated, the anticipation and preparation leading to their children leaving home did not adequately prepare many women for what they experienced at the point of separation:

> I just know how I as, hopefully, a fairly intelligent woman, um, had no idea of the impact it would have on me. And that's the thing. It crept up and hit me! You know that it's going to happen and you have these expectations of what it's going to be like so you prepare yourself, but when it actually happens it's completely different to what you expected. (Angela)

When Angela's son left to set up home with his partner she said her separation from him was 'completely different' from her expectations. Similarly, Janice described the time she took her son to university:

> You knew they were going and that he wouldn't be coming home and it's maybe easier to do that when they're still in the home. It's the actual, when you're there at university. As I say, I can still see him now, leaving him on those steps and us driving off and he was fine, but I think he knew we were upset, which did have an effect on him. Um, I think it's just one of those times that you'll never forget. (Janice)

Although all of my research participants articulated awareness that their children would one day leave home, as Janice said, 'it's maybe easier to do that when they're still in the home'. So, although women anticipated this time in their children's, if not their own, lives, its preparation had taken place within the relatively safe space of the home before children left and where women remained immersed in the daily practices of mothering. As discussed in the previous chapter, women's mothering was to a great extent dependent upon the presence of their children, whose needs they continued to meet. As Gill Valentine (1999: 51) comments: 'in our everyday lives we constantly position ourselves in relation to others' and as I have argued, the relational nature of the mother/child dyad is dependent upon presence rather than absence. As such, making plans for children's futures took place in the shared space of the home. In the actual physical 'doing' of leaving, what was imagined no longer 'made sense' for several of my participants. Living with inadequate and incomplete models of motherhood which inform women's mothering experiences and expectations means that a woman's sense of self-as-mother might be disrupted during the child's transition to adulthood. This was evidently the case for my interviewees when they talked about their experiences of separation from their adult children.

Leaving her son at university for the first time created visual memories for Janice that she said she would 'never forget'. Similar experiences were articulated by other women in the study. Nancy for example described the time she left her daughter at university:

> Oh! It was just terrible! ... I remember, um, as we drove away that day, um, seeing her walking up with her friend, both with long red hair, just walking off into the sunset, sort of thing, and we drove away. Oh, it was awful! Just the most awful feeling. (Nancy)

In her discussion of 'the unruliness of fluid emotion' Lupton notes that 'we feel the emotion accumulating within us, against which we may struggle to exert control, or else give in by letting it "out" of the body' (1998a: 85). At the point of separation and in its immediate aftermath many interviewees talked about similar feelings to those Nancy describes. Subsequently these accumulated within them, causing them and others to 'let out' their emotions through crying. As Ingrid said, 'my daughter burst into tears, we all did', and Denise said 'everybody was crying floods of tears, you know?' Janice described herself as 'a blubbering wreck' and Rita said 'we got in the car and tears started rolling down my face'. Paula said 'I cried all the way home'.

Other participants had 'exerted control' over their emotions when leaving their children, feeling they should hide their tears from their children (and from others). Several participants said they did not want their children to know they were upset and controlled their crying until after separation:

> We took him to university and settled him in his room but that was terrible, oh, terrible, you know? I managed not to cry in front of him [laughs] but I could easily have let the side down there. (Bridget)

> I managed not to cry until I got into the car to come back and then I cried all the way down the motorway! And my daughter kept saying, 'he'll be alright, mum'. 'I know he will. What about me?' (Fiona)

For Bridget, keeping her emotions under wraps and thereby not 'letting the side down' was undertaken so as to prevent her son from being upset. As she said: 'you don't want them to be feeling anything like that. You want them to be happy'. She did not submit to her emotions at the point of separation. She also indicates some knowledge of the public performance of emotion, what is perceived to be allowed and so can be 'done', and in turn what cannot. Both women articulate a 'management' of feelings. As Lupton (1998a: 50) said of her own participants: 'the reactions and feelings of others were a vital dimension in regulating the ways in which [interviewees] expressed or suppressed [their] emotions'.

Interestingly, and although Bridget was attempting to shield her son, she later received a letter from him in which he disclosed his experience of very similar feelings to those of his mother. My participant Fiona experienced a shift in perspective of whom she was crying for. Initially her son's well-being was prioritised, but in the immediate aftermath of separation her thoughts shifted towards herself, 'what about me?', and the feelings of loss she experienced; the meaning of her son's leaving in her own life thus manifested when she parted from him.

Separation from children was often accompanied by deep feelings of loss and my interviewee Angela, in a similar way to Bridget, experienced emotions she felt she needed to express but at the same time was unable to 'let out':

> It really does come up and smack you in the eye, it did for me anyway. I just felt terribly, terribly down, an enormous sense of loss, you know? There's an African word, 'keening'[1] I think it is, and they ... The noises that they make, and the wailing and the ... Yeah, I think that describes it, I mean, I didn't do that, but that's how I felt inside, that I needed to let it out. It was horrible, it was horrible. (Angela)

Angela's reference to ritual is indicative of the socially sanctioned expressions of emotion within contemporary UK society. Thompson's description of 'disenfranchised grief' (Doka: 2001, cited in Thompson, 2002: 8) helps to decipher my participants' confusing and contradictory emotional experiences: 'experiences of grief which are in some way not socially accepted, and which may therefore be more difficult to deal with because of a lack of social support or the benefits of established rituals'. I would argue that this is linked to the absence of a social script for the time of separation between mothers and their adult children, evidenced in their interview data. Leaving home is couched in a discourse of 'letting-go' rather than in one of continuance of the mother/adult child relationship. Indeed, as Fiona's husband said of her son, 'you've got to let him go'.

Women as a group are often unaware of other women's experiences and in times of transition which are not socially recognised can, as these examples attest, define their feelings in terms of individual pathologies. It is, however, little wonder that women who lived with their children for sixteen-plus years as my participants

---

1   Keen: Verb. To wail in grief for a dead person (*Oxford English Dictionary*, 2006).

had, should experience such raw emotion at the time of separation from them. Bridget for example said, 'I know this sounds completely crazy ... but actually it felt as though I'd lost a child. It felt like a bereavement'. She continued:

> I thought, this is mad! You know, here my son is on the other side of the world, doing all the things that I had always hoped he would do and grown up to be a lovely chap who I'm ever so proud of, um, and yet I'm feeling as if he's died and gone to heaven, really [laughs], which must look terribly illogical from the outside. (Bridget)

Bridget interprets her feelings as 'illogical', but she was not the only interviewee to describe the experience of separation in this way. As Nancy said, for example, 'well, my daughter's leaving, well, it was just like a bereavement, just this empty feeling in my stomach, one of loss'. Janice talked about returning home after taking her son to university, 'it was just as though there'd been a death'. Fiona encouraged her son to travel after university and was involved with his travel plans, yet underwent a distressing experience when he actually left which, like Bridget, she did not explain to her partner or to anyone else. As she described her experience of separating from her son at the airport, she drew on imagery of the maternal body:

> When I saw him off and I knew I wasn't going to see him for a year ... I just felt as if I had a big black hole in here [indicating stomach area] you know? It was just as if he'd been torn out of me ... That's how I felt when I left Heathrow Airport when he'd gone ... It was just awful ... It's like the umbilical cord, isn't it? (Fiona)

Lupton (1998a: 167) asserts that 'the experience of emotion involves the interpretation of physical sensations mediated through a body image that is culturally contingent'. In asking me, a mother and therefore an assumed empathic listener 'it's like the umbilical cord, isn't it?' Fiona was calling on a mutually experienced and culturally interpreted phenomenon in order to explain to me how she felt. When Fiona saw her son off at the airport, she knew she would not see him again for a relatively long period of time and often the length of time that would separate women from their children was a topic of conversation in the interviews. Bridget described how she felt about her daughter's leaving to work abroad:

> That was horrendous. She and I are very close, um, and it's such a long way and she wasn't going for ten weeks to university, she was going for fifty weeks and, um ... I just thought; I'm not going to see this child for a year! (Bridget)

Women's sudden realisations and emotional experiences were accompanied by a muting of their feelings because of a lack of legitimacy; as argued, their feelings of loss were 'disenfranchised' (Thompson, 2002). Participants' experiences also point to the lack of an appropriate language with which to express the emotions we might at times experience. In her discussion of love, for example, Stevi Jackson (1993: 207) states that it 'is in essence indefinable, mysterious, outside rational discourse. Its meaning is held to be knowable only intuitively, at the level of feeling, and cannot be communicated in precise terms'. Although referring to romantic love, Jackson's statement resonates strongly with my research participants' experiences of separation from their children; as 'indefinable'. Clearly then, my interviewees were not prepared for the conflicting emotional experiences of separation from their adult children. Some were shocked by the depth of feeling and, in some instances, did not think they would recover. Indeed, two women disclosed in their interviews that they had briefly entertained suicidal thoughts, such were their experiences of despair when their children left.

The Aftermath of Separation

As indicated, once separation between mother and adult child occurred several women experienced an emotional trauma akin to bereavement. I suggest that during this period each inhabited an intermediate or transitional position, 'a limbo state', as Angela called it, wherein their sense of self and feelings of well-being were disrupted.

> So we got in the car and tears started rolling down my face and by that time she'd turned round and walked away anyway ... I felt pretty awful and, even though my husband didn't say it, I think he felt pretty awful too. Even now he'll say 'isn't it quiet in the house'. (Rita)

Acute feelings of loss and emptiness were experienced by several interviewees. As Rita shows, for women whose children went to university or travelling, the journey back home after 'seeing them off' was emotionally loaded, and one that ended with a return to complex feelings about the home and about themselves as mothers (and in some instances fathers too, I return to this issue in the conclusion). As Valentine comments:

> The home is not only a physical location but also a matrix of social relations. It is the location where our routine everyday lives are played out. Not surprisingly, our homes – perhaps more than any other geographical locations – have strong claims on our time, resources and emotions. (2001: 71)

I discussed earlier how research into young people's home-leaving reveals their perception of the home as an unchanging place of safety and security. Indeed, this is how my interviewees articulated the home that they provided for their children. However, it would seem that once children left, the meanings women formerly attributed to the space of the home were no longer applicable, nor did they make sense. As Vanessa indicated, being caught up in the euphoria of her daughter's educational achievement masked her own feelings of loss until she returned home:

> The first one, she went to Oxford so, you know, it was great excitement when she went. I didn't have the, the real miserable feelings, um, because it was a new place. I mean, it was just beautiful and exciting. She was just thrilled to be there as well, um, and she's a very live-wire. So when we left her there and we came home it was like ... the whole place felt dead. (Vanessa)

Vanessa's description of the 'dead' space of the home acts as a metaphor for its new silence. This was a common thread throughout women's narratives; in the absence of the child, the space of the home was destabilised and experienced differently. As previously outlined, the majority of interviewees were responsible for the domestic and caring aspects of their households; the everyday routines that formerly structured their home lives. Meal times were often drawn on in the interviews as indicative of a time that family members routinely spent together. Valentine proposes that 'the performance and regulation of shared eating habits and practices of the self are two important ways that we can imagine our cultural space in the world' (1999: 51). She comments that when we

> Sit down to eat with others we consciously or unconsciously articulate our cultural place in the world. The importance of this lies in the fact that through these performative [...] acts and practices of the self, we express a common or shared identity with others and caring human relations. (1999: 54–5)

Responsibility for particular routines and everyday practices are thus imbued with meaning. As such, cooking a meal and setting the table in readiness for the family to eat suggests that when children's absence alters such routines a woman's sense of self and identity as 'mother' might be disrupted, ultimately shaking her sense of well-being and self-worth. In their turn then, the experiences of my interviewees are an indication of 'how meanings of home are structured by life course events' (Holdsworth and Morgan, 2005: 73), as Heather's recollection clearly shows:

> It's at meal times that I miss them most, you know, when you make a meal, you set the table and you sit down and there's just me and my husband. Um, and it's ... it just seems really, really empty then. (Heather)

Susan Gregory (1999: 60) comments that 'the provision of food and the organisation of meals are a pivotal feature of home life'. As Heather indicates, the absence of her four sons altered the meanings of these routine times of the day. Following Marjorie DeVault (1991), Gregory also interprets women's engagement in daily domestic tasks as 'an active endorsement of her gender identity' (61). For my interviewees, these tasks also affirmed their identities as mothers. Their engagement in the everyday of the domestic sphere was 'a key element in the construction of [the] self' (Morgan, 1996: 182). In some instances, a previously shared family occasion alerted women to the difference the child's absence might create. This was not always experienced in the way they imagined:

> It was funny when we first sat down to meals around the table, because we usually all sit together and my son's place ... I thought, how am I going to feel when he's not sat there? We never said anything, well, maybe I just commented. But we all moved round a bit so that the most awkward chair, that my husband had, nobody sat in it, just because it was awkward to get in, you know? So we just immediately just moved to somewhere and my son's place was filled. And I thought that was good, because then we weren't sat there thinking, oh, where is he? What's he doing? Is he eating? All that kind of thing. (Linda)

Linda earlier indicated her own readiness for her son to leave home. Occasionally children's behaviour was similarly interpreted by participants to mean they had separated from the family before their actual move out of the home. Gregory notes that sharing family meals also reinforces 'the family group and each member's place in it' (1999: 67). Ideological notions that home and family not only indicated togetherness and unity but also a kind of familial hierarchy clearly affected the way that some of my interviewees perceived their children's behaviour prior to their leaving the family home. Toke Christensen (2009: 439) notes that increasingly 'children's bedrooms are equipped with a wide range of media technologies' and comments on the 'many hours' children spend occupied with these media, either alone or with friends. Barbara and Frances both remarked on this aspect of their sons' lives:

> To me, he wasn't part of the family. He wouldn't sit and watch telly with you or anything and it got to where he wouldn't eat with us, because he was living a different life on the phone or the internet with his friends. (Barbara)

> It's not as if they'd ever sit in on a night and chat to us, because they didn't. They were out with their friends or their friends were round here and up in the bedroom. (Frances)

However, many women also expressed that one of the things they missed post-separation was the noise and bustle their children's lives had created in the family household, thus contradicting earlier statements inasmuch as they felt children had separated from the space they called home before actually leaving it. Some of my participants ultimately indicated that the behaviours that accompanied their children's in-house separation transformed into an element of women's everyday lives that they had lost once children left home:

It's just them that I miss and all their friends coming, that's the other thing, and the phone never used to stop ringing. I think it's the company, you know? It's different now. (Sally)

That's one of the things I miss, like I said. Them all going up and down the stairs and on the computer and things like that. It makes a difference to the house. (Frances)

Angela said her son's bedroom 'was a hard place to go into'. Gina talked about how her daughter's bedroom made her feel once her she had moved out to live with her partner. Although she nursed her daughter through four years of depression and described her home-leaving as 'almost a celebration', Gina nevertheless experienced feelings of loss and emptiness once her daughter left:

The empty room, yeah, I think that's the time when it hits me more than anything, when I go to clean it, that it is just that empty shell. It's a little bit of your life that … you'd left in the room. It almost sums up that feeling that you have, a little empty shell as you go in. (Gina)

Gina's metaphor of the empty shell incorporates her feelings; the room contained only past memories of her life with her daughter. Many women talked in similar ways about the home environment and the difference children's absence made to their everyday lives; the 'emptiness' of the house was a common phrase. Fiona said: 'god, the house just seemed so empty when I came back, which is silly, because I wasn't on my own'. She continued:

My son's bedroom is in the loft and he has his own bathroom up there, um, and I used to just sit on his stairs, just sit there and cry or just sit on his bed. You can smell them, their smell. I used to go in his room just to feel close to him. (Fiona)

Angela as well said it was: 'a smell thing, very much a smell thing. You know, I could smell his aftershave'. For Rachel, a particular song evoked memories of times spent with her three daughters; she talked about spending Christmas without them: 'New York City,[2] it's just the most wonderful Christmas song. So I was just listening to that and crying and saying "oh, we used to sing this together"'. Children's belongings 'left behind' in the home similarly acted as reminders: 'when we got home, sort of like, he used to have this table with all this stuff … I had to move it because it was just … yeah, his presence had gone' (Janice). The home is, then, 'much more than a repository of artefacts; it is in its own right and *par excellence* an artefact to which deeply buried meanings are attached' (Seely, 1956, cited in Holdsworth and Morgan, 2005: 78, original emphasis). On their return

---

2   *Fairytale of New York*, The Pogues and Kirsty MacColl.

home, the sensory furnishings[3] of their children's lives reminded my participants of the absence of their children; at times they heightened the sense of loss they experienced, at yet other times they were a source of comfort. The same rooms, objects, smells and sounds were thus transformed, ultimately unsettling women's previously held meanings of home.

The differences children's absence made to the everyday-ness of the home were felt acutely, as Janice indicated when she talked about the day after taking her son to university: 'I have memories of thinking the next day, will he get up? Shall I ring him? You know, it was all the motherly things I used to do'. Being relieved of 'the motherly things' that previously structured the home, and in turn their own and their children's lives, emerged from the interviews as a painful part of the process of separation between mothers and their adult children. Reflecting on separating from her son during his infancy, when she left him with her mother in order to go out to work, Heather said: 'the physical separation was awful when he was little, um, but it's, it's not as lonely as the separation now that they've grown up and taken their lives with them'. So how did women cope in the aftermath of their children's home-leaving? And who was there to support them through this time in their lives?

Support Networks

> Bridget: We had our kids within a few months of each other. She's got three and I've got three and, um, we know each other quite well. Well, very well and it's been just brilliant to be able to be very open with somebody about it.
>
> TG: And has she had similar kinds of feelings to you?
>
> Bridget: Oh yes, yes. Which makes you feel as if you're not mad!
>
> TG: And is that how you felt?
>
> Bridget: I think I could have done, yes. I suppose because it's not talked about very openly and very often. You don't turn on the radio and hear people talking about it.

The interview exchange above between Bridget and myself is drawn on here to illustrate that many of the women in my study expressed feelings of loneliness and confusion which they described as sometimes bordering on madness after their children had left home. This was because, as Bridget articulates, the experience is not 'talked about very openly and very often'. Because women's feelings

---

3   Adapted from Umberto Eco (2005) *The Mysterious Flame of Queen Loana*, in which the protagonist contemplates the 'sonic furnishings' of his childhood.

around their children leaving home remains relatively unspoken, indeed Fiona commented, 'this is a silent experience', several of my interviewees thought their feelings were unique to them.

I suggest that the lack of acknowledgement of her experience goes some way towards explaining the silence that surrounds this time in a mother's life course. In turn this links with my earlier argument regarding the inadequacy of models of motherhood women can access. It is also indicative of the previous discussion where women are judged (and judge themselves) pathologically lacking if they fail to control what they consider to be their unruly emotions. As Bridget said, 'maybe for somebody who hasn't been in that situation or who's just looking on, it might not even occur to them that you can actually have those feelings'. Indeed, several of the women were not aware how their own mothers experienced their daughters' leaving home:

> I was really glad to go. I can remember my mother crying at the airport and me thinking, oh, what's the matter with her? Because when you think back, it doesn't really enter your head what they're feeling. It's for you, you're thinking about yourself, yeah. (Paula)

As Fiona said, 'I think we're destined to repeat that, aren't we? I suppose our own children won't realise how much it hurts us when they leave until their own children leave'. In consequence, women felt they were the 'only ones' to experience such emotions: 'I thought, maybe it's just me. Am I stupid?' (Rita). The emotional turmoil was experienced in isolation, a distressing time that in some instances provoked several negative feelings:

> It wasn't about me preventing my sons from doing what they wanted to do, it was about a gap in me, um, so yeah, I felt isolated, because I felt silly and I felt selfish and I felt I shouldn't be ... Somebody said to me, 'if you truly love them, then you let them go', you know? And I thought, 'oh god!' ... I wanted to say, 'I don't want them to go and I wish he'd come back!' (Angela)

The 'gap' Angela identified 'in' herself shows how her son's leaving forced her to acknowledge how much she relied on him to sustain her sense of being in the world. The social pressures and cultural norms she was confronted with also resulted in several other interviewees feeling their emotional experiences at this time were not legitimate. This effectively silenced them, suppressed the feelings they had and stifled expressions of such emotions:

> There isn't anybody else really, exactly in my situation. I think it's sometimes hard to talk to people when they don't know what you're talking about. They think you're a bit daft or something. They can't understand where I'm coming from. (Sandra)

It was the case then that involvement in my research offered several participants the first opportunity to voice their feelings, like Rita said, 'this is helpful to me because I've just got nobody to talk to about it and people I know anyway are not aware of how you feel' (Rita). In some instances friends were sympathetic, but again the need for someone to share your experience was highlighted:

> I told my friend how I felt and she can't empathise because, like I say, her older daughter's fifteen and the other's twelve, so she's not experienced it yet and unless … unless somebody's experienced it they don't know how it feels. It's like having a baby. Nobody can tell you what it's like. It's got to be your experience. Nobody can experience it for you. (Fiona)

Like Fiona, many women drew on the experience of childbirth as a way of conveying how they felt post-separation from the now-adult child. As Angela said, 'you can talk about it, but you can't make people feel'. Linda thought that 'if they've not had the same experiences as you, I think it makes a difference'. Knowledge of 'what it's like' then was often used as a criterion for understanding the emotional experience of separation from the adult child.

There was occasionally an assumption amongst my research participants who were unpartnered at the time of the interviews that partnered mothers would find children leaving home easier to deal with: 'I think people whose kids leave but they're still in their marriage, it's a totally different thing' (Sandra); 'if you've got a partner, you share that loss' (Gina). This was indeed the case for some of the partnered women I spoke to, like Nancy for instance, who said, 'with my particular partner I just think I'm very lucky because we can talk about these things'; Frances also commented 'it must be a lot easier for me to see the boys go than it is for somebody without a husband'. Several of my other partnered interviewees however indicated a broad sense of a male lack of understanding: 'it's fatal isn't it, when a man says, "oh I understand" and you think, oh no you don't!' (Bridget). Just as Harrison's (1998: 108) observations that the male partners of the women in her study were 'unwilling or unable to break the mould of "inexpressive male", even when direct appeals [were] made' so too did several of my participants' male partners fail to meet their emotional needs:

> I'll often say something and he'll say, 'well, what do you want me to say?' and I think, that's not really the response I want. He's not very good with that sort of thing at all … He just leaves you until you're ready to talk. But often you need somebody to talk to when you're feeling that way. You need some support, don't you? … He's hopeless, you know [laughs]. What's the point? So I'll just ring my sister or something. (Sally)

Few of the partnered women told me that they experienced the depth of understanding from their husbands that they were looking for at the time their children left home. Some also indicated that children's leaving meant they were left without the support mechanism they previously relied on:

> I've never talked about it with my husband. He doesn't get into deep conversations. He understands how it must be for me because she's, like, the only other female person in the house, um. I found that quite hard, actually, being left with two chaps! (Rita)

Women often talked about the kinds of close bonds with daughters that Rita experienced. However, it was not always so strictly gendered between mothers and their children. Several women enjoyed closer bonds with their sons in some instances, like Sally for example, who said, 'with the boys going, I've lost a bit of comfort and support in that way, because they were more supportive than their dad'. Fiona commented similarly:

> I do miss my son because I mean, my husband's supportive and my daughter is, but this time that I've had off work while I've been stressed and everything, I would've been able to talk to him about things more. I don't know … it's a different relationship. I can't explain why, really. (Fiona)

At the point of separation from children, some of my participants male partners were upset and tearful, however, it would seem that in the period following, with few exceptions, these same did not articulate their feelings: 'whether he's upset internally, I don't know, because he's a man and he doesn't want to show it' (Sally). Jean Duncombe and Dennis Marsden (1998: 213) found that the women they interviewed attempted 'to make men talk openly about their feelings partly for men's own peace of mind but also to promote the sense of intimacy they themselves value'. In the case of several of my own interviewees, this kind of intimacy was not forthcoming in their relationships. Consequently, women turned to female friends for comfort and support. Harrison (1998: 99) observed how the women she spoke to were able to 'do intimacy' with women friends, 'which required acts of disclosure, expressions of private thoughts and feelings, and the sharing of common experiences'. It would seem that interpreting the feelings of other women whose children had left home as the same as or similar to their own was integral to the depth of support my participants felt they received at the time their children left home. It was also the case that this was available to only a small number of this group of women.

Although I earlier called on the discourse of support networks, in reality this term has limited usefulness for my participants as it would appear that this group of women did not have a 'network' with which to engage at the time their adult children left home. Furthermore, the prevailing discourse of 'letting children go' effectively rendered them unable to voice the feelings of loss they experienced. During several interviews women talked about the need for a support group for mothers going through the process of separation from their adult children and I return to this issue later.

Other Mothers

In her research into married women's female friendships, Oliker found that 'women established bonds of best friendship by a mutual self-disclosure and empathy that most found unparalleled even in marriage' (1989, cited in Harrison, 1998: 100). As previously illustrated, Harrison had similar conclusions herself. Many of my interviewees displayed an underlying belief that the bonds of friendship are predicated upon women's shared understandings, which meant that they could talk 'differently' to friends and discuss how they 'really' felt:

> I suppose because I knew, um, that she was just feeling exactly the same as I was and she is very expressive and very open and some of the things that she was saying, um, I just identified with so completely and probably the other way round as well. It was such a strong, um, bond. It was a really good support mechanism, it really was. Where would we be without our mates? (Bridget)

Separation from their children caused my participants to experience a dis-location in their sense of self which disrupted their ontological security. Those with friends who also experienced a child leave home were able to create a solidarity of feeling and an affirmation of the self, for example as 'not mad'. For these few, 'contact and mutual discovery' (Urwin, 1985: 173) helped them to re-locate and move forward. Discussing accounts of women's mothering experiences within the realm of the private Ribbens notes the significance of mothers' friendship networks:

> The exclusive picture of housewives as isolated may thus neglect an extremely significant aspect of some women's experiences as mothers, not least because such networks imply the possibility that, beyond the private sphere of the home, there may also be a female social world that is not part of male public worlds. (Ribbens, 1994: 31)

Ribbens further poses that such networking for women creates 'gendered social worlds'. In her study of women's early motherhood experiences, Urwin (1985: 168–9) similarly suggests that women's friendships and the value of getting to know other women's experiences via a 'culture of mothers and babies' led her research cohort towards a 're-evaluation of [their] competence at mothering' creating a space for an alternative dialogue through which to challenge 'expert' discourses.

Although not absolute, there is a marked tendency for friends 'to be of the same age, have similar class positions, to be the same gender, and to occupy similar positions in the life course' (Allan, 1996: 91). This was so for the women I interviewed, who overall reflected Allan's assertion. I would add that being mothers was integral to the friendships they were able to forge and that these were built on assumptions of 'being like each other', intersected by location, class, gender and motherhood. Harrison found in her study of friendship amongst middle-class married women that

> The constraints that came with marriage, part-time work, motherhood, and household responsibilities also produced a variety of opportunities in which to develop their friendships both individually with close intimates and collectively with larger groups [of women]. (Harrison, 1998: 93)

Similarly, the women I interviewed were able to forge meaningful relationships with other women because of, rather than in spite of, the heterosexual matrix in which they lived/continued to live. Their situatedness in the gendered social order created the space for friendships to be forged although, of course, the opportunities to form these were governed by the networks they were able to access. As aforementioned, all of the women spent some time during their early mothering years as dependants within the male bread-winner/female home-maker living arrangement. In these instances, the social worlds their children occupied therefore provided the grounding for lasting friendships with other mothers.

Social class position and the areas in which women lived means their friendships are for the most part formed with similarly located women. The catchment areas of schools, for example, reflect a specific demographic, and geographical immobility during the my participants' early mothering years meant they were more likely to make friends amongst women of a similar social background. As Ribbens observes regarding mothers' networks:

> Not only are differences of view perceived as threatening (representing an Otherness that carries the potential for refuting our own beliefs), but also they are counter-productive to our endeavours to construct a coherent and useful framework by which to live our lives, and to bring up our children. If we are seeking such a framework, we will instead need to interact and develop our ideas in conjunction with those who will help us to confirm and elaborate those ideas, rather than those who present us with a completely different set of core constructs from which to start. (Ribbens, 1994: 43)

As Ribbens illustrates, women seek similarities in the networks where they perform their mothering in order to confirm their mothering practices. The routines of children's lives provided my interviewees with an arena in which to meet other women, stimulating interaction and ultimately engendering friendships. Oliker (1998: 20) defines intimacy as 'the sharing of inner experience, mutual self-exploration and the expression of emotional attachment'. In some instances then, my participants were able to draw on a discourse of 'intimate friendship' (Oliker, 1998: 27) when describing their relationships with other women.

Rachel started a playgroup with a friend in a rural area when their children were young and continued to work with the same friend when both sets of children had grown up. In this way, her children were the foundation stone of Rachel's friendship and the same was the case for other women. Bridget recalled the move from her hometown because of her husband's work: 'I woke up the first morning that we lived here and I thought, oh, I don't know anyone!' Her solution was to join the local toddler group with her children where she soon formed new friendships, some of which continued into the present day. She voiced the feelings of others when she said her children had provided 'a very good bridge' to friendship.

Participants who mothered alone as well as those who lived in heterosexual relationships indicated they found comfort in talking to other women. This was couched in terms of being able to gain and to give support and achieve a shared understanding. Gina talked of a friend living in circumstances similar to her own, whom she had spoken to before her own daughter left home. She was able to understand more clearly her friend's experience, once her own daughter left:

> We've been through a lot together and she's got two children, separated from her husband, so we do talk quite a lot about it. She's got a child at home and the other one's left. He went in the navy so she experienced him going away, um, and I think she found that possibly harder than I felt. I can relate to the way she was feeling more now that my daughter's gone. (Gina)

For the most part, where support was available for my interviewees, it came from one (or two) close friends or relatives (sisters/female cousins) with similar experiences. Allan (1996) warns against an overemphasis on gender to understand how friendships work. However, my participants told me that speaking to other women about how they felt at the time of their children's home-leaving sustained their sense of well-being and prevented overwhelming feelings of isolation and loneliness, demonstrating that the most reliable and understanding confidante was a similarly located woman who also experienced a child leave home. It was also the case that only a small minority of my interviewees had spoken to anyone about this experience and, in consequence, their involvement in the research provided many of them with the first opportunity to talk about their feelings.

Moving On

As established so far, children as adults had effectively moved on to new ground, whilst their mothers returned to the homes they had once shared with their children as dependents. Their home lives no longer included the day-to-day caring tasks that previously structured their lives and which I suggest previously confirmed their motherhood identity.

Although in their earlier childrearing years the home had been the arena of partnership difficulties for some women and in some cases also a site of violence, at the time of my interviews with them, their perceptions of the home fitted Valentine's (2003: 63) description of 'a safe, loving and positive space' for themselves and their children. After children left, however, the home reverted to a 'three-dimensional structure' (Valentine, 2003: 63); a house, rather than the home they had previously experienced. Women's feelings in the aftermath of separation were often most strongly evoked in the home where many women initially experienced feelings of desolation. I have suggested they inhabited a liminal status at this time. As Hockey and James (1993: 8) observe however, a 'marginal social status can become a source of strength for those so classed, a position from which resistance, struggle and change can be embarked upon'.

It was evident from their narratives that over time my participants had begun to settle into their 'new' lives and began to make themselves 'at home' without their children. The final chapter discusses in more detail other transformations women experienced at this time. For now the focus is on ways in which women began to make changes in their lives that inculcated feelings of 'home' back into their households and, in turn, into their feelings about themselves as mothers who lived separately from their adult children.

For participants who still had one or more children remaining in the family home, the experience of separation from one child evoked thoughts of the departure of others. Paula, for example, said, 'well, I'll know what to expect next time, won't I?' Janice contemplated the aftermath of her daughter's future leaving in the following way:

> I wouldn't start moving her bedroom round straightaway. Maybe like a period
> of time, maybe like a mourning period where you come to accept they're not
> coming back and staying so then, then you take over and then it's yours again.
> (Janice)

The initial aftermath of children's leaving was experienced, like Janice describes, as a 'mourning period' followed by a period of adjustment during which women were more able to address to the breach their children's absence initially provoked in the home and, ultimately in their lives. My participants began to think anew of the changes children's absence made to their day-to-day lives and homes that in turn engendered an element of 'ownership'. A reclaiming of territory was evident in Janice's and other women's narratives, where the house began to re-form into a home again, albeit with a changed occupancy. Yet again, this time-period was often replete with mixed emotions:

> I went into the back bedroom, his bedroom, and started sorting stuff out and it
> must've taken me a week because ... I would come across stuff and break down
> and cry and think, oh god, you know? All his music, his scripts and scores and
> stuff that he'd written, well he left all that and ... But it was quite cathartic and
> it was quite nice to have somewhere to put the spare bedding and towels and I

arranged them all and I felt better to a certain extent, because I had reclaimed some of that space. (Angela)

When she actually finally went, um, the house felt awful. I just hated it for about three weeks, I think. I didn't like it at all. I couldn't settle. I was listless, you know, just really, um. I couldn't see the benefits of it, you know? And there are benefits. The fact that the house is so tidy for one. It doesn't need cleaning half as much, it's lovely. (Barbara)

The cathartic experience of clearing and reclaiming space that once 'belonged' to their children suggests that women moved towards a time when they were able to accept the separation from their children as well as perceive themselves as the mothers of adults from whom they lived apart. In Frances' case, this began three weeks after her daughter left; my interview with Angela took place eleven years after her son left but it was evident that her feelings were still quite raw. In her interview she also described how her readjustment to his absence in the home (although still 'incomplete') had taken several months. Robert Niemeyer and John Anderson (2002) argue that a central feature of the grieving process is the reconstruction of meaning. Thompson discusses two aspects of 'meaning reconstruction' in the advent of mourning which together inform our sense of self:

Seeking meaning by looking back on the loss experience and its impact on the frameworks of understanding that are part of our identity and sense of personal well-being ... and seeking meaning by looking forward, attempting to rebuild our lives and the meaning systems which also contribute to our ontological security. (2002: 7–8)

My participants described a readjustment of the home's spatial and temporal boundaries indicating that over time they became accustomed to life without their children. They began to reconstruct their own lives as the mothers of adult children from whom they lived apart and changes to the household were often talked about in terms of having to engage in less domestic labour and the time women were able to garner: 'well, you've got more time, haven't you? Life's a lot easier without him, really!' The fact that interviewees continued to perceive themselves as the providers of domestic labour is not the issue here, although undoubtedly they considered themselves to be responsible for the majority of tasks within the home, both practical and emotional and I return to this in a later chapter. My purpose here is to indicate that the perceptions women held of themselves as mothers were entwined in the nurturing and caring role they inhabited when their children lived at home, where I suggest domestic and emotional labour created the framework that sustained a sense of self-as-mother.

The immediate experience of separation was then followed by a period of re-adjustment during which they began to reframe their lives:

> I thought I'd miss them so dreadfully, that I would be so miserable. Then I realised that I wasn't because they were still alright, they were still around. They hadn't just gone and were never coming back. They still did want to keep in touch and I thought, oh yeah, this is ok. (Rachel)

Evident here is Rachel's initial fear that she had 'lost' her children. This was a common thread throughout the interviews. Rachel later realised this was not so, her daughters still wanted to 'keep in touch', they had not 'gone and were never coming back'. Moving towards an acceptance of separation from now-adult children was, to varying degrees, a difficult process to manage but the majority of women indicated that acceptance of their new situation, which involved redefining their relationships with their children, was underway. The next chapter considers in more detail how the reconstructed relationship of the post-separation mother and child was to a large extent dependent upon their continued interaction and communication across the geographical distances that separated them.

Concluding Remarks

> She has separated, you know, from me.
> […]
> Because she's had that time away I think, and has made decisions.
> […]
> She seems to have severed that link. I can only see her in her own place now.
> […]
> She seemed so definite in her mind about what she wanted. It was a real leaving home. (Helen)

Helen perceives her daughter to have severed her links with her mother. Her narrative moves Helen forward to a time of acceptance, indicating how she experienced the separation between herself and her daughter via her daughter's 'real leaving home'. Helen shifted across the three phases discussed in this chapter; she was prepared for her daughter's leaving, experienced separation from her and accepted her daughter's move out of the home. This indicated to Helen her daughter's now-adult status. I suggest this culminated in Helen's own transition to becoming the mother of an adult child. Also evident is that this was not experienced as a brutal severance, and in participants' experiences of separation from their adult children there was only one incidence of an unexpected and painful breach in the mother/child relationship.

Women did however progress over this seemingly rough and at times hazardous terrain and for the majority of them at least, there was an acceptance of both their own new status and that of their daughters and sons. This is not to suggest they were entirely free of the emotional entanglements in which they were embroiled during their children's and their own transitions. However, there was a sense of moving forward attached to many women's comments when they talked about how they felt in relation to their children leaving home at the time the interviews took place.

As evidenced in my research data, a mother's separation from her adult child can be an emotionally charged experience and yet it remains in many respects unspoken. Women's expectations of this time are thus incomplete; as my interviewees indicated, no one told them what it would be like. Instead the actual experience of separation underpinned and enforced their transition to becoming the mothers of adult children. Being granted the freedom to articulate their feelings to others would have been enabled by a heightened awareness of the importance of this time in a mother's life course. I do not suggest that women's experiences of separation from their children would have been substantially different if there was greater awareness of this period of time. However, women's experiences recounted here do reinforce my argument that we lack an appropriate concept of motherhood which lifts women out of the role of facilitator of dependent children's needs and moves them forward alongside their adult-children in more positive and dynamic ways.

Children's movement out of the family home is couched in a discourse that goes some way towards preventing women from speaking of their feelings of loss at this time, as participants' mixed emotions attest, and I have argued in this chapter that women need recognition and affirmation from those close to them that their grief at this time is legitimate. Furthermore I would argue that the separation between mother and child needs to be discursively reconstructed in terms of interconnectedness and interdependency, an element of the mother and adult-child relationship I shall address in different ways in the chapters that follow. The continuity of the relationship between mothers and their daughters and sons was an integral part of women's ability to manage the process of separation and move towards accepting their new status as the mothers of adult children. Although separation was complete, so that young people lived independently from their mothers in spatial terms, and for some this meant they now lived oceans apart, mothers and their children nevertheless remained interconnected; the child had moved from the home so that the relationship with the mother needed to be re-figured. In their turn, women had shifted their perspective on the house and home they now inhabited without their children. The next chapter discusses the issue of post-separation communication between women and their adult daughters and sons in order to consider its importance in the maintenance of reconfigured mother/child relationships and, in consequence, women's motherhood identities.

Chapter 5
Post-Separation Communication

Introduction

> All that coming together and drifting apart makes it possible to follow simultaneously the drive for freedom and the craving for belonging – and to cover up, if not fully make up for, the short-changing of both yearnings. (Bauman, 2003: 34)

Although focused on romantic rather than familial relationships, I use Bauman's words here because the incompatibility of 'freedom' and 'belonging' he identifies invokes a similar paradox to the one in which my interviewees found themselves enmeshed: although they wanted freedom for their daughters and sons, they simultaneously craved a continuation of the mother/child relationship and a sense of belonging, which I suggest hinged on their desire to feel needed. As established previously, my participants were immersed in a conceptual framework which promoted independence and autonomy as the main goal of their childrearing. At the same time, they acknowledged that 'keeping young people close is the mother's role, in line with the principal defining feature of modern motherhood, which is emotional attachment to children' (Brannen et al., 1994: 182). The construction of their identities as mothers therefore rested upon a contradictory set of discourses, the incongruities of which were only made manifest at the time of the child's emerging adulthood and home-leaving.

As already discussed, the notion of freedom interviewees desired for their adult children and identified earlier as a maternal aspiration, was accompanied by a confusing mix of emotions evoked when young people moved out of the family home. These elements highlight the divergence between the imagined event of children's home-leaving and its actual occurrence. Hence women's motherhood was a double-edged performance; an emotional balancing act that involved 'the difficult, vexing dialectics of the two irreconcilables' (Bauman, 2003: 34) as they attempted, albeit in different ways, to let go of their daughters and sons and at the same time remain connected to them in order to hold onto their motherhood identities. Ultimately women experienced an enforced shift in their own 'ways of being in the world' (Ribbens, 1994; Edwards and Ribbens, 1998), via their transition to becoming the mothers of the adult children from whom they lived apart.

Women experienced their children's home-leaving via three interconnected phases: preparation, separation and acceptance. Coming to terms with the absence of the now-adult child was entwined with the knowledge that the child was not in fact 'lost' to the mother; the pair remained interconnected, albeit across differences in space and time. Hence mothers and young people continued, in Bauman's words, to come together and drift apart, although for the most part not in the same physical space. How their relationships could be enacted was subsequently transformed, as distance became a metaphor for the re-negotiation of the meanings of the mother/ child dyad and ultimately the performance of motherhood itself. Contact with their daughters and sons was embedded in women's ability to sustain a sense of self-as-mother under changed conditions of communication.

This chapter pursues the significance of communicating via different technologies: the land-line telephone, the mobile/cellular phone and the internet, for my research participants' reworking of the mother/child relationship post-separation and the construction of new meanings of motherhood. Underpinning my argument is the notion that advances in technologically-mediated communication have run in parallel with the changes in young people's employment patterns and expectations of mobility. As Robins (1997: 402) notes, such rapid transitions have undermined and reconfigured 'modernist ideas concerning space, time, reality, nature'. Before going on to consider my research participants' relationships with new technologies, I offer a brief discussion of the possibilities for communication between people who are separated across geographical space.

Communicating over Space and Time

Before the advent of technologically mediated communication, interpersonal and face-to-face contact occurred in 'environments in which two or more individuals [were] physically in one another's response presence' (Goffman, 1972: 2; see also Berger and Luckmann, 1966). Post-separation contact across geographical distances relied on the postal service and later, telegrams, each of which provided non-interactive, one-way communication, underscored by the time that elapsed between sending and receiving. The land-line telephone, mobile phone and computer have since facilitated immediate 'interpersonal communication at a distance, either by electronically transmitted speech or by written text' (Moores, 2000: 141). Indeed, as Freed comments:

> We've progressed from single-strand copper wires carrying telegraphs in Morse code to twisted pairs of copper wires carrying voices, faxes, data and video. Telecommunication advances into coaxial cables and now optical fibres are offering a range of interactive services never before possible. (Freed, 2001: 1)

Although, as Sarah Holloway and Gill Valentine (2000: 768) remind us, technological development is geographically uneven and 'the wired world is not inclusive, as many countries of the South are less integrated into these networks than their counterparts in the North', access to the World Wide Web (whilst not denying the existence of spatial unevenness within the UK as well) has become part of the fabric of daily life. As Robert Kitchin (1998: 386) states it 'offers users a range of interactions, allowing them to explore the world beyond their home'. Indeed, its use in the home outstrips that of commerce and academe (Batty and Barr, 1994). Nowadays, the majority of the population in the UK have access to the internet, either at home, an educational establishment or the workplace. Alongside this we have witnessed an upsurge in the availability of internet access in public spaces such as libraries and internet cafés. To be sure, the internet café culture is a growing phenomenon that offers a domain where people can connect with those they are geographically separated from.

The ubiquitous ownership of the mobile phone also promises that we can make contact, and be contacted, wherever we are; we no longer have to be fixed to a particular place in order to interact with others. Bauman (2003: 61) informs us that 'cell phones signal, materially and symbolically, the ultimate liberation from place'. The TV advertisement for *Vodafone* transmitted into our homes during the summer of 2006 offered its viewers a glimpse of the places mobile phones can take us. Viewers watched (and interpreted) as two white women walked through a forest, one middle-aged, one younger (mother and daughter), their heads were close together as they talked (the giving and receiving of maternal guidance and advice). At the edge of the forest (the end of adolescent turbulence) the daughter crossed a bridge alone (separation from the mother) and we were shown the mother's anxious face as she silently watched her daughter leave the forest (maternal concern, protectiveness and powerlessness). The young woman stopped at the end of the bridge (passively awaiting fulfilment) and a young white male flew through the clouds and took her hands (heterosexual coupledom). As they gazed into each other's eyes and flew off together, the soundtrack played, *I'm on another world with you*. In the final shot, the same young woman is walking down a busy street talking on her mobile phone. The voiceover asks the viewer: 'where will your conversations take you?' (the advertisement can be viewed at www.vodafone.com).

The imagery of this advertisement promises 'liberation from place' with the possibility of our presence simultaneously here and elsewhere. As such it provokes a blurring of the boundaries of the real/virtual dichotomy. As Holloway and Valentine (2003: 107) comment, 'this ability of things to influence our emotions (bringing comfort, confidence, sensual pleasure, evoking memories, etc.) is after all, the basis of most consumer advertising'. In current advertising for technology, with its cast of 'familiar' characters, such playing with our emotions is evidently at work. In a similar vein to *Vodafone*, for example, the advertisement for *Tesco Internet Phones* portrays a mother at home contacting her daughter in another town. The camera pans out to expose a map of Britain, then the world and finally the moon (!), each with *Tesco* icons indicating where the internet phone can be utilised, the ultimate message being its ability to immediately connect people across geographical spaces. Helen Fulton (2005a: 5) comments that 'the extent to which we feel ourselves to be part of an audience depends on whether we feel addressed by a media text'. I suggest that the airing of these advertisements during the summer is key to their impact as this heralds the end of compulsory full-time education, is post A-levels, pre gap year and so on.

As Rosemary Huisman (2005: 286) comments, 'advertising writes stories which link products or objects with subject positions of desired attributes, such as those of being manly, neighbourly or adventurous and so on'; in other words, the products on sale are imbued with social and personal meanings. In the advertisements discussed above, the discourse of heterosexual normativity is pervasive, alongside a normalising of the westernised autonomous and mobile lifestyle (except, perhaps, for the mother-figures in these advertisements, who presumably remain at the edge of the forest/in the family home, anxiously waiting for the telephone to ring. The problematic of mothers' autonomy is more fully explored in the next chapter). Thus *Vodafone* and *Tesco* invite us to 'taste the pleasures of narrative and figuration, of recognizing stories and images of which one is part' (Haraway, 1997: 169). In so doing, they not only inform us that geographical distances between family members are now commonplace, but also that contact with others across such distances is not an obstacle since we can enjoy a simulated or 'virtual visit' to them at any time. As Cheris Kramarae states:

> The claims for what the Internet has done or will do to change our lives for much the better are widely available in the media, in news stories, advertisements, and editorials. Clearly many people in many countries are going about their work, their communication, and their relationships in somewhat different ways because of their use of the Net. (1998: 100)

These TV advertisements, and others like them imply, as Kramarae notes, that the techno-goods on offer will service our relationships and ultimately the way we live our lives, because they bring us 'close to' those we live separately from. Travel in 'cyberspace' is presented as a mundane and daily occurrence, as indeed it has become for many, whereas two decades or more ago such journeys dwelt in the imaginations of science-fiction writers such as Gibson (1984), who originally coined the term in his novel *Neuromancer*. I am employing the term 'cyberspace' here to refer to the non-place I suggest we all 'inhabit' when using technologically-mediated forms of communication for human interaction, e.g. landline telephones, mobile/cellular phones and the internet. I am thus following Mike Featherstone and Roger Burrows who define cyberspace as:

> A generic term which refers to a cluster of different technologies, some familiar, some only recently available, some being developed and some still fictional, all of which have in common the ability to simulate environments within which humans can interact. (Featherstone and Burrows, 1995: 5)

As Freed (2001: 1) states, 'once a change is naturalized, the new order of life is naturalized in us from birth'. The repetitive nature of advertising and the 'simulation of the real' (Fulton, 2005b: 303) normalize distance and render communication technology devices necessary possessions for the continuance of daily life as we continue to live and understand it. In her discussion of technoscience, Donna Haraway (1997: 100) identifies cyberspace as a 'technical-semiotic zone [that] script[s] the future'. Certainly the scripting of these advertisements and blurring of the dichotomies of present/future, local/global and real/virtual promotes a shift in the definitions of contact, distance and time alongside a reconfiguration of 'touch'. They also grant immediate gratification: we just need to push the right buttons. Technologically-mediated communication therefore allows human interactions to occur immediately across time, space and place, engendering an imagined merging of tangible and intangible connections to those we are geographically separated from, be they in the next street, town or country. From a western perspective they have, as Toke Christensen (2009: 433) comments 'become an integral part of society and everyday life'.

New technologies enable communication across geographical distances and as such posit a reconceptualisation of human relationships. In light of this, the remainder of this chapter follows my research participants' use of the landline telephone, the mobile phone and the internet in order to consider whether their use of such technologies reconciled the two disparate notions of rupture and continuity they experienced in the aftermath of their children's leaving.

Does Distance Make a Difference?

> I suppose, like a lot of parents, I liked to know they were safe, and the only way they could possibly be safe was if they were with me [laughs] and it's still true today! I think worrying's a way, as long as it doesn't become over-obsessive, it's a way of ensuring the children are safe, isn't it? Because if we didn't consider all the things that could happen then they would, you know, fall down the first manhole they came across, wouldn't they? (Angela)

Many women identified, as Angela does, the conflation of closeness and protection as 'part of' motherhood. As Holloway and Valentine (2003: 7) suggest, 'risk and safety are increasingly central to the construction of childhood'. Evidently in her children's adulthoods this notion continued to underscore Angela's maternal feelings and concerns. Although both sons lived locally, her comments indicate how their absence from the home created feelings of anxiety for her regarding their safety in the 'unknown' space outside the front-door; a habit of Angela's earlier mothering practises. Although conveyed in an amusing way, Angela's expression of motherly protection and concern, made manifest in episodes of worry and anxiety, was a common feature of the interview data. Worry and anxiety were not however, perceived as weaknesses, but as part of the make-up of motherhood and defined as indicators of maternal care. In this way, closeness to the mother translated as safety for the child, a basic principle of motherhood alluded to in earlier chapters, and inherent in the concept of being there. Gina, for example, said of her daughter's move into her own home in a nearby street:

> She wasn't moving far away so I think, in that respect, it helped. You felt you could still be there for her if she needed you to be. Because you're quite protective of all children, but when they've not been well, I would've been quite concerned, having known that she'd been suffering from depression, if she was going away, perhaps to university, and living in a flat on her own or something. I would've been concerned about her mental health, but because she was close I felt, well, if she needs me, I'm not far away. (Gina)

Presence is then coupled with safety and security and in turn also renders the practical and emotional tasks of motherhood easier to perform, particularly when, as Gina's experience highlights, children's teenage years had been challenging. Having easy access to daughters and sons because they lived locally obviously had an impact on how women felt:

> I think because my eldest son's near it's better probably. He pops in all the time and I still do bits and pieces for him. He comes for a meal every week so if he forgets something, or wants something, or even if he's just been in the village, he'll just pop in and say 'hello', you know, so we see him quite regularly, really. (Frances)

Similarly, Serena said, 'I know that I can see them at any time, yeah. So for all they've spread their wings and they've got their own places they're, um, yeah, still quite close'. Alma contemplated the difference created by her daughters living in separate places from one another:

> The only problem is if either of them needed me in a hurry, I could be at my youngest daughter's in 15/20 minutes, whereas with my eldest daughter, you're two-plus hours away, so that's the difference but … that is the only drawback, I suppose, the fact that there is that particular distance. (Alma)

Alma helped in a situation with her younger daughter's abusive boyfriend. As she indicates, she was able to reach her within minutes to provide the help and support her daughter needed. This culminated in a short stay in Alma's house where she provided her daughter with maternal protection and security. Having children who lived locally did not necessarily mean women were unable to acknowledge the adult status of their daughters and sons:

> It's nice that my daughter's not too far and yet I think if she was in the village we'd maybe be too close. I think, in a way, the distance is nice and it makes me feel that she is completely independent, type of thing. … We do see each other but we are, you know, two separate families. I always think of them as, although

of course they're part of a wider family, but they are a complete family of their own. A separate unit. And it's a strong unit, you know? (Helen)

A grown man, yeah, my son'll come in and say, 'you should see the state he's left that kitchen in' about his flatmate. Just the kind of thing I used to say to him. So, yeah, it's changed him I think. He has to take a bit more responsibility, I suppose. (Serena)

Adulthood took the form of responsibility for the self in the case of Serena's son and for Helen, her daughter's setting up home with her partner and baby provided evidence of an adult self via the formation of a separate household. The nuclear family unit was linked with the notion of adult children's 'settling down' by several women, when it appeared to validate a young person's independence and a perceived completion of separation from the mother. This also had an impact on women's future decision-making, discussed in more detail in the next chapter.

Physical proximity for many interviewees was articulated as easing the perceived practical and emotional performance of motherhood. In its turn, this highlighted the difficulties envisaged and experienced by separation across wider geographical spaces. Because her daughter lived approximately forty miles away, Barbara told me 'it is difficult when you're not physically close'. Although at the time of the interviews Janice's son had returned to live locally, he originally went to a university sixty miles away. Nancy's daughter's university was almost four-hundred miles away from her hometown:

I can't concentrate if either of them have a problem of any kind, you know, then it affects me and my husband will say, 'don't let it get you down' and I say, 'no, I know, but I can't, it's on my mind, I want to resolve it, what can I do?' because you've just done it all their lives and, even though they're in adulthood, you still want to help, you know? (Janice)

It was just this awful feeling, you know, worrying about them, hoping they'll be alright, hoping that they'll cope, hoping that they're happy. Just hoping for them, really. Not worrying about yourself so much as worrying about them, and having to do it from a distance. (Nancy)

As already established my interviewees subscribed to western notions of autonomy and independence as the goal of their mothering and as essential indicators of adulthood (Guhman, 1999) yet long-distance worry and concern for children's ability to cope alone, that is, without their mothers, was evident. Worry and anxiety are also exposed here as maternal rather than paternal concerns. As Brannen et al. (1994: 205) state, a mother's 'predicament is manifest in maternal worry – based on a combination of responsibility and impotence'. My participants' experiences of maternal impotence seemingly occurred because of geographical distances that created a barrier to the performance of motherhood as defined and previously practised by them. As Janice said, 'you've just done it all their lives', emphasising the difficulty in letting go of the responsibilities that become embedded in the intertwining life course of mother and child.

Geographical distance was perceived in practical terms by some interviewees. It did not, as Maggie told me, 'represent much of a problem except when you have to get in the car and drive through the night but, you know, that's just one of those things that you have to do'. Similarly, Rachel felt she could reach her daughters easily as it was 'a hundred miles to one of them and forty or fifty to the other. You can go up and down in a day. I think I still feel like they're quite accessible'. In some instances then, perceiving children to be easily accessible alleviated anxieties women might experience.

Unlike Rachel and Maggie, children's physical absence in the home overrode both Janice and Paula's ability to rationalise the manageability of the relatively short distances between them and their sons:

> My son's at Sheffield University and somebody once said to me, 'god, you'd think he was a million miles away' and I said, 'well, it doesn't matter, when they're not here, they're not here', you know? When they're not at home, they're not at home, full-stop! (Paula)

> Leeds was only an hour away but … he wasn't in the home, he wasn't coming home on a night, so he could've been in London, it would've been exactly the same type of thing. It's strange really, the distance didn't have anything, you know, I didn't think, oh, we're an hour away, type of thing. It was just that he wasn't there. (Janice)

Although Paula and Janice articulate their inability to cope with absence across nationally defined distances, as Rachel and Maggie show, the difficulties that arose when daughters and sons living outside their hometown but still within the UK were manageable in practical terms as all of my interviewees were financially secure enough to either drive/be driven or use public transport in order to visit and be visited by their children. However, when young people's plans took them outside of the UK, geographical distance took on another set of practical and emotional meanings: 'my son was homesick and it was horrible, because he was right on the other side of the world' (Fiona). Fiona's inability to comfort her son was reinforced by the great distance that separated them. Bridget's daughter previously worked in Africa and, at the time of the interview, was studying in America. Her son was studying in China:

> I think there is an added something about them physically going such a long, long way. I mean, if they were in London or Leeds, even, I mean, maybe we wouldn't have seen them for several weeks at a stretch but … it just, sort of, feels different I suppose. It sounds very simplistic, but it's just such a blooming long way and, um, there isn't the option of popping to see them for a day or a

weekend or whatever, you can't do it and, yeah, it just feels very, very cut off.
(Bridget)

Physical separation across wider geographical distances here carries with it the notion of severance; Bridget was physically 'cut off' from her children. She did not have the option of 'popping in' to see them, and plans for visiting had practical as well as financial ramifications. Different ways of conceptualising distance and varied interpretations of near and far were thus evident in women's narratives; geographical distance between mothers and their daughters and sons was then differently experienced and managed. However, changes occurred over the time this group of women mothered and these led Bridget to observe: 'everybody nowadays is expected to be mobile, whereas at one time it wouldn't have … it would have been very unusual, wouldn't it?'

Changes over Time

My mum's two uncles emigrated at the end of the First World War and so my mum never met them. My grandma and her brothers never saw each other again … As soon as her brothers emigrated, that was it and she had letters and photographs but my grandma never went out of East Yorkshire! So the thought of going to visit her brothers in Australia was just beyond comprehension, so, really, the world's a much smaller place now, isn't it? (Fiona)

Fiona drew on 'past/present family biography' (Tulloch and Lupton, 2003: 119) to make an historical comparison with her own situation. Changes in mobility occurring across generations can be traced through her reflections on the experiences of her ancestors. In their study of risk-taking, John Tulloch and Deborah Lupton (2003: 119) found that the conditions under which mobility is undertaken in the UK are currently 'more fortunate, since the industrial concentrations and confines of "place" have been breached'. The ability to leave the UK for other continents is indicative of the reaches of travel nowadays. An article in the UK *Observer* newspaper (06/08/06) for example, reported on the massification of tourism that has in effect changed the culture of air travel: 'what was once the rare indulgence of a privileged elite has become everyday […] It used to cost several thousand pounds to go to New York; now it is as cheap as chips'.

Alongside changes in global opportunities, and because of them as well, young people are increasingly taking 'gap' years either before or after university and travelling/working abroad. This was the case of several interviewees' children. Women were well-acquainted with global change and welcomed it as providing the possibility of widening horizons for daughters and sons.[1]

---

1 A television programme aired in June 2007 and entitled *Mind the Gap Year*, documented a number of recent tragic accidents and young people's disappearances; the

Recognition of the world having changed is of primary importance here. Women's awareness of the ease of access to travel alongside the increasing availability of cheap flights rendered distance less problematic than during their own youth. As Fiona indicates above, it was male family members who previously emigrated, whilst females were 'left behind'. I would add therefore that one of the major transformations in travel opportunities for young people in the west is the acceptance and expectation that daughters as well as sons will grasp the opportunities for travel/work abroad and will, for the most part, do so with maternal backing and approval:

> I want them to have adventures … I like the idea of, you know, the swallows that shoot off to Africa and then they come back again. As long as my daughters keep shooting off and coming back I'll be happy. I've actually got three swallows tattooed on my back and I told them that's why it was. That's what I want them to do; to feel free to go as far as they like, but don't forget to come back. As long as I know they're there, I think. (Rachel)

That people are no longer confined to a particular place for employment and/or other experiences was often acknowledged by my interviewees. Judith for instance said of her musician son: 'he might work in America. He might work all over the place, I don't know, and when that time comes, I'll just have to get used to it'. Judith's son initially left home for university within the UK. She did not expect him to return to live locally but rather believed that he would travel further afield in order to pursue his musical ambitions and that this was something Judith would 'get used to'. Similarly, and although very positive about her three daughters' future travels, Rachel hinted at the possibility they might not return. Another fear for some women was that geographical distance might also mean loss of contact and communication: 'I just hope my sons don't just drift away, you know, with living away' (Sally).

Anxieties regarding young people travelling and working abroad emerged in women's perceptions of their children traversing previously unexplored territories. As Paula said of her son's intention to work in America, 'I'll worry more! It's the unknown, isn't?' and when Nancy talked about her son's travelling in Australia and New Zealand she said, 'it's a whole unknown quantity, really … when he's in a base, I feel happier. When he starts moving around I feel more ill at ease'. The ability to fix her son geographically lessened feelings of worry and anxiety for Nancy. I suggest that this was at times linked to women's inability, perhaps like their mothers before them, to envisage the whereabouts of adult children whose location in the world was for the most part outside their own experiences.

---

ongoing trial for the murder of student Meredith Kercher in 2007 is frequently reported on TV and in newspapers; the *Guardian* (03/10/09) recently reported the disappearance in Panama of 29-year-old Alex Humphrey. Public knowledge of such incidents might mean that travel loses its appeal as well as its maternal support.

Nancy was, however, one of two interviewees who had worked outside the UK as younger women. Her son's travelling abroad caused Nancy to contemplate her own mother's experience:

> I worked abroad for a while. I taught in Germany and travelled around there. My mother wouldn't be able to envisage that scenario because it was out of her experience, but she would still have those maternal feelings, wouldn't she? (Nancy)

Nancy imagined her mother had the same 'maternal feelings' she experienced herself, centred again on worry and anxiety. As she said, 'what you worry about changes, that's all, and you've no control over what's happening to them'. Although the majority of women expressed similar concerns to those discussed so far, interviewees also articulated they wanted experiences for their children that differed from their own: 'I always wanted my eldest daughter to travel, because it was something I used to dream of' (Dawn); 'it was an adventure for me for her to go away' (Rita). In this way, the location of children was unproblematic in so far as maternal ambitions were being satisfied by young people's pursuance of their individual goals. Overall geographical distances between women and their children were accepted as a fact of their new way of life, to which they would become accustomed:

> If my son does what he wants to do as a career, he's not going to come back to [hometown] because there's nothing in this area. So he will always live away. Um, if he's lucky, he'll probably travel the world, doing what he wants to do but … so he'll be … always away from here. But that doesn't mean to say, you know, that there's not that bond between us. There will always be that bond. (Judith)

Judith had accepted that after leaving university and in order for him to achieve his aspirations, her son would 'always live away', but as she indicates it was not perceived that the bonds between them would be broken. The maintenance of maternal ties with adult children was integral to the emotional management of the geographical distances between my participants and their daughters and sons. To this end, women's interpellation into technologically mediated communication helped to maintain these bonds across the distances that separated them. Although Christensen (2009: 441) argues that mobile phone use 'is highest when the children are young and decreases as they grow older and become more independent', in what follows I will reveal that once my participants' 'independent' children left home, the mobile phone, as well as other mediating technologies, emerged as frequently used communication tools. I suggest that in its turn, women's involvement with such devices sustained their identities as mothers.

The Landscape of Communication

> I wrote letters home, but I only phoned very, very occasionally. Um, and that went on when I was at college. Then I worked in Essex to begin with, then in Germany. All of that time it was mainly letters and just a very isolated phone call. No mobiles. No emails. And that was how it was done and you ... So things are very different now. (Nancy)

> When I spoke to my eldest son the other week, I couldn't believe he was thousands of miles away. It just sounded as though he was in the next room, it was so clear. I think it'd be very hard if we couldn't do that ... It must've been a lots worse for people in the past, when people emigrated and things like that. (Sally)

Historical comparisons are again made here this time by Nancy and Sally who draw attention to the changes in communication mechanisms that have occurred over time. In his discussion of intra-familial mobile phone use in everyday life, Christensen (2009: 437) comments how calls and text messages contribute 'to the creation of a general sense of closeness between family members when they are physically separated'. Indeed, Sally explained how unproblematic contact with her son made his absence more manageable and easier to cope with. Her engagement with 'distance-transcending technologies' (Wood and Smith, 2001: 70) meant her son felt close by, he was almost tangible, thus adding to her acceptance of his absence. Interviewees also highlighted the changes in communication possibilities that occurred within their own lifetimes. In reflecting on their own experiences of leaving home, comparisons were again made between their own and their mothers' feelings at the time of mother/adult child separation:

> But, you know, how did my mum feel when I went into the army? We didn't have a phone in the house. I mean, I joined the army at 18, but it's interesting, I hadn't given this any consideration, but my daughter had a phone in her room and she had her mobile, so I knew I could get her at any time. So, how would it have changed my feelings if there hadn't been that level of contact? (Ingrid)

Although it is not possible to know the answer to Ingrid's question I would nevertheless propose that the ability to be in contact with, and be contacted by, absent daughters and sons alleviated some of the feelings of anxiety and worry my participants might have experienced otherwise. James Lull (2001: 1) emphasises 'the significance that communication processes hold for real people as they engage the entire range of material and symbolic resources at their disposal'. Post-separation contact with daughters and sons was essential in the lives of my interviewees and their engagement with communication technologies ensured this was possible. In redefining 'the meaning of the technology' (Holloway and Valentine, 2003: 123) the mobile phone and other technologies took up a significant presence in my participants' lives and, I would add, those of their adult children.

The phrase 'keeping in touch' is commonly articulated, even though we are unable to physically touch those we are geographically separated from. Indeed, one of the issues women talked about was how they 'kept in touch' with their daughters and sons now they no longer lived in the family home:

> I've realised my first words to my eldest son are, 'where are you?' and I always say it. I said it last night to him. I want to know where he is so I can imagine him there. (Paula)

Paula's question to her son is one we can imagine is asked every time we hear the words, 'I'm on the train'. As she said, it was the first thing she asked her son. Anne Markham (1998: 88) comments that individual identities can be 'maintained through technology'. When talking on the phone to her son, Paula, like other of my interviewees, created a sense of place into which she could fix him and, in imagining him there, eased her anxiety in the knowledge that he was 'safe' in the 'uncertain' world outside the home. I suggest that at the same time she fixed herself as the mother of her son, easing her own anxieties regarding her changed maternal role.

Contacting her son through the wires of technology alleviated some of Paula's anxieties, but for some interviewees the location of their children was not always conducive to this. The majority of people in the world are, as Cheris Kramarae (1998: 109) notes 'without basic telecommunication, and Internet access time and computer equipment are relatively much more expensive for those in South Asia and Africa than for those living in most Northern countries'. When my participant Bridget's daughter left home to work in Africa, her crossing of geographical and cultural boundaries meant she and Bridget glimpsed first-hand the spatial unevenness and unequal distribution of communication technologies. In a lived contradiction of the advertisements I outlined earlier, Bridget and her daughter were confronted with obstacles to communication not previously experienced: 'no telephone, no email' (Bridget). Instead they relied on letter-writing, which in itself posed major difficulties:

> Letters were very unpredictable and, as it happened, the first letter that she wrote to us took the longest to arrive. It took four weeks to get here, so I didn't know if she'd got my letters, I didn't know if she was ok, didn't know anything about where they were or, um, I didn't know what she was doing. I just knew nothing! She just kind of disappeared, really, and I found that really, really difficult. … When we got the letter, oh it was wonderful, 'oh, she's alive!' [laughs]. So I wrote lots of letters that year. (Bridget)

Bridget found her daughter's later move to America much more tolerable: 'I suppose because we'd done it once before and because the communication's so much easier from there'. Steve Jones (1998: xii) suggests that 'electronically distributed, almost instantaneous, communication has for many people supplanted the postal service'. Apart from Bridget above, and Nancy who said, 'I don't think I've exchanged any letters with my daughter or my son except to send them something, you know, and you put in a letter', none of the women I spoke to used letter-writing as a form of communication. Lupton (1995: 99) identifies the relationship between computer and user as 'symbiotic'. She suggests that human interaction with such technologies renders other equipment, such as the pen, 'awkward as writing instruments'. Indeed, as Heather said, 'I never write to them, no, I never write letters'. It was the case as well that the nomadic lifestyles of some adult children once they left home also meant there was no 'physical' place letters to which letters could be addressed. Computer mediated communication therefore became a more than adequate substitute.

Heather used email to contact her four sons which, like letter-writing, is reliant (for the most part) on text via the internet. Unlike letter-writing it is immediate: the here-and-now can be transmitted instantaneously:

> When one of my sons was travelling, it was email. When he was in Canada, because he worked in a ski resort for about five or six months and then he went travelling, um, through Canada, through the Rockies and into the States, so it was always email then and ... I think we had a couple of telephone calls, that was all. (Heather)

Heather also said that during her sons' travels he would 'email about once a week and that was quite nice because we saved them all as well, um, to pass on to his grandma and granddad'. The transformation of emails from electronic media to printed object meant they performed the same function as letters; they could be passed on for other family members to read, strengthening wider familial ties. They could also be kept. One of the differences between electronic communication, such as email and mobile phone texting is that, although like letters they are text-based, they are not tangible nor, keep-able objects (unless printed off, as in Heather's case). Internet mail boxes and mobile phone files 'fill-up' and messages have to be deleted. They do not/cannot therefore concretise memories of times past.

Email did however act as a mediator of everyday news of their children's lives for several of my participants. Dawn's daughter, for example, was buying a house in America: 'so at the moment I'm getting emails with pictures'; Nancy talked about her son's travels: 'he emails us photos and things'. Having access to images of their children's lives points again to the mitigation of the loss of proximity computer mediated communication might make possible in some instances, that of rendering the 'unknown' less mysterious and therefore less daunting. Nowadays, 'other places' are, to a great extent, no longer outside our scope of vision and because we can 'see' them, they might no longer hold the mystery they once did for previous generations. From the perspective of my participants, such images also performed the function of bringing them 'closer to' their absent daughters and sons, engendering meaningful exchanges in which they felt included; they remained 'part of' their adult children's lives, wherever they were in the world.

In commenting on an overlooked characteristic of computer mediated communication, Fernback and Thompson (1995: 9) suggest there is 'the possibility, even likelihood, that as CMC grows in popularity, there will be less need for face-to-face interaction'. Certainly my research participants had taken full advantage of this means of communication once their children left home. I am reluctant to claim, however, that a mother's desire for interaction with her child in the same physical space (as well as the adult child's need for face to face contact with the mother) could be overridden by CMC. I would rather suggest, as Markham (1998) has done, that technological devices in some cases might formulate harsh reminders of the geographical distances that exist between women and their children. I also would argue that practising 'virtual' motherhood will never become a substitute for mothering in the 'real' world.

Following Elisabeth Grosz (1994), Lupton (1995: 98–9) asserts that 'inanimate objects, when touched or on the body for long enough, become extensions of the body image and sensation. They become psychically invested into the self'. Referring to the mobile phone and its users Ingrid declared: 'it's so much of an accessory now … people have become so dependent on it'. In these terms, the mobile phone is indeed becoming an 'extension of the self in wider space' (Holloway and Valentine, 2003: 101). Although obviously alarmed by what she perceived as its insidious nature, Ingrid did own a mobile phone herself so that her daughter could contact her: 'I guess because my daughter has this thing about exams, and she needs to feel confident'. In this instance, as in others too, the mobile phone was a link to the mother for the child, where a supportive boost of confidence was immediately accessed.

Instantaneous messaging via the mobile phone often allayed anxieties, as Janice said of her son: 'he realises that if he just texts or gives us a quick ring, everything's fine'. In almost echoing the advertisements outlined earlier, Frances said, 'with text messages, you're in touch whenever you want, aren't you really?' At times the mobile phone took on an almost iconic status:

One of my stepsons is not brilliant at keeping in touch either but, you know, mobile phones have been the *salvation* of contact really. (Heather)

But the mobile phone is a *godsend*. I didn't really want to hear her voice, I just wanted to get the message, 'I'm ok' or, 'I've made a friend called so-and-so, we're going out tonight'. Those were the messages I wanted, yeah, yeah. How they managed in the olden days without them I don't know. (Rita)

Rita again refers to the past management of separation; as she intimates, advances in technology are perceived to have made geographical distance less relevant as far as communication is concerned. She also voices her desire to know her daughter was engaged in the everyday activities of making friends and 'going out'. Rita, like other interviewees, wanted to hear about the mundane to enable her to fix her daughter in a place of relative safety. In so doing she was able to alleviate some of her anxieties. I suggest that having access to snippets of the lives of their daughters and sons via email, mobile phones and text-messaging reassured women that their children were engaged in the ordinary, everyday activities they previously performed before they left home. The quest for adventure and freedom women claimed to want for their children was therefore clouded by an underlying desire for their lives to be safely grounded in an everyday 'normality' taking place in the 'uncertain' space of the world outside the home.

As Bauman (2003: 63) comments: 'the advent of electronically assured out-of-placeness makes travel safer, less risky and off-putting than ever before', suggesting that 'it cancels out many of the past limits to the magnetic power of "going places"'. However, regardless of the 'location awareness [that] is built into cellular phone systems' (Rheingold, 2002: 98) on occasion, our reliance on it and indeed trust in its infallibility did occasionally cause my participants to experience feelings of unease:

> I just don't want them to … I just have the idea that, if my daughter did [travel] the only way I would know where she was is her mobile phone number, and you don't know where that mobile phone is. And if it didn't get paid for, or got lost, you actually wouldn't know and you could lose someone. You actually wouldn't know where on earth someone was. Scary! (Rachel)

Nevertheless, Rachel's children and those of my other interviewees were encouraged to 'go places'. Women's travels in cyberspace in order to be close to their adult children allowed 'meaningful human activities [to take] place' (Markham, 1998: 88). In most instances, interviewees were able to use available technologies as forms of contact with absent daughters and sons, maintaining their relationships and sustaining feelings of the self-as-mother.

In her discussion of computer usage Lupton (1995: 98) asserts that 'rather than the computer/human dyad being a simple matter of self versus other, there is, for many people, a blurring of the boundaries between the embodied self and the PC'. A similar 'blurring' emerged from interview data regarding techno-goods such as the internet, land-line telephone and mobile phone. Indeed, although communication technologies are (not yet) built into our flesh (but see Jones, Williams and Fleuriot, 2003), mobile phones were almost-integral appendages for my interviewees. They allowed byte-sized chunks of their adult children's everyday lives, although this was not always a reciprocal arrangement.

Two-Way Interaction?

> I got a mobile for when he went away because I thought, at least I can text, you know? I don't have to speak to him all the time and I can get messages. He does

send me messages so, it's not the same as speaking, but at least he's thinking about me, you know? (Paula)

In their discussion of on-line interactions, Andrew Wood and Matthew Smith (2001: 80–1) note that 'it is the *sender,* who possesses greater control of self-presentation to others' and that 'the *receiver* can overestimate the qualities' of the sender. There remains therefore, 'an uncertainty about whether or not the message was received and interpreted in the way it was intended' (original emphases). In Paula's case, the intention and interpretation of text messaging between her and her son are probably the same; her son intends Paula to be consoled by his messages and, indeed, she is. Accepting text messaging as an adequate form of communication proved an important watershed for Paula, helping to ameliorate past tensions:

> He went back to university in September and, um, for the first three weeks he didn't ring me at all and I rang him two or three times and he said, 'what're you ringing all the time for?' and I said, 'I'm not'. He said, 'I'm fine, you don't have to ring me all the time' [laughs]. Well, I just sat and cried. ... I wanted to ring every day. I'd sit here on a night thinking, don't ring him, don't ring [laughs]. (Paula)

Embedded within her son's decision to text Paula there might be gleaned his covert intention to fend off what he perceived as her intrusion into his life. Paul Levinson (2004: 89) states that the mobile phone means that 'there is no place anyone can be away from family now', adding that previously 'to leave the home was to leave both the physical space and most of the communication. Nowadays the cellphone keeps the family's communication intact when the home is left behind'. Levinson relates his comments to the lives of young people prior to home-leaving. As he suggests, possession of the mobile phone does indicate the possibility of an increase in parental 'surveillance'.

As Holloway and Valentine (2000: 763) observe, 'children's identities are constituted in and through particular spaces'. As already established, the space of the home was construed by my research participants as a place of safety for their children. With the advent of mobile phone ownership, public spaces might have been rendered less 'dangerous'; the child is contactable and, by default, 'safe' as the mobile phone in her pocket simulates an extension of the reach of the home/ mother. In his discussion of 'remote parenting' for example, Christensen (2009: 436) comments that the mobile phone 'provides a general sense of security [and is] one of the strongest motives for purchasing a mobile phone'. According to Owain Jones and his colleagues (Jones, Williams and Fleuriot, 2003: 169) 'child-technology interaction subtly reconfigures not only childhood and its spatialities but also the childhood-adult interface' in so far as mothers and their children are experiencing new ways of being connected. I would add that this applies to the periods both before and after children leave home.

It is possible that parents and their children might read different meanings into the potential for mutual contact provided by the new technologies I am discussing here. Brannen and her colleagues offer some understanding of this when they suggest that during the teenage years and before leaving home, young people seek independence from their parents and interpret parental concerns and anxieties as interference so that 'maintaining channels of communication has a different kind of significance for them'. They continue:

> It is the control aspects of the Janus-headed character of communication in parent-child relationships which concerns them more. While young people may interpret gentle enquiry from parents as signs of love and concern, more persistent demands for information may be perceived as unwarranted and unwelcome prying and interference. (Brannen et al., 1994: 183–4)

In a similar way to Paula, my participant Linda facilitated the means by which her son could contact her, paying for land-line phone installation in his university accommodation, and paying for credit on his mobile phone. Nevertheless, her strategies for ensuring communication were unsuccessful:

> I'm just in dispute with him at the moment because he was playing his first paid-for gig with his friends, with the rock band, and I did expect him … to text us or to tell us how he'd got on and I've texted twice and I've emailed once and he's still not been in touch, really … I did say, 'right, well, text tonight' and, um, he hasn't done. So I'm a bit disappointed. (Linda)

In both of these instances, mothers' interest in their sons' activities was seemingly unwelcome. This obvious resistance to cooperating with a mothers' desire for continued communication is indicative of a shift in issues of power and control. Mothers and their adult children had equal access to technologies such as the mobile phone. Both groups were then able to initiate, refuse or terminate communication via cyberspace; each then had the freedom to communicate and the freedom not to.

Communication became the prerogative of Paula and Linda's sons in terms of when and how much contact they were willing to commit to once they had left home for university. As discussed earlier, children's home-leaving forced a disjuncture in the meanings of 'child' and 'adult' and as such created a dilemma for some of my interviewees. Maternal (over)concern might then be perceived as control by children, and mothers' inability to let go of practices that might be defined as 'controlling' thus placed the child as adult in a particular position from which they re/acted accordingly.

As Teri Apter (1990) argues, at this stage in their life course, young people desire acknowledgement of their adult status from their parents and in consequence recognition of their ability to be responsible for themselves in some respects. Indeed, in his research into young people's interactions with their parents via the mobile phone prior to home-leaving, Christensen (2009: 442) found that 'parental calls can be interpreted by adolescents as interfering and challenging their desire for independence'.

It was apparent from their narratives that some of my research participants were unable to meet their children's 'desire' for independence because it was at odds with how they perceived their mothering role and so in turn, their children; mothers might in this instance however interpret their own actions as a continuance of their role to meet children's needs. Holdsworth and Morgan (2005: 104) found from their research with young people that leaving home might allow for 'more control over how [children] interact with parents in time and space'. As can be discerned from my own and others studies then, a shift in the balance of control between mothers and their adult children is seemingly instigated by physical separation which begins when the child still resides in the family home and, I suggest, might well increase once they leave it.

Although independence was the goal of women's childrearing strategies, this does not automatically translate as young people's lack of communication, or their negation of responsibility for others. Overall the majority of women I interviewed reported very few problems regarding their children's acceptance of responsibility for the reciprocation of communication, although as Paula and Linda's experiences indicate, sons were at times less committed to maintaining contact on any kind of regular basis:

> I think all the while my daughter has tried harder with the contact than my son has. I don't think that it's that he doesn't care. I think, in a way, he's a typical young male. I think, generally speaking, and there are always exceptions, I think females try and keep up the contact more than males do. (Nancy)

Nancy excuses her son's lack of effort in maintaining relationships as part of his masculinity: 'he's a typical young male'. As Brannen et al. (1994: 193) comment, 'mothers seem to accept their sons' reticence as part of their make-up'. Although some participants were aware that their sons could also be non-committal at times regarding their well-being, during telephone conversations 'non-verbal cues' (Wood and Smith, 2001: 71) sometimes became a mother's way of 'knowing' what was going on in children's lives:

> My youngest son went into the Navy in September and up until Christmas he seemed ok but then, when he went back, I was talking to him on the telephone and I knew there was something wrong. You can always tell with him. Well, I can tell with the pair of them because of their voices. (Sally)

Sally's son was finding life in the Services difficult for a variety of reasons. She reassured him, saying 'we'll talk about it when you come home, so don't worry about it'. She also expressed relief that her son's disclosure was made to her not his father:

> Now I just took it in my stride, but it's a good job he didn't talk to his dad, because my husband said to me when I told him, 'there's no way he's leaving!' and I said 'don't say that to him'. So I was glad he'd told me and not his dad because when he spoke to him on the phone later on he said, 'what's this about you maybe not staying?' and I was going, you know, shaking my head and saying, 'just tell him we'll discuss it when he comes home'. (Sally)

Sally's success at creating a 'talking relationship' (Brannen et al., 1994: 205) with her sons, which she nurtured throughout her childrearing years, was evident in the strengthening of the close ties between them and the ability of her sons to offload and share information with her. In this instance, Sally felt that the difficulties her son was experiencing necessitated face-to-face as opposed to through-the-wires discussion because of their sensitive nature, an aspect seemingly overlooked by her husband. Sally and her husband both wanted their son to stay in the Navy, but their different approaches to reach this outcome are evident here and display a gendered and 'traditional' parent-child/mother-father dynamic: in order to achieve the same outcome, the father attempted to lay down the law at a distance, whilst the mother sought to offer support in the safe space of the home; this had been the pattern of Sally's familial relationships throughout her marriage.

Jamieson (1999: 488) comments that recent 'empirical research finds parents claiming they want to have closer relationships with their children than they had with their own parents'. Jones, O'Sullivan and Rouse (2006) similarly concluded their discussion of parent/child relationships. Nurturing 'openness' and mutual disclosure prior to children's home-leaving was practised by my interviewees; they described this as a different model of mothering from that of their own mothers. Many of them couched their relationships with their children in terms of friendship, manifesting in 'girlie chats' with their daughters for Gina and Rita, and 'the next step beyond friendship' between Barbara and her daughter and son.

Although Jamieson (1999: 488) identifies the adoption of a 'confiding relationship' with teenage children as a strategy of middle-class motherhood, my interviewees did not predominantly identify as middle-class. Middle-class values do, however, continue to discursively shape childrearing practices and goals. The emergence of 'democratic parenting' (Giddens, 1992) is an indicator of this. Indeed, my research participants told me they had worked towards a more egalitarian relationship with their children than the one experienced with their own parents. Brannen et al. (1994: 205) comment that mothers' strategies to construct relationships of disclosure with their children act as an 'insurance policy in terms of ensuring the maintenance of contact with young people in the future'. However, one of the major anxieties my interviewees highlighted was 'loss' of the adult child following separation. Thus the pursuit of a disclosing relationship within the home did not necessarily result in feeling secure that the same kind of contact would be maintained once their children left.

Diane Reay (2004: 59) observes that 'within families, women engage in emotional labour far more than men and [are responsible] for maintaining the emotional aspects of family relationships'. It was apparent from the interviews I conducted with this group of women that for the most part, mothers rather than fathers instigated contact with their absent daughters and sons (see Rakow, 1988 for further discussion of gendered differences in landline telephone use). At the same time they ensured that male partners were included, thus continuing their role as mediators of father/child relationships 'it's usually me who rings and then my husband will talk to them as well' (Heather); 'my daughter and I do keep in close contact, whereas my husband might just ring her once a week' (Rita). Ingrid said:

> I ring at least once a week, um, and I always make sure dad's around. I'll maybe ring her once a week from work, but don't tell anybody! Then I always make sure we ring again, possibly at the weekend so her dad can talk to her or, if it gets to Friday I'll say to him, "have you rung her this week?" so we have that weekly contact each, as mum and dad. (Ingrid)

Some interviewees did however talk about fathers' initiation of contact:

> I ring my daughter about a couple of times a week but I ring her, like, about 8 o'clock, but my husband will just think, oh, I'll giver her a ring, and just ring in the middle of the day, just for five minutes chat … He seems to ring more than I do, really … I think so. Because when I ring her, we talk for about half-an-hour, for a good chat, whereas he just rings, 'oh, I just thought I'd see how you were'. So he probably has more contact with her now than he did when they were younger, because he was never about when they were younger. (Denise)

Denise's husband did not engage in proactive fatherhood during his children's early years and instead immersed himself in the breadwinner role. At the same time that her daughter left home, Denise's husband retired whilst Denise remained full-time in the workplace. She told me she felt her husband had 'missed out when the children were young'. Once their daughter left home he became a more 'involved' father, albeit this taking form in 'five minute chats' over the telephone. In their discussion of relating via the internet, Wood and Smith (2001: 81) comment that 'online interaction may provide a forum to find a voice that might otherwise remain silent'. I suggest the 'silence' of the fatherhood role Denise's partner previously inhabited was able to find a voice via the telephone, engendering a 'new' and also 'virtual' relationship with his daughter.

Heather was recently remarried and the stepmother of three sons. She also had a son from her first marriage, from which she was widowed when her son was eleven weeks old. All four sons had left home for university and she thought that the disparity in their communication post-separation was based on differences in their upbringings:

> My son's really good, yeah. I think it's just the different sorts of family culture. He doesn't ring every day, um, but he'll ring maybe two or three times a week

and always wants to know the far end of everything, whereas my stepsons are content to know that everything's alright. (Heather)

Fiona said that when her son was at university, 'he'd always tell me when he was going away so I always knew where he was'. Heather and Fiona both repartnered after mothering alone for some years. I suggest a reciprocal relationship between mother and son was created during their early childrearing years which might not have emerged had they remained in a couple relationship. This was so for several of the women who mothered alone. In a similar vein to Holdsworth and Morgan (2005: 99), my data revealed close lone mother/adult child relationships. Where I diverge from the findings of these authors is that my interviewees revealed examples of both daughters' *and* sons' commitment to maintaining strong emotional bonds with their mothers.

Mothering through the Wires

In some ways I'm redundant, but in other ways, um, when you get on the phone and they've got problems, um, you still get that awful feeling in your stomach, you know? You wish you could do something, and you can't always. … It makes you feel gutted, really, when you know they're worrying about things or that things aren't going right for them. I'm on the one hand trying to do my counselling bit, trying to make suggestions, you know? (Nancy)

Women's emotional support for daughters and sons continued post-separation and was often conveyed through telephone wires. In considering how women managed and experienced motherhood as they shifted towards the 'weightlessness'[2] of mothering brought about by the lifting of the domestic burden they previously carried, Nancy's statement highlight the difficulties encountered by some interviewees when they dealt with problems in the lives of their adult children when face-to-face interaction was not possible.

Nancy's daughter experienced many difficulties in her working life and, in her turn, Nancy experienced feelings of powerlessness because of her inability to help her daughter. She felt that if she lived nearer, her daughter's problems would be alleviated and was contemplating a 400-mile house move in order to live close by, thus reiterating the conflation of spatial closeness and maternal protectiveness I discussed earlier. However, distance in this instance was also a metaphor for the kinds of problems that cannot be solved by another person: 'we used to suggest things when she was feeling down, you know, "could you try this? Could you

---

2   In *No Logo* (2001) Naomi Klein applies the term 'weightlessness' to the movement of heavy industry from the West to developing countries, thus the owners of production simply 'carry' the label of their companies.

try that?" And we got really frustrated because she'd probably have an excuse' (Nancy).

Within western constructions of motherhood there is an underlying supposition that a mother's duty is to protect her (dependent) children. Thus, being unable to perform this aspect of her motherly duties created feelings of failure for Nancy. Although the mother of an adult child, this did not alleviate Nancy's desire to meet her daughter's needs. The emotional gratification her daughter might have felt following her conversations with her mother found their opposite in Nancy herself, who said her daughter did not act on her advice. After each of their telephone conversations she waited for the next instalment regarding her daughter's work troubles and, as she said, 'my heart sinks sometimes, when the phone rings'.

Other women had similar experiences of powerlessness in their long-distance relationships with their adult children. Vanessa's daughter, for example, was living with an abusive partner but, unlike Alma and her daughter's situation discussed earlier, Vanessa and her daughter lived some distance apart. The telephone was the medium via which her daughter appealed for and Vanessa communicated maternal advice and support:

> She rings me up in the early hours of the morning so, in one sense, I feel happy that she can do that. I said to her, 'don't get in a state, just ring, it doesn't matter what time'. I can't go back on that, so I have to keep the phone on and I get woken up. … You know, you give all sorts of advice, but the next morning she doesn't want the advice at all. She just wants everything to be smoothed over. It's very hard to know what to do, really. I feel like punching him on the nose! (Vanessa)

Although she was comforted by the fact that her daughter could disclose her difficulties to her, at the same time Vanessa remained powerless; her daughter wanted to offload her problems onto her mother, but she did not heed the maternal advice she was offered. Brannen et al. found that the mothers they spoke to were placed in similar situations to those of Vanessa and Nancy, in that they were given information by their teenage children (prior to their home-leaving) on the understanding that they would not 'act' on it:

> For mothers, knowledge means power without authority; they continue to be the responsible parent, but cannot act on information, even when they disapprove of their sons' or daughters' activities. Through creating channels of communication, mothers endeavour to exert influence though without appearing to constrain. (Brannen et al., 1994: 205)

This was particularly so for my participant Vanessa. Although she wanted to be proactive and protect her daughter from her boyfriend: 'I want to go and rescue her', she was constrained from doing so by her daughter: 'if you do that, you'll lose me'. Vanessa's dilemma is similar to the findings of Jones et al.'s (2006: 383) research, where parents' interventions into their daughters' and sons' relationships posed the risk of 'losing' the adult child. I suggest that this becomes particularly risky once children have left home. In several instances, the need to preserve the mother/child relationship involved my participants' resisting impulses to take action.

Communication from daughters and sons was often interpreted as a sign of the central role women continued to play in children's lives. This was also indicative of the transformation of relationships over time between mothers and their children. In this scenario, the mother/adult child relationship is built on the basis of reciprocal trust and support, of which mutual disclosure plays an important part. I suggest therefore that because of this, the interconnectedness of the mother/child relationship was not imagined as diluted by the distances that existed between them. Rather, mothering had to be transmitted, which changed the way it could be practised and also, of course, the way it was received:

> He rang me from New Zealand to tell me that he couldn't sleep because he'd done something really stupid and he needed to talk to me about it, needed to tell me. He couldn't keep it a secret. And he's on the other side of the world and I'd never have found out ... He'd got drunk and spent a ridiculous amount of money in dens of iniquity in Auckland! [laughs] ... It was just upsetting him so much and ... the only person he could talk to about it was me [cries]. (Fiona)

Wood and Smith (2001: 75) argue that 'interacting in any given context is a subjective experience. [...] It is not inherent characteristics of the media that make the experience impersonal or not, it is our own perception that helps make it so'. I suggest however that for my interviewees, the subjective experience of mother/child interactions underwent an enforced transition in their technological mediation. Cyberspace became a place where mothering as praxis was re-negotiated and thus transformed. I am in agreement therefore with Williams when he comments that in cyberspace there can be no 'cuddle for the crying child'. He continues:

> What we lose in cyberspace is the depth of emotional experience, warmth and understanding which comes from embodied gestures such as being 'touched' by another human being through face-to-face contact and physical co-presence in the real world [...] Embodied gestures touch us deeply and communicate a shared sense of trust, intimacy and vulnerability which is grounded in the contingencies of our fleshy mortal bodies. (Williams, 1998: 128)

Several commentators on cyberspace have defined it as an escape route from the self in real space (Jones, 1998; Markham, 1998; Reid and Kolko, 1998; Rheingold, 1993). However, I would argue that my interviewees were not escaping from the real world self, but in effect were running after a sense of self that was disrupted post-separation from their adult children. To this end, communicating via different technologies became an essential part of their lives as mothers. Although their mothering underwent an enforced change through its technological mediation, women were able to effectively manage and maintain their relationships with their daughters and sons via the different technologies available to them. Attempting to transmit motherly advice and comfort through the wires can at times however be less than satisfactory, not least because prior to home-leaving, physical proximity was an everyday part of the mother/child relationship that rendered it an embodied experience performed mainly in the domestic arena:

> I know we talk on the phone a lot, but I just do miss her. When you're talking on the phone it's so condensed, you've got everything to get into a short space of time, trying to say everything, whereas in the day-to-day, you brush against each other as the day goes on, don't you? So it's very different. (Bridget)

The configuration of the mother/child dyad is one of close physical proximity that translates as maternal protection for the dependent child. On reaching adulthood and on home-leaving, this coupling is prised apart creating a disjuncture in the former, and I suggest silent, meanings of mother and child. Although previously the gate-keeper of the private/public boundary and thus protector of her children, the child's adult status transforms the mother's function, as Dawn said: 'my daughter was flying, you know? I had to open the door and let her fly'. Thus the differences geographical distances created were often profoundly felt when interviewees talked about communicating with their daughters and sons once they had left the family home.

As Bridget implies, face-to-face interactions which necessitate the embodied presence of an other, are not replaced by the ability to talk on the telephone, which was perceived in many women's narratives as a poor substitute for physical presence involving all of the senses. As Moores notes (2000: 135), 'all social interaction – including that which takes place between co-present participants – is "mediated by" the signs of language or gesture'. In the case of my participants, the signs and gestures that previously made up face-to-face interactions with their daughters and sons were previously caught up in their everyday lives together. Their meanings became more pronounced when recalled in the aftermath of separation, when mediation devices were unable to compensate for what was missed and so acted merely as an appeasement of absence.

In calling on the terminology of spatial as well as emotional proximity, Bridget illustrates how absence and presence are both embodied phenomena, a situation Beth Kolko and Elizabeth Reid (1998: 221) identify in their discussion of on-line communities: 'a separation of the embodied self from the sensory consequences of physical space'. For Bridget and other interviewees, the physical and sensory indicators of thought and feeling were missing from their technically-assisted interactions with their adult children. Brushing against a child in the nearness of 'the day-to-day' was recalled by Bridget as very differently experienced from a 'condensed' telephone conversation that takes place across geographical distance. In its turn, this throws into relief the reconfiguration of the mother/child relationship and the transformation of motherhood when practised at a distance. As Fernback and Thompson state:

> The least complex and most informative means of communications is to meet face to face. Direct, personal conversation has multiple levels of communication. In addition to the words that are spoken, vocal inflections, body language and even the setting carry meaning. (1995: 11)

Once children left home, my interviewees were forced to replace daily face-to-face interaction with word/text-based communication in order to maintain close contact, which at times proved limiting and frustrating. Although the distance-shrinking abilities of technology had to some extent enabled them to carry out some of the motherly practices that were part of their sense of self-as-mother, and their engagement with technology provided 'real' experiences, these were virtual. So, despite the fact that images were on occasion sent via the internet, sensory experiences were for the most part missing, and so missed, from women's encounters with their children in cyberspace so that they were forced to 'interact using words/text rather than bodies' (Markham, 1998: 79).

Clearly, my participants' emotional management of separation from their adult children was assisted by the ability to communicate across geographical spaces enabling an engagement in motherly practises such as caring, support, the lending of a 'listening ear'. This heralds a major shift in motherhood as praxis in that when children leave home mothering continues under circumstances previously not possible. However, I would argue that technologically enhanced communication came a 'poor second' to the intimate relationships my research participants had for the most part previously shared with their children.

Concluding Remarks

> The future is unfolding around us. Over the next decade we will be able to see all sorts of differences that we can barely imagine today. Vodafone is working hard to mobilize tomorrow's world, but we need your input. You are our partners in innovation, helping to shape a future that offers the mobile services we want, and brings us closer to the people we care about, wherever they are in the world. Together we can build a future that turns this vision into reality. (www.vodafone.com)

This chapter has highlighted the issue of post-separation mother/child communication, because coming to terms with the shift in their identities as mothers of adult children from whom they lived separately in part rested upon my participants' ability for continued communication and interaction with them. Post-separation motherhood was for much of the time practised by them across geographical distances and women's retention of family unity was evident, for example they strove to ensure that fathers and their children remained in touch. More importantly however, I found embedded within my participants' narratives a profound commitment to the continuity of the self-as-mother. This was dependent upon the knowledge that their daughters and sons were safe in the 'unknown' space outside the home. Unlike those who use cyberspace to transcend the 'seeming fixity of the "real world" self' (Kolko and Reid, 1998: 218), I suggest that my interviewees were attempting to ensure and fix their 'real-world' motherhood identities via cyberspace as they attempted to reconcile the two opposing phenomena of rupture and continuity they experienced post-separation from their adult children.

The statement above from the *Vodafone* website conflates closeness in cyberspace with physical proximity suggesting in the same way as does their TV advertisement discussed earlier in the chapter, that mobile phone possession and usage render us part of a 'future vision'; we can be 'mobilized' in more ways than one. As such, we are enticed by its promise to bring us closer to those we care about and, in consequence, by its normalizing discourse. There can be no doubt that communication technology is here to stay. Oddly, the conflation of proximity and care evident in such advertising rhetoric resonates with women's narratives regarding notions of motherhood and protectiveness/care, yet I have exposed in this chapter that these carry very different meanings for mothers themselves in the absence of their children. I therefore agree with Williams when he bluntly states, 'virtual reality, as the term suggests, does not stand a cat in hell's chance of capturing the subtlety and sophistication of life in the real world' (Williams, 1998: 129).

I want now to return to the advertisements outlined earlier and focus on the 'mother figure' in each, in order to call attention to the fact that she is in fact *not* mobile. With striking similarity to the mother of Lee's novel, discussed in Chapter 1, the mother figure of these advertisements remains at the edge of the forest/in the home, whilst the young person is mobile/has moved away. However, although I have argued here that women sought to construct and fix a motherhood identity for themselves via cyberspace, I do not suggest that their lives once their adult children left home remained static. Rather, I argue that they desired affirmation of their identities as mothers. So, unlike the mother figure of mobile phone advertising, I am not implying that my interviewees' lives remained 'on hold'. In the next chapter, I pursue how women's identities as mothers, which rested upon their continued interactions with their adult children, impacted on the plans they made, and the aspirations they had, for their own futures.

Chapter 6
Mothers' Futures

The previous chapter highlighted the importance for my research participants of maintaining in contact with their absent daughters and sons across geographical distances. I argued that this indicated a desire for the affirmation of a maternal identity. However, and unlike representations of the mother figure previously discussed, I also suggested that the lives of the women I interviewed did not remain static once their children left home. In this chapter therefore I explore what these women did next. In other words I reflect on my participants' experiences post-separation from their adult children, investigate their life circumstances, and consider the chances and choices that were available to them once they successfully mothered their children to adulthood and experienced them leave home.

Comings and Goings

> It's as though they've left home, but you've still got to organise your life around them and when they're home. We always say to them, you know, 'don't worry, we'll organise things around you'. … So we still do prioritise them, I think. I mean, you think, I can do all sorts now, and then you find you can't because they're always coming back! [laughs] They still rule your life! (Sally)

My interviewees indicated that over time they began to settle into home-life without their daughters and sons. A major aspect of this acceptance, elaborated in the previous chapter, was their continued interaction with children across geographical distances. Mothers and adult children also continued to see each other during visits/holidays and so on and, as Sally indicates, such visits often affected the 'new' home-life established after they left. When young people made visits to the family home, for example between university semesters, or for shore-leave as in the case of Sally's sons, my participants' households were often disrupted: 'you know, you get into this routine that she's not around then, all of a sudden, she's back again!' explained Rita. She further described some of the mixed feelings she experienced during her daughter's visits:

> I can be desperately lonely one minute then absolutely sick of her the next [laughs]. It's really weird when she comes back, you know. It's a novelty for a bit, then it all wears off, um, so it is a very fine line between, you know, really missing her and being fed up with her. (Rita)

Other interviewees described changes to the household when children visited and the ambivalent feelings this often aroused. At such times, several women stated they found themselves once more responsible for domestic and other chores they were relieved of when children had left:

> Two days into him being home I'll be saying, 'oh my god, what a mess!' … Do you know, I'm so busy when he comes home, I ferry him here, there and everywhere, 'can you just take me to work?' So I'm backwards and forwards while he's at home, never seem to have two minutes to myself. When he goes back it's phew! I've got more time. It's all or nothing. When they're here there's all this stuff going on, and then he goes back and it all stops. It's really quiet when he's not here and yet I love him to be home. (Paula)

Although they lived elsewhere, the majority of daughters and sons retained a space in their parental home, usually their bedrooms: 'it's still her room and it's not touched' (Serena); 'she knows that her room's still there' (Gina). Although children's rooms were described as 'there' for daughters and sons, often interviewees expressed surprise at children's continued attachment to the home, its rooms and their contents:

> My daughter doesn't come home very often anyway. She hasn't been here for about a year and this year we wanted to decorate her room and I was quite surprised because she wanted to have a say in what colours we chose and I said, 'but you aren't here anymore'. But she was quite adamant. She wanted to have a say, and that quite surprised me. (Nancy)

> I said something about my eldest son's room when he was getting his own place and he said, 'no, that's still my bedroom!' I suppose, you know, with him coming home, you know, it is still his bedroom. I would think it would only be, like, if he gets a partner or he gets married, that he'll then not want his bedroom, you know? (Sally)

Even though Sally's son lived in his own flat in a town in the south of England, and Nancy's daughter lived with her partner in a flat in Scotland, thereby giving the impression that these adult children had 'really' left home, both maintained a place in their parents' house, highlighting their interconnectedness with the parental home/parents. As discussed, this is indicative of what young people imagine the parental home to be. Indeed, Holdsworth and Morgan (2005: 78) cite one of their research participants' description of his parental home: 'something that you can identify with is waiting for you on your return'. In her discussion of the meanings of home that emerge across different academic disciplines, Kenyon lists the following:

> Home as a projection and realization of self-identity and social and cultural
> status; home as a place of retreat, safety, relaxation and freedom; home as a
> space of privacy; home as a social support mechanism; and home as a place of
> familiarity and continuity. (Kenyon, 2003: 105)

As Kenyon further comments: 'home can be both an ideal and a reality' (105), and
her observations of the meanings of home, both real and imaginary, were echoed
in my research participants' narratives. Although Janice's son, for example, owned
his own flat in the same town as his parents, she described his visits to the parental
home as suffused with his need for stability and continuity:

> My son'll just stay for an hour and that's maybe all he needs. Just come back
> into the … his home, as it was. The cats are there, you know, that home-life, and
> he chats with us and reads his mail … He still, you know, calls in and comes
> round a couple of nights and one night he comes for his tea and, more often than
> not, we see him over the weekend, he'll come round for his Sunday dinner and
> it seems to go back to how it was before he left. I think he likes things to be as
> it was, sort of thing. (Janice)

Janice's son appears unable to consider that his parents might have moved on during
his absence; as Janice intimates, he 'needed' his visits back to an 'unchanged'
domestic space. Vanessa as well said that when her daughters visited they 'just
drop into place … if I've moved things or taken things down, "where's that picture
of so-and-so I liked?" you know? So they like things to look the same, to hark
back'. Vanessa offered some understanding of young people's reactions to changes
in the home when she reflected on her own experience:

> I always remember when I left home and I went back and all the old *Rupert*
> books and things like that, that I'd had for years stuck in the big cupboard
> between the bedrooms, they'd all disappeared. I think my mum had had a clear
> out, you know, and I was actually really hurt that she'd actually got rid of them.
> (Vanessa)

These examples illustrate how my interviewees' daughters and sons regarded the
home, and in consequence, the mother, as constant and unchanging: the mother's
life was viewed in terms of stasis and their own in terms of dynamism, since
they were the ones to have 'made the move' when they left the parental home.
A young person might then perceive her/himself as 'owning' change and the
mother's expected invariance thus contains the proof of the child's adult status:
in effect, the young person has moved beyond the childhood self the home and
mother represent. However, and as indicated previously, over the time mothers
and their children were apart, *all* of their lives had moved on. Consequently the
mother/child relationship shifted, sometimes uneasily. Visiting the family home
highlighted children's own ideas of their mothers' lives as static and in some

instances they were confronted with changes to the home environment which they 'raged against', and which their mothers either resisted or accommodated:

> When my son calls round he likes us all to be in, he doesn't like it when I'm at the gym ... he gets despondent when I'm not in and I say, 'yeah, but I can't give up what I want to do' ... So in a sense, I get a bit hardened now. Because they still want you to be there ... You know, my husband will say, 'well, you do go every Thursday' and I'll say, 'yes, I know, and I'm going to carry on going every Thursday'. And I get what I'd call emotional blackmail from him, you know? (Janice)

Janice became 'hardened' towards her son's despair at her absence from the home, indicating she no longer felt responsible for meeting *only* his needs. Ribbens McCarthy, Edwards and Gillies (2000: 785) explore how 'the presence of dependent children [leads] to an overall key moral imperative concerning the requirement for responsible adults to put the needs of children first'. As my participants' narratives indicate, this was the stance they took. As Janice clearly shows however, her feelings of responsibility shifted during the time that had elapsed since her son left home. She resisted being held in place, not only by her son, but also by her husband. Spatial separation thus acted as an engine for change, as mothers and their children (and partners) came to regard each other differently:

> I think the relationship with the boys is different, um, that you're not sort of ... running their lives anymore, sort of, making provision for them anymore. But I still feel very much their parent and I think they feel that much more that, um, that they're adult people coming home to their parents so that, um, the things that they talk to you about change as well, I think, um, you know, they talk about their own relationships that are outside the family, outside the household, much more. (Heather)

Time apart for Heather and her sons created a space for the reconfiguration of family relationships and acknowledgement of changed and changing identities once they were together in the same physical space. Heather said she was no longer 'running' her sons' lives, thus the relinquishing of a mother's 'control' and move towards her children's uptake of responsibility for themselves meant Heather perceived their visits as 'adult people coming home'. In turn, this provided opportunities to share and discuss issues in all of their lives. Making the most of 'quality time' (Heather), mothers and adult children began to relate on what some participants perceived as a more reciprocal and egalitarian basis. As Frances said, 'now my son's gone, if anything, we seem to have a better relationship because we make more of the time that we have. We make sure that we both sit down and we have a nice chat and see what each others' doing'.

Although I do not claim that my participants were fully released from feelings of responsibility towards their children, I do suggest that their spatial separation initiated a shift in mothers' perceptions of children's status: they began to 'see' the adult. But not in all instances was such spatial separation maintained; some women also experienced their children's return to live in the family home on a long-term basis.

Long-term Returners

> As the introduction of tuition fees hit home for UK students and employment opportunities shrank, the 'progression' from school to university to independent adult ceased to represent the key life course transition which it used to be for many 18-year-olds. (Hockey and James, 2003: 115)

Hockey and James highlight how the transition to adulthood that higher education once made possible is no longer guaranteed for increasing numbers of young people, thus exposing that an 'ages and stages' approach to childhood, adolescence and adulthood masks the complexities of home-leaving and, indeed, the multiple departures and returns leaving home might entail (Allatt, 1996; Hockey and James, 2003; Holdsworth and Morgan, 2005; Noller and Callan, 1991).

The return to the parental home following undergraduate years, as Hockey and James (2003) suggest, is becoming a common occurrence for young people. Other life circumstances also impact upon this decision and in the case of my participants, six experienced the return of the child to the family home to live, albeit on a temporary but fairly long-term basis (Angela, Bridget, Heather, Janice, Nancy and Vanessa): of these six young people, three returned after university, two from travelling/working abroad and one following the breakdown of a relationship. At the time of interview Angela's and Heather's sons were still living in the parental home, whilst the other children had left for a second time.

Although not all participants' children who returned had originally left home for university, similar assumptions to those suggested by Hockey and James (2003: 115) could be applied across this group of young people: 'provisional student identities are predicated upon the comfortable but constricting category of "childhood" which continues to remain open to them on their return to the parental home'. Indeed, as Serena told me of her own return when her first marriage ended: 'I just had a time when I lived at home with mum and dad again. And you soon slip back into daughter ways, with my parents looking after me'.

Interviewees cemented their availability to their adult children by building bridges of support, underpinned by the concept of 'being there', previously identified as a reconfigured continuance of the needs discourse in which mothers were immersed during their early childrearing years. In its turn this confirmed my participants' maternal identities following their children's home-leaving: 'the kids will, um, always need help of some kind, and I always will be there for them' (Judith); 'I shall always be there for the girls' (Alma). As such, Hockey and James' assertion of a return to childhood which the move back to the family home seemingly offers, and which the terms 'kids' and 'girls' to some extent also implies, was then an option open to interviewees' adult children. Given this, one might expect a degree of accommodation between mother and child if the latter returned to live in the parental home for any length of time.

However, this assumption was unwarranted since, of course, the 'children' in question were returning home as adults so that not only had the power balance between parents and children potentially shifted, but adult children's expectations of the kind of life they might lead had too, thus frequently leading to conflicts over territory, both literally and metaphorically. As Janice said of her son's return, 'it sounded good at the time in theory, but in practice it's very different'. Ultimately, returners and their mothers were often in tension with each other in the space of the home they had once more amicably shared:

> You had these feelings of, um, um, she'd come back and taken the place over again. Do you know what I mean? It's a bit like, you know, because she's older and more grown up, she wanted to do things the way she wanted to do them. Um, and I had got used to the peace and quiet ... But I felt that all I was doing was clearing up, you know, going round and sorting her life out again. My life wasn't my own at that point, you know, it was back to looking after someone again. (Vanessa)

Vanessa became accustomed to life without her daughter at home. When she returned Vanessa resumed her role of sorting out her daughter's life, although clearly found it difficult to accept that her daughter might desire to do things her own way, indicating perhaps a difficulty in accepting her daughter's adult/independent status. Although an instigator of some tension, the continued meeting of children's needs often underscored mother/adult child returners' relationships. In these instances it would seem, as Lawler comments, 'to be difficult for children (even adult children) to see their mothers as having a "self" outside of the subject-position "mother"' (Lawler, 2000: 155). I would add that it might also be difficult for mothers to perceive themselves differently in the presence of their returning children.

Long-term return home was a cause of practical and emotional disruption. Once again the child's movement, this time back into the home, enforced a realisation of time passing and of shifts in the way the home was inhabited. As Janice observed, returning home was not an easy option for the mother, or for the child as adult:

> He'd been away for five years ... so coming back was quite a trauma for him and, really, the rest of us because we didn't realise that over the five years you had, well, you had moved on ... he'd had his, like, freedom as you might say. He needed that back and it's right, he did need that back. Equally, we needed that space, um.' (Janice)

Although financial reasons underpinned the reasons for Janice's son's return to the family home, the reality of their living together again proved difficult for the whole family so much so that in the home that once accommodated the whole family, Janice said she needed the space her son occupied on his return. Angela's son had returned home after a relationship breakdown, she told me 'he always said that this was his safe place and he knew he could come back and he knew that we'd understand'. Yet, and in a similar vein to Janice, she experienced a lack of fit on his return and talked of the difficulties of living with her son-as-adult:

> It isn't equitable to have three adults all with their own agendas living under one roof. *It's not my little boy living with me, is it? He's an adult* and he's come back to use, if you like, the facilities of his parents' home before he moves on, and we always knew that. (Angela)

I have shown in earlier chapters how my interviewees underwent a personal transition at the time of their children's home-leaving which placed them in the seemingly precarious position of accepting themselves as the mothers of adults from whom they lived separately. Angela and Janice both found this a particularly difficult and distressing time. However, acknowledgement of the temporal status of their sons' return home and their impending second departure acted to further reinforce the recognition of their sons as adults. Indeed, Angela's comments highlight the shift she made in the perception of her son's status that enabled a letting-go of the responsibility that previously defined her mothering:

> For three years I haven't known what he was doing, maybe this time I'm more accepting of the fact that he's an adult. Maybe when he left home the first time he was my little boy leaving home. I've tried to think about this. But this time, he's come back as an adult ... He's not dependent on me anymore and therefore I don't feel so anxious about him. I'm not responsible for his welfare. I'm not responsible for him, am I? (Angela)

Mothers and their adult children might then experience contradictory emotions when the latter return home that veer between the resumption of left-behind roles as children and parents react as if no change had occurred, as well as expecting to experience the impact of both parents and children having moved on. Children might continue to desire the territorial and material stability of the parental home, whilst expecting to display, and have accepted by parents, adult behaviours that invade the parents' space, alongside expectations of how that space and they are treated. The mother might expect to continue to 'parent' as opposed to 'merely' materially provide, but at the same time she has come to terms with her child no longer being young and dependent, but adult and as such, independent. Adult children's visits and returns home then caused disruption in their mothers' lives. In turn, the difficulties interviewees encountered further reinforced a sense of themselves as the mothers of children who were adults. In the remainder of the chapter other aspects of women's lives that continued after children left home are considered. The first of these is a discussion of women's employment.

Women and Work

Over the time that my research participants were bringing up their children, women's relationship to paid work outside the home changed dramatically. As Anne Witz (1997: 239) states, 'the steadily increasing participation of women in paid employment during the latter half of the twentieth century is arguably one of the most significant aspects of the transformation of gender relations'. Judith Phillips (2000) indicates that women of the age of my participants (44–57 years) were amongst the first to encounter these changing trends. Although the majority of my participants were married in their early twenties and many of them did not work during their children's early years, all worked outside the home in either a full- or part-time capacity at the time of the interviews:

> I didn't have that feeling, where does my life go from here? Which I'm sure, for some women it does, if they're not working. But I didn't have that because I was already in a job. I didn't have that feeling, well, where does my life go from now? Because, well, I knew where my life was going from there, I had a job. (Nancy)

Nancy indicated how employment as a teacher became a stabilising presence she drew on to provide direction to her life course. Thus she as well as other interviewees confirmed what Borland (1982: 122) suggests: 'the cessation of the maternal role should be cushioned by the already existing work role'. Nancy also said: 'I've quite enjoyed my working life', indicating how work provided her with a sense of fulfilment that was separate from her mothering role.

In her study of middle-class women who combine motherhood with a career, Caroline Gattrell (2005: 86–7) comments that 'women, just like men, develop work orientations which are central to their social identity'. Gattrell observes the saliency of women's being able to establish 'a separate social identity from that of the domestic roles of mother, wife/partner' (87). Her focus is on mothering during children's early years. My interviewees' relationship to paid work emerged as an area of major importance to them once children left home. Many highlighted how work inculcated a positive sense of self: 'I still made a life for myself. I still did my degree, proved to myself I can do it. I've got a good job, you know' (Rita).

In my participants' narratives, the notion of 'making a life for oneself' was often attached to the working persona that existed outside the category 'mother'. This was amplified upon children's home-leaving: 'I want to focus more on what I want to do, um. I want to focus on things like doing this new job I'm doing, um, you know, and work on that, get that right' (Alma). Employment outside the home offered women an element of autonomy and independence, though not only from mothering responsibilities: 'I think now I've started this new job, that's what I see myself doing, is working. I've got this thing that I need to be independent and I don't want to rely on a man financially again' (Serena).

Paid work outside the home thus emerged as an important facet at this time in the life course. This is consistent with other studies in this area. Julie Skucha and Miriam Bernard (2000: 29) for example, found that paid work provided their study cohort 'with a social identity in addition to their familial one, social interaction with colleagues and clients, a sense of independence and […] a source of income'. Engagement in the world of paid work was articulated as fulfilling and satisfying by the majority of my interviewees, not least because their employment status boosted their self-confidence: 'during my working life I began to discover things about myself; that I was extremely competent and well capable of doing whatever was put in front of me' (Alma). Paid employment thus enabled women to perceive themselves as skilled workers. As Bergman (2005: 12) comments, 'the cash wages which women earn motivate and finance many of the changes that have occurred in their lives'.

In some instances it was apparent that employment outside the home was also envisaged as an extension of the mothering self. For example, now that one daughter had left home, and a second was contemplating her own leaving, Gina was considering leaving her post as an early-years lecturer in an FE college and returning to nursery teaching:

> I am already thinking of going back to teaching little ones … it's maternal
> instinct, you see. I just need to be with children. I just need to feel needed, you
> know, just feeling that you're needed and being wanted. (Gina)

Gina felt she had lost the element of 'need' in her life as her two daughters grew up and more so in the aftermath of the elder daughter's departure from the home. In expressing her desire to feel needed, Gina associated 'maternal instinct' with 'little ones', evoking my earlier argument regarding the incongruous nature of mothering the 'child as adult' and thus the inability for Gina to derive the same fulfilment from her role as the mother of adult daughters. Indeed, when I met up with my participants a year after my interviews with them, Gina had returned to primary teaching.

Although paid employment was articulated as a source of satisfaction by the majority of my participants, there was also some sense that being in mid-life meant it was difficult for women to move on from their current positions. Mid-life as I am using it here encompasses those between the ages of 35 and 60 (Featherstone and Hepworth, 1991; Hockey and James, 1993; 2003), thus my research participants fit this demographic. Angela said, 'it's not that easy to change jobs at 57, you know, people don't want you when you're 57'; Vanessa, who was 58, commented 'I've got to continue working where I am because nobody wants you at this age, doesn't matter how good you are. I mean, that should change with this, um, EU thing that's coming in next year, you know, against ageism.'[1] Alma, however, who was 55 at the time of the interviews, took a more proactive stance with regard to a recent change in her employment status and Judith, also 55, was contemplating a job move:

> I thought it was time for me to move on. I thought: I'll be regarded as a piece of the furniture. I probably needed a new challenge as well. It's very easy for things to become so routine that, um, you become staid in your outlook. So I'm pleased I made that decision at that time. It had to be. It had to be. You've got to take these opportunities as they come, there's no point in thinking 'if only'. (Alma)

> When I took this job on I thought this was until I retire and now I'm thinking, no, it's not going to be, because now it's time to move on again. So, you know, you get used to those changes I think. (Judith)

All interviewees were engaged in paid work for some time before their children left home. During the interviews their employment emerged as an important factor in their lives on which they drew to sustain a sense of self and well-being that existed outside, but also alongside, their mothering selves, and that continued after children left; relationships with male partners was another.

Women's Partnerships

Ann Oakley and Alan Rigby (1998: 106) note that 'most women (around 90 per cent) have children either in marriage or within a cohabiting relationship with the father of their child. However, one in five mothers are caring for children in one-parent households'. From an international perspective Northern Europe contrasts with southern nations, as Holdsworth (2004: 910) observes in her comparative analysis of young people's home-leaving under three different welfare state regimes; Norway, Spain and the UK. Marriage remains a dominant way of creating new families in the south, whilst northern Europe is 'associated with the decline in marriage and increase in cohabitation, divorce, re-marriage and extra-marital fertility'.

Each of my interviewees followed a traditional path to motherhood and lived in heterosexual relationships during their childrearing years. When I met them, less than half remained in their first marriages/relationships. These data are in keeping with those of Jones et al. (2006: 379) wherein their own sample of 70 cases, '59 per cent of the parents' partnerships were intact; 21 per cent had re-partnered and 11 per cent were lone parents'. As these authors state, 'the indication is that transitions a generation ago were already risky, and that normative patterns

---

1   The Employment Equality (Age) Regulations 2006 - SI No 2006/1031 - came into force on 1 October 2006 (www.dti.gov.uk accessed 27/10/06).

provided no protection from this risk'. There was much variation within partnership typologies that emerged from my own data. One of these was solo-living.

In their discussion of household statistics, Arber, Davidson and Ginn (2003: 10) comment that 'solo living is closely associated with lack of a partner, since the majority of older people who are widowed, divorced or never married live alone'. Interestingly solo-living is here associated with 'lack' which carries with it negative connotations.[2] Helen, who was not in a partnership when I interviewed her, said, 'everybody's answer is, "oh you need a man, that's what it is. Get yourself a man". They think a man's the answer to everything! [laughs]'. Gina said:

> I've never, sort of, been particularly bothered about going out and meeting somebody else. I've got friends whose marriages have split up and they've been out on the town, you know? It's been a real big thing. They've got to have a partner and somebody to be with them, whereas I've, sort of, been quite contented just being a mum and not having anybody else there. (Gina)

Equally, Alma told me she enjoyed living alone:

> I'm quite happy as I am, I enjoy being on my own. ... I have enough interests to keep me occupied for as long as I wish and ... it is good. I'm quite self-sufficient. I don't need anybody else. I mean, if I want to go anywhere, I'm quite happy to go. I don't have to have somebody to go with. I think I've now developed sufficient confidence to be able to walk into a room where I know virtually nobody and feel quite at ease, and it's an achievement. I think so anyway. (Alma)

Judith was in a relatively new relationship at the time that I interviewed her. She told me that following her divorce, a friend had become 'a right little matchmaker' who she told, 'if it happens, it happens. It's not one of those things I'm out and out for, another guy, I'm alright by myself'. Similarly Rachel, who was also in a new relationship, talked about going out for the evening with her daughters and their boyfriends: 'I could do that on my own. I don't have to have a partner to do that'. These narratives are not dissimilar from those in Kate Davidson's (2001: 311) study of late-life widowhood. The women she interviewed 'were not prepared to relinquish the freedom and independence they had enjoyed since coming to terms with living alone'.

Seemingly, the 'lack' of a partner during their later childrearing years and at the time of my interviews with them, was not perceived negatively by these participants; rather their single motherhood had proved to be a source of self-discovery. As Alma said of her marriage, 'all the time we were together I probably

---

2 Lack: absence, deficiency, want, need (*of* something desirable or necessary); the state of being in want; the fact that a person or thing is not present (*Oxford English Dictionary*, 2006).

didn't realise how much my husband was suppressing me'. Similarly, Helen and Judith both separated from their husbands when their children were young:

> I was quite dependent on my husband … I was quite happy for him to do all the money and, um, things and I just tended to go along with whatever he wanted. So that when he went and I was having to make decisions … I found it difficult at first. Even for things like ringing up for car insurance. I'd never done anything like that. But over ten years, I've got more independent and stronger in my mind and personality. (Helen)

> I kind of woke up when I got divorced … it, it changed my life in the way that I looked at things … you get a strength from … from being on your own, really, because you get independent. You've got to do things you wouldn't normally do. (Judith)

By their own admission, each of these women adopted passive roles as married women. Following divorce they managed their households, brought up their children and held down full-time jobs, practices which engendered changed perceptions of themselves as active, capable and independent women and mothers. In consequence, and in a similar vein to Carol Smart and Bren Neal (1999) who found that women were concerned with issues of independence and becoming 'your own person' once divorced, my interviewees experienced the emergence of a different self when their marriages ended. Judith drew on her time alone to set the parameters of her new relationship: 'I was determined that, if I got into a relationship of any kind, I wasn't going to be the doormat again'.

Although time spent as lone mothers confirmed women's ability to manage, after their children left home, solo living was not as desirable in the long-term for some interviewees. During her early childrearing years Gina had been content to mother by herself. However, the imminence of her second daughter's home-leaving provoked thoughts of meeting a new partner:

> I don't think I'd ever get married again. I just don't have much confidence in that. But socially and that, just to have a close friend who you can socialise with and go places with, I think it's something that's far more of a priority than I would say it ever has been whilst the children were little. (Gina)

Sandra left her husband once her son had left home, following which she experienced deep feelings of loneliness:

> I don't like doing things on my own, don't like going places on my own, don't like spending hours and hours and hours and hours on my own … I'd love to meet somebody. I would love to meet somebody to share my life with. I don't know if I'd want to live with somebody, I don't know if I'd go that far. (Sandra)

Although Gina and Sandra were keen to embrace new relationships, both said they would not re-marry/co-habit. The circumstances of their married lives that they disclosed in our interviews provide some reasons for this. Gina's husband left her with two very young daughters making no further contact with them, although he lived close by. Sandra left her abusive husband when her son left home for university. She told me: 'I feel as if I've missed out ... I want somebody to sit and snuggle up with while I'm watching a film'. I suggest that Sandra's desire for physical and emotional support was underpinned by 'the rhetoric of heterosexual love and protection which encourages women to see men as their saviours' (Oakley and Rigby, 1998: 123–4). Even though 'romantic imagery may often disguise exploitation' (Duncombe and Marsden, 1993: 237), the disappointment of her first marriage did not deter Sandra from seeking a new partner. As both women indicate however, any new relationships they engaged in would be negotiated on different terms from those of their former marriages.

Repartnered Women

Of the ten research participants who were repartnered, seven were cohabiting at the time of the interviews. All ten had children of their own from previous relationships. Of these, three gave birth to subsequent children with their new partners and three were step-mothers to partners' children (all six of these women lived with their partners). When asked how children's home-leaving impacted on relationships with their male partners, this was often articulated as having created a space for experiences usually ascribed to the early stages of romantic relationships:

> I want to be able to make decisions for the two of us and do things together. I guess that's what I missed about not having that time at the other end of our relationship and having the children first. It's just a reversal, really, you know? ... We're both starting to appreciate the time we've got now as a couple. We've waited long enough for it! (Ingrid)

> We've just, at the moment, maybe in the last year or two, pretty much in the last year actually, we're starting to get a life that's just us two because we've never had it. I always had my eldest son, you know, and there's always been children around ... I can have a relationship with my partner instead of just being mother and all that that entails, you know? (Lois)

Children leaving home clearly provided an opportunity for couples to pursue experiences that, unlike their always-married counterparts, they had not yet shared. As Lois intimated, children had been a constant presence. She thus perceived that mothering occluded some aspects of her relationship with her partner. Another element to emerge was that of gaining feelings of security from repartnering that ameliorated the uncertainty of a future without children in the home. Heather, for example, reflected on meeting her partner shortly before her son left home:

> I think the future feels much more certain than it would have done if I'd been on my own. ... If I'd been on my own once my son had gone, I could've done absolutely anything, but probably wouldn't have known what I wanted to do, whereas now it just ... it's just different, um, that what my husband and I do, we'll do together. (Heather)

Judith said: 'I suppose I could've been sat here on my own, um, thinking, you know, what is there in life for me? You know, sort of thing, what do I do?' Judith mothered alone for several years. She drew on notions of coupledom to describe the difficulties she perceived she might have encountered had she remained single after both her sons left home: 'all my friends are married so I always find that, if go out with my friends it's usually during the week, it's the weekends where you're sat on your own'. A further element that emerged from Judith's interview was that repartnering might also alleviate her sons' concerns regarding her wellbeing:

> I think my sons would probably have felt guilty about me being alone, which I wouldn't want them to feel, um, kind of, especially my younger son, you know, because he's more in tune with my feelings, really. He would've been thinking he ought to come round here and see me and make sure I was alright and all this kind of thing. So for them, my partner's been a godsend, really, um, because they know he'll look after me. (Judith)

Although their children leaving home undeniably caused emotional disruption in my participants' lives that was for some of them still ongoing at the time of my interviews with them, repartnered women were able to override some of these feelings: 'I miss my sons terribly but, because my husband and I have never had our time together, you know, we never had a sort of honeymoon time or a time when we had no children, it's quite nice' (Heather).

Whereas for this group of interviewees, living with partners was built upon notions of coupledom and togetherness, other repartnered interviewees chose to retain separate households. Oakley and Rigby (1998: 106) suggest that 'formal marital status is increasingly a poor guide to actual living circumstances [...] Married couples may be living apart, and non-married women may be living with partners in long-lasting relationships' Roseneil (2006: 5) also observes that 'more people in Britain are living longer periods of their lives not just outside marriage and the conventional family, but also outside a co-residential partnership'. This was so for Dawn, Rachel and Serena:

> My partner has his house and I have my house. Um, when my house gets too full I move into his house. If all the girls are home at once there aren't enough beds for them so I just move into his house. Just take my clothes and move in. ... I've

got my children and I sleep with my partner but I live here. We're all doing it. It's actually not bad at all. (Rachel)

I've been with my partner three years now, about three years. It's quite lovely because I live here, he lives in his house and we go out and have a wonderful time … then go back to our own houses, and it suits me lovely. (Dawn)

These are examples of the type of relationship mid-life and older women (and men) might choose to enter into, and of which Serena said, 'it's just ideal the way it is … I'm not looking for any more than that'. Although the focus of some research attention (Levin, 2004; Roseneil, 2006), it is only recently that formal recognition of this type of partnership arrangement within the UK has appeared in household statistics (Roseneil, 2006). In Sweden, however, 'living apart together' (LAT) has for some time been accorded legitimacy: 'namely *särbo* (where *sär* stands for 'apart' and *bo* for 'live')' (Borell and Karlsson, 2003: 50). As these authors state:

The acceptance of the concept *särbo* gives an ontological status to a type of relationship that involves separate domiciles, but is not a transitional form leading to cohabitation, within or outside wedlock. By being named, and thereby defined in relation to other family forms or intimate relationships, this type of relationship becomes a distinct alternative that people can consciously make a choice about. (Borell and Karlsson, 2003: 50)

My research participants Dawn, Rachel and Serena lived in the same town as their partners. Retaining their own homes was not then due to the constraints of geographical distance. Instead, reasons given for their choice not to cohabit were linked to their being able to make independent decisions. In their own homes they were not compromised by having to defer to another's opinion, and this was considered a valuable part of their identities as 'single' women. In the absence of 'dependent' children in the home, (by which I mean those younger than 16) Dawn, Rachel and Serena were able to define their own needs more clearly. Alongside the lack of legitimacy for this type of partnership runs the absence of a formal script for its enactment; women are therefore free to 'write' their own. Reflecting on her two marriages for example, Serena said these involved:

Joint decisions about, you know, what furniture you're buying and so on. I've never had that time where I could do that on my own. Now that I can just about manage it financially, it feels good to be able to buy things for my house and pay for jobs and that. So I don't think I'd like to lose that, not yet anyway! [laughs] … I think I'm just enjoying my life as I am now, him in his house with his boys, me in mine with mine. And I'm not dependent. I don't think I could go back to being dependent. I love him and I love his company and perhaps one day we'll

end up together, but I don't foresee it because I don't want to live with him and
take on his children. (Serena)

Serena's partner's two sons lived with him: 'and no signs of them going'. Clearly,
Serena did not wish to take on the responsibility for the care of her partner's
children. As Arber and her colleagues note, 'maintaining their own household
enables older women to avoid some of the asymmetrical distribution of household
labour and unequal demands of caring for a partner' (2003: 9). I would add to
this women's avoidance of caring for their partners' children, like Serena or, as in
the case of Dawn, an aged parent: 'my partner lives with his mother ... he's the
main carer for his mum'. Resistance to taking on extra caring responsibilities was
not however the only reason women gave for living apart from their partners, as
Serena showed in rejecting the dependency she viewed as implicit in a cohabiting
heterosexual relationship. The findings from my research resonate with those of
Roseneil, whose interviewees:

> Expressed a strong sense of individual agency, and a determination to be in
> control of their own lives. Whilst their partners were important to them, this
> group of interviewees shared a more or less explicitly articulated commitment to
> maintaining separateness from their partners. (Roseneil, 2006: 11)

Each of my interviewees who lived apart from their male partner still had a child
living at home, although Rachel's 17-year-old daughter lived for some of the time
with her father. Dawn lived with her 17-year-old daughter and Serena with her 21-
year-old son. Consequently, although all three considered themselves to be freed
from some of the maternal practices that formerly structured their lives during
children's early years, they nevertheless had an other present in their households
and all articulated that they enjoyed good relationships with these children. It
is therefore difficult to assess whether, once these children left home, all three
women would continue living apart from their partners.

This is not to diminish, however, their choice to live separately from their
partners. It was evident that Dawn, Rachel and Serena did not consider themselves
to be in a transitional phase; rather they lived 'gladly apart' (Roseneil, 2006: 11)
from their partners. As Serena said, 'the more I'm by myself, the more I like it. I
do think it would be hard to give up'. Dawn echoed this when she told me: 'I do
like my own space'. Each woman made decisive choices on how to conduct her
relationship with her male partner in the present time. Indeed, all three articulated
a future in which they envisaged a shared home with their partners, although
Rachel followed this with a cautionary note to herself: 'we do have some sort of
longish-term plans ... he's been married twice before as well as me, so that does
make you quite a realist'.

In keeping with the study undertaken by Borell and Karlsson (2003), autonomy
was a prime motivator for those research participants who lived separately from
their male partners. I suggest that in repartnering but living apart these three

women felt in control and that this was borne of previous knowledge accumulated from their live-in partnership experiences. This resonates with the experiences of Judith and Helen discussed earlier.

Although the end of a relationship might initially be fraught with difficulties, women's narratives here illustrate that taking on new challenges increased their self-esteem and in turn their ability to manage alone. Perhaps for the first time, Dawn, Rachel and Serena controlled their everyday lives and laid down the rules of engagement regarding their relationships. I suggest that the freedom they were enjoying was built upon their retreat from the domestic arena where they were expected, and expected themselves, to meet the needs of others. As Borell and Karlsson suggest, and my interview data support, 'a household of their own is a place in which personal control is ensured, a resource women can draw on to balance their need for intimacy with their need for privacy' (2003: 59). Several women remained married throughout their childrearing years and up to their children leaving home; I discuss their experiences next.

For Better or for Worse?

In the aftermath of children's home-leaving, women who remained in their marriages were offered a space for consideration and reappraisal of these relationships. In the case of Alma, this meant leaving her marriage of twenty-nine years once her youngest daughter left the family home:

> Once the girls had got themselves so that their careers were off the ground, they were settled, they were as happy as I could be sure that they were happy, then I thought, that is it. It is now time for me to go. And I did. ... when they had gone, there was nothing at all to keep us together, none whatsoever. After I left I just felt such an overwhelming sense of relief, I just thought, there's no way I can contemplate spending the rest of my life opposite you. That is it! (Alma)

As Alma later said, 'it's happening more and more. I know no end of people who almost the same thing has happened to. As soon as the children have flown the nest couples realise just how little they have in common'. Indeed her observation is confirmed on the Parentline Plus website which states: 'when their child leaves home, parents may look at each other, [and] realise that there is nothing left' (www.parentlineplus.co.uk), a situation Vanessa faced:

> When it got to the last one going to university, my husband came in and said, 'right, well it's just us now. What are we going to do together?' and I turned round and said, 'we're not doing anything at all. I've done my bit and I'm going to have some space now'. I literally wanted out. I'd thoroughly enjoyed it, you know, with the youngsters, but there's no way I wanted to be on my own with one

man, um, who hadn't really wanted me around prior to that … He just assumed
I'd just, like, click back into place. But I wasn't going to. (Vanessa)

Duncombe and Marsden found that women 'foresaw problems when husbands
naively anticipated that the earlier, more intimate coupledom would automatically
return after the children left'; as one of their respondents stated: '"it's too late!"'
(1993: 226–7). Vanessa had, however, remained in the marital home. Knowing
that there was little left in a couple's relationship once children left did not always
result in women ending their marriages:

> When you've had people around you all your life, um, and you've got a possibility
> or a prospect where you could be living on your own as a woman, for the rest of
> your life, then it's very daunting because, um, it can be very lonely. (Vanessa)

There were connections between Vanessa's negative perception of solo-living and
those of Gina and Sandra. Vanessa also considered how her outlook on life post-
separation from her daughters would have differed had she decided to end her
marriage earlier: 'I think it would probably have been better for me. I think I
would've, um, done things more, um, that I wanted to do. I would be able to be
alone now and not worry about being lonely'. Her speculation is confirmed if
compared with women who mothered alone for significant periods of time, as
discussed above. Like Vanessa, Angela had stayed in an estranged relationship
with her husband after both sons left home:

> I do live on my own here, I have my own bedroom, I have my own safe place. I
> wouldn't, I wouldn't actually see where things would be that different because
> there are no constraints. I'm not answerable to anybody. Um, this is my house,
> where I've lived. This is what I've created. We both have … I've lived with it
> for such a long time. It's become a way of life … I suppose I jogged along, you
> know, reasonably safe financially. I worried about if I left, where would I live?
> Would I have enough money? You know, all those kinds of things and I suppose
> I just accepted it; this is who I am. (Angela)

In their study of marital disruption following the last child leaving home,
Hiedemann and her colleagues (Hiedemann, Suhomlinova and O'Rand, 1998:
228) suggest that 'longer-term marriages are expected to be reservoirs of jointly
held economic and emotional capital based on long-term investments not easily
abandoned'. Indeed, financial constraint and investment in home-making were
voiced by Angela as underlying her reasons to remain in her marriage after her
sons left. Fear of financial insecurity outweighed her desire to live independently
from the marital home. However, it would seem that the emotional investment
Angela and Vanessa both made in family life left with their children, in whom
that commitment was invested. It is also the case that their estranged partnership
situations were in the minority amongst the women in my study whose marriages

had remained intact during their childrearing years and after their children left home.

In their discussion of married couples' relationships over time, Duncombe and Marsden (1993: 225) identify two phases of love: 'the early, heady romantic stage of being "in love" and the conventional image of a mature and stable "companionate" love'. Several of the always-married women I interviewed talked of the transformed communicative and emotional landscape of their relationships. They indicated that a shift occurred after children left home: 'it's like you go back, you think, oh god, this is how it was when we were first married' (Janice); 'our relationship's probably better than it ever was since we first got married really' (Denise); and Bridget talked about a renewed closeness with her partner, 'I think my husband and I are closer to each other now than we have been, um, we probably talk to each other more than we ever have done … We are having to, sort of, re-discover who we are without the kids'.

Hiedemann et al. (1998: 220) observe that 'the empty-nest[3] phase has been labelled as a period of euphoria in marriages that have survived the demands of childraising'. This was sometimes evident in the narratives of my always-married participants; as Bridget said, 'not only because we've got to, but because we've got the opportunity to as well'. Other participants also commented on the opportunity for relationship-discovery children's home-leaving brought about:

> If I want to sit up the garden and have a glass of wine my husband will more than likely join me, there's nobody coming home going, 'what time's tea? … There's just you two and you can watch what you like and the house keeps clean and it's just the workload, it isn't an issue when there's just two of you, you know, things are easier. (Janice)

> We both love walking, you know, so we get out and do our walks. That's nice when the kids aren't at home anymore … we come home and you don't have to cook a meal for anybody. It's definitely got more relaxing in some ways, when the kids have been away. (Nancy)

Once children left home my interviewees were increasingly able to determine their own day-to-day schedules with partners, something that previously, as Linda Gannon (1999: 13) notes of her own cohort, was 'precluded by being responsible for the care and feeding of [children]'. Having the space, time and opportunity to renegotiate relationships were positive features of this group of women's lives

---

3 Hiedemann, Suhomlinova and O'Rand (1998: 225) define 'empty nest' as 'the departure of the last child from the household'. Fifteen of my interviewees still had children living at home as the only stipulation for women's participation in the study was that they had experienced a child, or children, leave. Thus mothers with children remaining at home when a child leaves were previously overlooked.

post separation from daughters and sons and viewed as an opportunity to resume previous activities that were once part of the pre-child couple relationship:

> Luckily we've always had a good relationship so we're able to do more of the things that we used to do now. We used to do a lot of sailing when we were younger so we've even talked about starting sailing again, you know, things like this that we used to do. Things that went on the back burner, that we weren't able to afford, you know? The boys took precedence. There were their football matches, their cricket matches, you know, everything like that. So now we've thought, it's our time again. (Frances)

It was also the case that children's home-leaving created a space for my participants to pursue independent interests. Helen compared her unpartnered situation to that of a partnered woman: 'I'm in a better position than somebody who's maybe married and, you know, wants to do something on their own and can't because their partner might not want them to'. Indeed, although not overtly restricted in the way Helen speculated, in some instances women proceeded cautiously with their independent activities:

> I do think I've changed and getting more, it's me, to a point where I'm thinking, don't do it too much or my husband'll be, you know? I'm like, well, my son's off my hands, I'll go and do this, or I'll go do things I like doing and I have to cut back on that because I think, well, best do things together, yeah, because otherwise it's like you could … I suppose, revert back to when I was in my twenties, you know, just that I'll go there, or I'll go round and see that friend, just have a good natter. And then I think, oh well, that's leaving my husband, and I won't do that, just because I've got that freedom. (Janice)

The majority of always-married interviewees talked positively about the changes they experienced in their relationships with their partners. More often than not this was having time to spend together without having to meet the everyday needs of their children. Thus reclaiming time and space was a key element of women's relationships with male partners after their children left home. As Frances said, 'we're on a revival and we're getting back to doing things for ourselves again. It's just, you know, getting our lives back, really'.

In some instances, major changes within women's partnerships coincided with children's leaving, so that family lives that had previously followed traditional patterns of female homemaker/male breadwinner, were overturned. Due to her husband's redundancy, for example, Denise told me that in her household 'the roles have reversed in a lot of ways'. She explained that her husband's new status meant he had 'changed completely'. So had she: 'now I'm the main … wage earner and he isn't and I've, I'm maybe more confident and more assertive now and he's lost a lot of it because of what's happened to him'. Women's earnings within dual-income marriages are often, as Gattrell (2005: 86) notes, 'characterized as almost incidental to household income, and less important than the man's'. Although she worked on a part-time basis throughout her marriage, Denise identified that the change in power dynamics in her home life was due to her capacity to earn the 'family wage', which provoked a shift in household relationships:

> You get to the stage where you feel a doormat, don't you? You think, am I only here to work and clean up and cook for you lot? You know, why am I here? You know, and … I don't know, everybody seems to appreciate me more and you think, oh, I should've done this years ago! [laughs]. (Denise)

Denise's ability to be 'more assertive' in the home environment was tied to her earning power in the workplace: 'for the first time I think, well, I don't have to answer to anybody now and if my husband doesn't like it, well, you know, it doesn't matter. I don't depend on him anymore' (Denise). Gannon (1999: 13) argues that 'men's lives [are] essentially their work lives, characterized by paid employment and much influence in the social, political, and family spheres', she suggests these are 'typified by considerable control'. Denise described her married life along these lines and talked about the inequality she experienced as a younger mother/worker. Whilst her husband worked full-time, for example, his domestic input was minimal and his involvement in neighbourhood organisations resulted in his absence from the home during their children's early years. Once he was made redundant however the couple renegotiated their relationship: 'we came to an agreement, I'd work full-time' (Denise).

The withdrawal of her efforts in the domestic arena coupled with her earning power seemingly resulted in Denise receiving more respect from family members. Her experience highlights not only the wider ramifications of role reversal situations but the continued privileging of the 'breadwinner' status, irrespective to some extent of the gender of the earner. As Pahl suggests, 'being a breadwinner is often regarded as a burden, but it can also be a source of pride and power' (Pahl, 1989: 125). Of course, this also points to the continued denigration of the work involved in the domestic sphere, not least the skills and commitment that childrearing necessitates.

Nancy, whose husband retired in his fifties, continued in full-time work as a teacher: 'it was like a reverse of the original, traditional roles, you know, him being in the house and me being the working person'. Like Denise, she noticed changes in her own attitude that indicated a letting go of her role in the household arena and acceptance of her husband's ability to manage domestic work:

> He's happy pottering around the house, doing the garden, doing his house-husband things, you know, looking after the home. I've changed as well because, when he first took on this role, I would come home and, um, he'd maybe be doing a meal and I'd be, 'no, you should do it like that', but I have learned to stand back … and not to criticise and let him get on. I just love going home and

having my meal on the table. My pipe and slippers aren't by the fire but, um [laughs]. (Nancy)

Tony Chapman (1999: 164) comments that the end result of the process of socialising women into a domestic role is that 'women feel responsible for the organisation of the home and, as a consequence, come to believe that they *know* the best way that tasks should be done' (original emphasis). As Nancy indicated, she had to 'learn to stand back' and allow her husband to 'get on'. Of course, one major difference to the household once adult children leave is that there is no longer a daily demand for childcare, something all of my participants had undertaken alongside paid employment before their children left home. However, financial implications cannot be overlooked and during the early years of participants' childrearing men's greater earning power reinforced the gendered division of labour within and outside the home (Bergman, 2005; Oakley and Rigby, 1998; Pahl, 1989; Witz, 1997). Nevertheless, both Denise and Nancy enjoyed their working lives, their more recent role as main wage earners and the restructuring of their relationships.

Phillips (2000: 42–3) observes that 'despite increasing female employment and the loss of the traditional male "breadwinner", there has not yet been a significant shift in men's domestic roles'. Similarly, the study undertaken by Oakley and Rigby (1998: 122), which focused on parenthood during children's early years, highlighted that 'the positive contribution men make in terms of domestic work, childcare and psychological and social support is a declining resource over time'. I suggest however that following children's home-leaving, we might begin to witness a greater number of role reversal situations like those of my interviewees and concomitant increase in men's domestic input. The complexities of women's relationships and the reasons that underpinned their choices of whether to remain in married/cohabiting relationships or whether to reject them, once their children left home have been the main focus of my discussion so far. To conclude the chapter I discuss the future plans my research participants' shared with me.

Looking Forward

Initially I just thought, that's the end … now I think, right, I've done that, I've got a few years left, now I'll do what I want to do, you know? (Denise)

I'm looking forward to getting just that little bit older and having fun! (Rachel)

Denise shows how in the initial period of her daughter's home-leaving she felt without direction. However, during her daughter's absence Denise clearly turned full-circle. She was ready to pursue her aspirations and make decisions about her future. The majority of women indicated that during the time that elapsed since children left home they were beginning, like the respondents of Wadsworth and Green's (2003: 214) study, to perceive 'the declining maternal role as a positive event'.

Women's perceptions that an ageing self 'suddenly' emerged at the time children left home was discussed previously. Above, Rachel shows that rather than perceiving her ageing self in negative terms, she fully embraced it and she told me she was looking forward to spending time travelling with her new partner. Several women had plans to travel: 'it's my ambition to visit Rome' (Vanessa); 'to visit exciting and exotic places!' (Bridget); to take 'different kinds of holidays' (Heather). Barbara talked about a holiday with her husband:

> We went on holiday for the first time together, on our own without the children, in the summer. We had two weeks in Greece and I thought, god, are we going to get on without the kids. Before we went, I was thinking, what will we do? Will we fall out? And we got on great! Just two people to look after, not four. (Barbara)

It was clear that, following the initial turbulence their adult children's leaving home had created, women began to explore the opportunities this had opened up for them. Often this was articulated in terms of 'freedom' (Dawn, Ingrid, Judith) and 'change' (Janice, Serena). Shifts in women's ways of thinking about their children's leaving home were evident:

> I did decide somewhere along the line that you couldn't sit and mope forever and that you need to see the plus points, and one of the plus points was going to different bits of the world that I would never have gone to otherwise. (Dawn)

> It's nice that we're seeing more of the country! I like him being in the south of England you know, being down there, because it's nice to see areas that we haven't seen before and it's a bit of a holiday when we do go down there. It's nice to be able, when we go there, be able to stay somewhere and not have to get bed and breakfast. (Sally)

Having children who lived/worked away from their hometown, either abroad or in the UK, in turn had created travel and other opportunities for my participants. The emotional and practical difficulties Bridget had encountered during the time her daughter worked in Africa were discussed in the previous chapter. Her daughter later moved to America and her son later began his studies in China. Bridget and her husband had visited all three countries. She considered that the 'plus points' of being able to travel to these places alleviated some of the distress created by geographical separation:

> It gave my husband and I, um, an opportunity to meet people that we would never have done otherwise. You know, if you'd gone as a tourist, that's a totally

different experience of the country and I think it's such a privilege that you sort
of think, oh well, actually! [laughs] Their going has given me, and I'm sure will
give me, all sorts of experiences I wouldn't otherwise have had. (Bridget)

For other interviewees too, daughters' and sons' experiences created opportunities
that might not have otherwise materialised:

My daughter and I have just booked our flights. We're going out there at Easter
to New Zealand and my son's going to get some time off and we're going on
a 'whale watch', um, so he's really looking forward to that. I, a while ago, I
wanted to go to Australia to see the relatives out there because they'd been over
here and, um, I wanted to go out there but then, um, my son going to New
Zealand, I though, um, you know, it's an opportunity. If I don't go now while
he's there, I won't ever go. (Fiona)

Fiona's narrative also points to the maintenance of familial ties across great
distances discussed previously, something she articulated as impossible for earlier
generations of her family. Participants evidently began to take advantage of the
opportunities children leaving home opened up to them which in its turn offered
some solace to the feelings of loss initially experienced in the aftermath of that
leaving; as Denise said, 'I suppose independence works both ways, doesn't it?'
As such, many interviewees shifted towards an enjoyment of the lives they lived
separately from their adult daughters and sons and anticipated a future taken up
with activities with their partners and/or friends:

My friend's daughter's fifteen at the moment and she's hoping she'll go on to
university and my friend's always saying, 'we'll get motorbikes and go round
Europe!' It's a friend I met at work that does the same thing as me and, um, she's
always saying we'll do all sorts together when the kids have gone. (Helen)

Hockey and James (2003: 103) state that 'mid-life is, demographically speaking,
the key period for grand parenting'. They critique contemporary images which
present grandparents as 'comfortably retired people with time on their hand to
indulge small children, their ageing bodies easily falling into step with a toddler's
ambling pace'. They argue that these are 'at odds with the look and lifestyle of the
forty-somethings who are *actually* grandparenting today' (original emphasis). My
research participant Helen was a lone mother from her daughters' early years. At
the time of the interview, all three of her daughters were in their early twenties;
the middle daughter had left home to live with her partner and child. Helen was
then also a grandmother as well as in full-time employment. She is testament to
the notion of 'how orientations to lifestyles in later life are redefining ageing'
(Fairhurst, 2003: 39). Helen not only challenged static notions of mothers' lives
once children leave, but also the stereotypes of grandmotherhood that Hockey and
James also critique.

Although several of my interviewees told me they looked forward to becoming grandmothers, this was not always the case. Ingrid, for example, was not ready to accept grandchildren into her life. As discussed earlier, once adult children left home repartnered women embarked on a 'honeymoon time' (Heather). As a repartnered woman, Ingrid said, 'I know that if grandchildren come along, that I'll want to be a big part of their lives, um, and I'm not ready for that yet'. Jerrome (1996: 90) indicates that to some extent the role of grandparent 'interferes with the pursuit of new mid-life opportunities'. I would add that this is especially so in repartnered relationships. Like Rachel, Ingrid was in fact planning to travel with her partner: 'my husband wants to go to all these countries that he went to when he was in the Navy and to explore them. So that's what we're looking forward to doing'. Once grandchildren came along, Ingrid perceived that she would forfeit some of her newfound freedom.

Retirement also featured in women's thoughts about the future. Although Nancy was due to retire two years following our interview, this phase of her life course was not particularly relished: 'I don't like to wish my life away. I don't want it to come any quicker'. She did envisage, however, that she and her husband would 'do as much as we can while the body allows, you know? Go off on holidays'. Barbara told me: 'my husband will actually formerly retire at 65, that's in three years' time. That'll be a big impact on us I think as a couple. I think that'll be the biggest thing we'll face'. In her study on age and gender in life after work, Eileen Fairhurst (2003: 38) found her respondents' notions of having to 'work at' relationships during retirement emerged as 'a matter for both rather than just one party in the marriage'. This was also evident in the narratives of several of my partnered interviewees. As she further comments:

> Individuals' acknowledgement and assessment of social change are situated through contrasts made between their current experiences and those of preceding or ascending generations. This is particularly evident in talk about lifestyles in retirement and intergenerational relationships. (Fairhurst, 2003: 33)

Rita's mother was a full-time housewife/mother throughout her married life, whereas Rita worked full-time for the majority of her married years. She drew on the differences between her own relationship and that of her parents' when she considered how retirement would be experienced by herself and her husband:

> They were very close, my parents and, because our life has been different, because we have been working and … we're really going to have to try and work on [our relationship in retirement]. That's why we do the allotment together. We do some things together, you know, and we've got plans, we've got ideas. We like walking, so we've got that to do together so I'm sure that will all come back together when we both, sort of, relax a bit from working because before we couldn't possibly afford to do that. (Rita)

Although enjoying the opportunities that children's home-leaving created, the desire to be physically close to their adult children often steered some interviewees' future plans. Nancy was considering a house move to Scotland in order to be nearer to her daughter. Similarly, when considering her son's mobile lifestyle and the thought that he might eventually decide to live in another country, Fiona said: 'perhaps after he's been away a year he might realise that he can do it and, um, I don't know, he might stay. I'll have to move to New Zealand! [laughs]'. Some women were also planning to move elsewhere, either within or outside of the UK, but often called on the notion of their children 'settling down' before making a move that would take them further away from their children:

> We do plan that, when both the kids are settled, possibly, it's an idea, to sell up and go live elsewhere, in a different country. But they would have to be well settled before we did that. Um, so that's us moving away from them. It's an adventure, and I like adventures, and the world isn't a big place any more. It would be nice for them to come and join us wherever we are, you know, it's a holiday for them and provides a little bit extra in their life for them. (Ingrid)

> I'm not going to Crete to get away from the kids but, you know, you're going because it's what you want to do, rather than what's best for everyone else ... once my son's got settled down then we'll probably go because ... we thought, really, it's not much further for ... it's four hours drive if you go to Newcastle, to Crete it's four hours flight. (Denise)

Ingrid justified her decision to move abroad in terms of it being beneficial to her children, and both she and Denise drew on the concept of the ease of travel between the UK and other countries discussed more fully in the previous chapter. Denise and her husband also planned to buy a flat in the UK as a base for their children and a place to return to. Similarly, Rachel told me of plans she and her partner had to buy a house in the UK and another in Rachel's home country of New Zealand.

Although also contemplating a house move, Maggie had rejected earlier thoughts she had of moving to France, deciding that this was 'far too far away from the children'. Instead she and her partner decided to stay in the UK: 'I think we'll end up somewhere central, easy access to all the children'. Similarly, Dawn's decision to move house within the UK was made with ease of access in mind: 'I wouldn't move far, well, I would move far, but it'd be in this country, within train distance'. As their narratives indicate, my participants had several plans, some modest, some more adventurous, but all of them in opposition to the notion of women's lives as a time of stasis once their children leave home.

Concluding Remarks

Previous chapters have elaborated how women fixed themselves as 'available' to their children via the concept of 'being there'. This chapter has problematised this situation by exploring the dilemmas some women experienced when daughters and sons visited/returned to the home. These are drawn on as indicators of mothers' shifting perceptions of their children's status as well as that of their mothering selves. Time spent apart from their daughters and sons forced a reconceptualisation of their children and of themselves which in turn shifted them further towards their acceptance and/or recognition of the child-as-adult and so, of course, of themselves as the mothers of children who were also adults from whom, for the most part, they lived separately.

My participants' narratives illustrate that children's home-leaving offered women a space in which a number of new experiences, choices and opportunities were opened up, and which many of them were beginning to enthusiastically embrace. Their engagement in paid employment, for example, emerged as an important factor in their lives, providing an identity that co-existed alongside their mothering selves and continued after children left home. Interviewees were also able to reappraise their partnership status once children left. This chapter revealed how women were actively engaged in making choices of whether to accept or reject the circumstances under which their relationships with men were formerly conducted and experienced. It also explored participants' travel plans and in some instances their plans for moving abroad. Nevertheless it was evident that women continued to indicate an unfaltering connection with their daughters and sons; as Sally said: 'they're still a major part of your life. They're still your children, whatever age they are'. It was clear then that considerations of their children's needs and a desire for ease of access to them remained important elements in the decisions women were making for the future.

Lives without their children at home were however, starting to take their own shape and children's home-leaving was often reconceptualised as a 'new beginning'. What this chapter has established, therefore, is that women's lives after their adult children left home were dynamic and processual rather than static and unchanging, and were being lived in opposition to the mother of Lee's 1960s novel, introduced in the introductory chapter, and the twenty-first century *Vodafone* mum, whose representation I problematised in Chapter 5. As Serena said, 'I do feel that I'm still changing and, I don't know, I'm happy with myself. I like myself. I do like myself. Which is a good start, isn't it?'

Chapter 7

Conclusion: Reflections on Motherhood, Absence and Transition

This book has explored women's experiences of separation from their adult children at the time of the latter's leaving home, an aspect of motherhood that I have argued has to date received little academic attention. The data produced was grounded in the meanings of child- and mother- hoods for my twenty-five research participants prior to, during and following the time their daughters and sons left home. In focusing on motherhood during a particular stage of the life course, I am exposing the need to reconceptualise the mother/child relationship to encompass within it women's relationships with their children once they become adult. To conclude the book, I summarise the contribution my argument offers to contemporary understandings of motherhood, absence and transition.

The concept of motherhood as a socially and emotionally experienced identity is an underlying feature of the work and I have identified and elaborated on women's reflections on motherhood and their feelings about themselves as mothers. The analysis of the interview data provides an insight into the practice of mothering at the time children leave and as such is a valuable addition to other work in the area of mother/child relationships, notably Ribbens McCarthy and Edwards (2002: 210) who ask: 'what room is left for mothering as centred on emotion, moral identity and a particularistic relationship that does not constitute a purposive projective with clearly identifiable outcomes?'

The boundaries constructed around mother- and child- hoods have received particular attention as it is these which inform mothers (and others) of what mothering is and what it should be. As Smart (1996: 48) suggests: 'motherhood is highly contrived and historically specific' and so, in consequence, is childhood. When I began to write a difficulty in using the terms 'child' and 'adult' emerged; these words invariably jarred and failed to convey the meanings I sought. This awkwardness highlighted the inadequacy of our understandings of the concepts 'mother' and 'child'. This resulted in my decision to use the terms 'child' and 'children' interchangeably with 'now-adult child/ren', 'child/ren as adult(s)' and 'adult child/ren' so that their usage emphasised the disjuncture that occurs in mothers' perceptions of themselves and their offspring (as well as the perceptions of wider society), once children reach a certain age and stage in the life course.

I have argued that motherhood is culturally perceived as a 'timed' event – the transition to motherhood which the birth of a baby signifies, a middle period of mothering, during which the child is simultaneously cared for and reared and an 'ending', when the child becomes adult and separates from the mother. This model negates certain continuities of mothering once children are adult. Motherhood is then performed within a specific framework that is heavily embedded in sociocultural definitions relating to time and place. As each of the chapters in this volume have established, these definitions do not convey the depth of meaning mothers attribute to their relationships with their children as they grow up and then leave home. Effectively, this is because there is an absence of templates for dealing with the transformation of mothering that occurs alongside the child's movement out of the home. I have argued that this is a silenced transition for the mother.

Gillies et al. (2003: 33) comment that 'a focus on young people as the sole object of change risks obscuring the important turning points and continuities experienced by other "family" members, concurrent with the process of "growing up"'. Although my own research took the young person's movement out of the family home as the catalyst of change for the mother, the focus of my enquiry fell on my interviewees' understandings and experiences of this time and I have fore-fronted not only the changes but also the continuities in mothers' relationships with their adult children.

To this end, I have suggested that a broader view of women's experiences is necessary and argued for a need to incorporate into constructions of motherhood the continuity of interactions with adult daughters and sons from whom mothers live separately. Thus the work adds to the work of Holdsworth and Morgan (2005: 2) who suggest that the process of leaving home is important 'to the individuals concerned – both those who are leaving or contemplating leaving home and those who are left behind'. By drawing on mothers' experiences of this phase of the life course I have illustrated how young people's movement out of the family home has wide-reaching and complex consequences for our understandings of motherhood and for women's mothering as praxis.

The work has also elaborated on the mother/child relationship to highlight how the emerging adulthood of the child impacted on each of my research participant's sense of self-as-mother. I have argued that children's movement out of the home disrupted the ontological basis of women's mothering identities. Each of the chapters has tackled this issue in different ways. In Chapter 3, for example, I discussed the difficulties my interviewees encountered when confronted with the emerging adulthood of the child that manifested at the time of their home-leaving whilst in Chapter 4 I analysed women's the management of separation from their adult children. The ability to maintain contact with children via the use of different communication technologies was revealed in Chapter 5 to underscore women's ability to sustain their motherhood identities. The final chapter considered how women's desire to meet their own needs more fully emerged in the aftermath of children's leaving and explored my participants' plans and aspirations for the future. The volume as a whole has highlighted how children's home-leaving instigates a reconfiguration of the mother/adult child relationship. The overarching conceptual framework was drawn from women's experiences of mothering their children to adulthood and one of the strengths of the volume is the application of women's interview narratives to a multidisciplinary range of theoretical perspectives.

In my discussion in Chapter 1, 'Becoming and Being a Mother' I highlighted the gap in our knowledge regarding what motherhood and mothering mean to women once their adult children leave. In this chapter I commented that although home-leaving is an expected event in the life course of the child, there is little acknowledgement of what the child's movement out of the home means for the mother. I argued that her experience is effectively silenced by the sociocultural constructions of mother and child and the privileging of the child's entry into adulthood via their home-leaving.

The third chapter focused on the notion of 'Modelling Motherhood' in order to reveal the disjuncture in sociocultural perceptions of mothers and their children via a juxtaposition of images of mother/child and mother/adult child. I suggested here that the power of mother/child representations has a major impact on contemporary understandings of women as mothers. As such, the age-related dimension of mother and child and their relation to each other becomes confused at the time of the child's emerging adulthood and forces a negotiation between static models of motherhood and the dynamic of change underlying the movement from child towards adult identities. I argued that available models of motherhood do not take women beyond the early and dependent years of their children's lives and that this lack manifests itself most profoundly at the time that children leave home. As such, I revealed how my participants were positioned precariously as the mothers of children who 'suddenly' became adults. In consequence they needed to re-think their mothering. The break in the continuity of mothering that the 'changing' child provokes causes to varying degrees the mother's mis-recognition of her child and, in consequence, of her self-as-mother.

In many instances, this ran in conjunction with and in contradiction to, the fact that each of my participants was acculturated into an understanding that the purpose of her mothering was the nurturance of independence and autonomy; as Ingrid said, 'you bring your children up to be independent and to go away'. This chapter thus exposed the intertwining of the personal and social aspects of women's lives as mothers as their mothering as praxis is reliant upon and practiced with reference to the models of motherhood currently available to them. In rejecting the model of motherhood experienced as daughters, women were left without a mentor or precedent on which to base their experiences at the time their children left home.

The chapter argued that the ultimate goal of 'successful' mothering in a contemporary UK context is the production of an autonomous individual and that this underscored women's accounts of the purpose of their mothering. Similarly, childcare 'advice' is couched in the rhetoric of development and 'becoming' adult, rather than in notions of 'being' a child. This was prevalent in my interviewees' narratives which highlighted a collective aim to produce independent adults. The achievement of this by the child signified successful mothering – the affirmation of getting motherhood 'right'. Paradoxically, once children were perceived to have achieved adult status, exemplified by their move out of the family home, mothers themselves were confronted by their independent adult-child. This was the cause of unease for many women, whose identities as mothers remained immersed in the understandings of mothering the child as dependent. I have suggested that women maintained and sustained their mothering identities through a refiguring of the discourse of 'being there' (Ribbens, 1994; Ribbens McCarthy and Edwards, 2001).

Chapter 3 therefore exposed the incongruity of the notion of mothering an individual whose identity rests upon the concept of 'independent adult'. This explains to some extent the negation of the emotional aspects of children's transition out of the family home and the mother's silent support of the child's 'independence'. More importantly however, I argued that the dilemma women experienced at the time of their children's home-leaving was linked to the inadequacy of available models of motherhood that inform collective understandings of what a mother (and in turn, a child) is.

In Chapter 4 I discussed my participants' management of the process of separation. I argued that my interviewees travelled a non-linear journey at the time of their children's home-leaving that culminated in an acceptance of their adult children's absence from the home. The chapter revealed that this transition was ragged and often difficult as, regardless of their interpellation within the discourse of the goals of 'successful' motherhood, many of my participants were ill-prepared for the reality of separation from adult children. In this chapter, the competing demands of 'head' and 'heart' were explored through my participants' experiences of the contradictory emotions of wanting children to leave in order to achieve culturally sanctioned goals of independence and success, alongside a desire for the closeness and proximity with the child that had until the point of separation defined the mother/child relationship and so, their mothering selves.

The concepts of preparation, separation and acceptance provided a chronology for the chapter through which I was able to describe women's emotional journeys at the time of their children's home-leaving, although as aforementioned, this was not straightforward or sequential. Indeed, although the child's move out often followed a linear pathway, which was particularly acute for interviewees whose children left home for university, women's own experiences of this time were disjointed. The preparation of the child for home-leaving did not go hand-in-hand with the mother's preparation for the actual experience of separation, nor for life at home without the child in it.

The privileging of the child's movement out of the home was highlighted. This suppressed women's ability to display the feelings of loss they experienced and an internal emotional conflict was evident in many women's narratives, exposing the tension between the mother's support for the child leaving with that of needing support herself. The latter is 'played down' when compared to the 'big moment' of the adult child's movement away from the home/mother. It was also the case that few interviewees were able to draw the support they felt they needed from male partners (where present). Rather it emerged that friendship with similarly placed women was a greater source of comfort. It was also the case that for the majority of my participants the research interview itself provided the first opportunity to talk in any depth about their feelings.

The emotional disruption caused by separation from the adult child was articulated by many of my participants as evoking emotions akin to those of bereavement. Unlike bereavement however, my interviewees' feelings regarding children's leaving were not accorded legitimacy; instead many of the women had coped with their feelings alone. As such, their narratives highlighted the silence that surrounds this time in a mother's life course and to some extent her own perpetuation of that silence. Although some participants recollected their own mothers' sadness at the time of their own home-leaving, they had not pursued/ understood its source; neither had they articulated their feelings to their daughters and sons when they left. Thus the creation and perpetuation of the silence regarding what a mother experiences when a child leaves home was evident in several of my interviewees' narratives. I argued that this is due to the naturalising and normalizing of the western child's culturally sanctioned quest for independence from the mother and the home.

The child's absence also radically altered the way the space of the home was experienced and often the emptiness of the house provided a metaphor for the emptiness my participants' experienced within themselves once their children left. The chapter thus argued that the caring practices that had once structured interviewees' day-to-day lives, and which was interpreted by them as symbolic of their love and care for their children, were relinquished when children were no longer present. As such, women were perplexed as to how they could demonstrate an important aspect of their mothering. The chapter also revealed that over time the majority of women began to 'reclaim' the territory of the home that once 'belonged' to their children. Although they experienced feelings of being 'in limbo', as Angela described it, this was coupled with a sense that my participants had begun to re-shape their lives. Ultimately, although a spatial separation had occurred, children's absence was not indicative of a brutal severance of the child from the mother but formed the catalyst for a reconfiguration of the mother/adult child relationship.

My discussion in Chapter 5 of mothers and children's 'Post-Separation Communication' explored the meanings of place and space. In this chapter I elaborated that mothers' contact with their absent daughters and sons across geographical distances was integral to the continuity of their relationships and in turn women's mothering selves. Undoubtedly, the fact that mothers were able to maintain contact with their children emerged as a major factor that shifted women towards accepting themselves as the mothers of children who were also adults and from whom they lived apart. This sustained the relationship with their children and, in turn, their identities as mothers.

This chapter asked how geographical distances between mothers and their children impacted on the mother/adult child relationship and, in consequence, on women's mothering as praxis. The sense of being on the periphery of their adult children's lives and thus no longer central to their well-being is one indicator of mothers' changed and changing roles. The chapter reiterated that motherhood is a relational identity that is most commonly understood alongside the presence of a 'dependent' child. In my interview data this translated into the conflation of safety and proximity, which the child's leaving home disrupted. As such, contact with their adult children helped women to combat the feelings of exclusion separation had provoked and the unrest women experienced in their 'new' role as the mothers of adults. Key to this was the incorporation of communication technologies into their everyday lives.

The land-line telephone, the mobile phone and the internet provided my research participants with a virtual space in which meaningful interactions with absent children could take place. Although articulating the desire for children to have life experiences that differed from their own, in terms of travel and adventure for example, mothers' contact with their children via cyberspace also provided them with the knowledge that their children's lives were safely grounded in everyday activities similar to those they previously pursued before leaving home.

Unlike those who travel in virtual spaces to transcend fixed identities of the real world (Jones, 1998; Kolko and Reid, 1998; Markham, 1998; Rheingold, 1993, 2000), I argued in this chapter that my interviewees used cyberspace to fix their real world motherhood identities in an attempt to reconcile the opposing feelings of rupture and continuity experienced in the absence of their children. I did not suggest in this chapter however that my participants' lives had remained static once their children left home. Rather I argued that the women desired affirmation of their motherhood identities. Thus I suggested that contact with their children helped sustain a sense of self-as-mother, albeit under changed conditions of communication.

The transformation of some aspects of interviewees' mothering was made apparent when women reflected on their adult children's visits or long-term returns to the family home. This was a focus of Chapter 6. Although it was clear that some adult children held onto static notions of their mothers' lives, underpinned by their expectation of and desire for her invariance, the chapter exposed a shift in mothers' perceptions of children's adult status had taken place which manifested when daughters and sons visited. Motherhood identities were experienced as in flux as women began to assert their independence from their children in order to pursue their own desires. This difficulty was particularly pronounced for my participants whose children made a long-term return, not only because of the mothers' more clearly emerging desire to meet their own needs more fully, but also because the returners were no longer identified as 'children' coming back home, but as 'adults'.

My discussion of the post-separation dis/continuities of the mother/child relationship that remained pertinent to women's lives and the decisions they were willing and/or able to make regarding their own future plans illustrated how women's lives were active and processual rather than static and unchanging. Rather than offering a nostalgic view of mothering which, as Silva (1996: 33) states, 'risk[s] stressing losses rather than contradictory shifts, gains and redefinitions', I am concerned to emphasise how women renegotiated their relationships with their adult children with whom they enjoyed interconnected lives.

Adult children leaving home altered women's perceptions of other aspects of their lives, for example the relationship to paid work and their partnership status and these were also discussed in Chapter 6. Women's relationship to paid employment was commonly articulated as having sustained a sense of self-worth and self-esteem that built upon an identity that existed outside of motherhood and continued after their children left. Likewise, the presence or absence of male partners in their lives revealed much diversity in women's partnership status and the choices and challenges they encountered once their daughters and sons left home.

Although their future plans were often underscored by women's continued consideration of adult children's needs, pursuing activities independently from children was articulated by my participants as an element of their lives they welcomed. Following the struggle to renegotiate and then reclaim a sense of self-as-mother, many of them were revealed in this chapter to be actively engaged in 'shaping mothering in ways that suit[ed] their own needs and interests' (Silva 1996: 34). Thus, children's home-leaving created a space for women to more fully pursue desires that existed separately from their motherhood, and so from their adult children.

Bringing Mothers Together

Overall, in embarking on a study of women who have successfully reared their children to adulthood the book has argued for the need to broaden discussions of motherhood as it appears to be only with hindsight, as my participants reflected not only on what being a mother had meant prior to children leaving home, but also on what it continued to mean to them, that they could begin to make more sense of their own experiences of mothering over time. It was also the case that an event I organised for my participants created a forum wherein experiences of their children leaving home could be shared.

> I really feel that with this there ought to be some recognition, you know. I'm not suggesting that we rush out and form self-help groups, but I think there ought to be something … it's not taken seriously, there's no recognition, is there? (Angela)

> Are other women feeling like me? I suppose that's what I want to know. (Rita)

> I'd like to know eventually whatever you put together. I'd like to, sort of, keep involved. (Rachel)

Three recurring issues emerged from my research with this group of women and are detailed in the extracts above: the call for this stage of the mother's life course to be acknowledged; a need to find out how other mothers feel about their children's home-leaving; and an interest in the outcomes of the research. These led me to present some of my findings back to my participants. As Griffin (2005: 192) suggests: 'interviewees frequently agree to be interviewed because they are interested in the topic; they will therefore also be interested in the findings'. I was keen to give something back to the women who committed their time and gave their stories to the research. Inviting them to an event that offered the opportunity of networking with other mothers provided an ideal solution that incorporated each of the above themes.

This event did not serve as a data producing tool. Rather its main function was an opportunity to bring women together, as in many of the interviews participants stressed the need to talk to others who had undergone the same experience. Another advantage of their participation in the research was then an opportunity to talk with other women about a previously silenced experience. The group were able to share their thoughts in a 'safe' environment which enabled a talking forum and a further outcome of the event was that the women organised more meetings. Moreover, women's comments throughout the day served to cement the relevance of researching this phase in mothers' lives. It was evident from their comments that the women appreciated and enjoyed the experience of participating in the research and the opportunity to offer their feedback. This event provides an example of users using the research positively and its success adds weight to the body of work that promotes the inclusion of participants as subjects involved in the research process and its outcomes, rather than as passive objects of research (Griffin, 2005; Skeggs, 1994).

Future Directions

Life course transitions in later life might at times be perceived as somehow natural or inevitable, which means they do not receive the academic attention they deserve. To this end, the work presented in this volume addresses some of the gaps within social science research that tends to build theory upon primary life course transitions, effectively ignoring what I suggest are the secondary or default transitions of others. The starting point for my research was the adult child's departure from the home but my focus was on the mother's experience. The aim was to make this phase of the mother's life course more visible in order to contribute to existing theoretical frameworks for the study of motherhood, ageing and gender.

Throughout the book I have made references to the growing body of literature that focuses on young people's home-leaving in order to reinforce my argument that to date, little in-depth investigation has been made into how this is experienced by their mothers. By examining this hitherto unexplored time in the mother's life course my findings thus contribute to understandings of motherhood and mothering in a contemporary UK context. The concepts of motherhood, absence and transition form the basis of the work and the empirical chapters provide in-depth discussions that range across the relationship between constructions of motherhood/mothering and childhood; the emotions and disruptions of the actual home-leaving process; advances in communication technologies and the implications of these for mothering 'virtually'; and the consequences of adult children 'boomeranging' between natal home and new home for women's emergent identities. A major finding is the identification of the conceptual, cultural and personal 'silence' surrounding mothers' experiences of their adult children's home-leaving. As such, the book contributes to a neglected research field, underpinned as it is by the rich narratives of my research participants. In turn, there is ample opportunity to take the subject matter forward.

The conceptual discussion of the way that models of motherhood and mothering coupled with mothers' experiences of simultaneously caring for and rearing their children, provides a means of understanding the complex experiences and reconfigurations in emotions, identities and biographies women face when their children leave home. By taking the substantive topic of leaving home as an illustration, and stressing the relational dimensions of this particular life course transition, the conceptual framework of motherhood, absence and transition that underpins the arguments of the book has theoretical generalisability. It provides a focus on issues such as relational aspects of the life course; ageing and gendered subjectivities; the emotional meanings of space and place; and constructions of western citizenship. In turn these contribute to ongoing and emerging debates and discussions on subjectivity and identity theorisation and the relationship between subjectivity and time.

There are relatively few studies that explore the significance of advances in communication technology for familial and interpersonal relationships. In the book I have argued that my participants were pursuing confirmation of their motherhood identity when their children left home. Their access to a range of techno-goods was integral to this as they were enabled in effect to 'mother virtually'. My findings thus offer an observation of the mother/adult child relationship that is hitherto unexamined and that in turn provides a contrasting perception of constructions of 21st century individualistic western citizenship. There is potential then for further research into the impact of geographical distances and the use of new technologies on the performance of familial/affective relationships. There is also a need to pursue more fully the relational dimensions of transitional phases of the life course.

Also illuminated in the book is that much of the literature addressing notions of intimacy points to the fragmentary and unstable nature of contemporary heterosexual relationships. These accounts tend to define the mother/child relationship as one of proximity, security and stability. I have problematised these notions because the adult child, at least from a western perspective, is destined, and encouraged, to travel further afield than previous generations. This then poses a challenge to debates that position the child as 'fixed', and not least because of their accompanying 'fixing' of the mother and further research would be welcome in this area.

The women who participated in the research were drawn from a particular locality which, although a diverse group, resulted in certain commonalities. My respondents were self-selecting within the reach of the immediate environment in which I sought participants. This means that the group might have looked quite different had I sampled from another environment. What the impact of this might be could in turn provide the basis for further study. I did not specifically sample for class, ethnicity or sexuality for example, all issues that merit more dedicated attention. Furthermore, it might be interesting to find out about fathers' experiences of their children leaving home in relation to shifting constructions of fatherhood and masculinity.

Final Comments

The findings from my research reflect the need to make not only an academic contribution but also to inform individuals dealing with this time of transition, both professionally and personally, in order to contribute to a wider public understanding of a previously unexplored life course experience. Despite the conflicting and contradictory messages in which motherhood is immersed, the twenty-five women who participated in my research had successfully navigated their way through the experience of their children's home-leaving. Though this proved a struggle at times, they nevertheless renegotiated and then reclaimed a place in their adult children's lives post-separation. Each created a new dialogue across space and time; that of reformulating notions of the self-as-mother in relation to the absent child.

Contemporary cultural constructions of motherhood, mothering, childcare and childrearing might continue to shore up contradictory notions of dependence and independence, however for each of my interviewees' at least, mother and adult child remained markedly interrelated and interdependent following the latter's home-leaving. In analysing the many different aspects of women's lives as mothers and emphasising the cultural, emotional and spatial aspects of motherhood in a contemporary UK context, the work presented in this volume thus contributes to the understandings of the meanings and practices of motherhood across the life course, not only for an academic audience, but for mothers themselves once their adult children leave home.

Appendix 1
Participants' Biographies

Alma (55) White British middle-class, with middle-class upbringing. She did not undertake paid employment when her children were young. At the time the research took place, she had two daughters, aged 29 and 27, both of whom had left home. Alma was single, having divorced her husband of 29 years following her second daughter's home-leaving. She had lived alone for 2.5 years. She worked full-time as a secretary.

Angela (56) White British. She did not answer the 'class' question, commenting: 'I attended a grammar school, as did all my brothers, sisters, cousins etc. and all my family went to university and have sound education backgrounds'. Angela worked outside the home in a full-time and part-time capacity alongside childrearing. At the time of the interview her two sons, aged 33 and 29, had left home but the youngest had returned after his relationship break-up and was living with Angela and her husband. Angela was a full-time FE college lecturer.

Barbara (44) White British working-class, with working-class upbringing. She did not work outside the home during her childrearing years. She had a daughter aged 16 and an adopted son aged 21, both of whom had left home. Her son was from her first and her daughter from her second marriage. She had previously lived as a single parent for one year. Barbara lived with her second husband and worked as a departmental administrator in a university.

Bridget (48) White British middle-class, with middle-class upbringing. She did not work outside the home when her children were young. She had a daughter aged 22 and two sons, aged 24 and 18. All three had left home for university and to travel/work abroad. Bridget lived with her husband, the father of all three children, and worked as a church administrator.

Dawn (44) White British middle-class, with middle-class upbringing. She worked part-time outside the home when her children were young. Two of her three daughters, aged 22 and 19, had left home. Dawn had experienced two periods of lone-mothering, for 18 months and for 6 years. She lived with her youngest daughter, aged 17, and was in a non-cohabiting relationship with a male partner. She worked full-time as a teaching assistant.

Denise (45) White British working-class, with working-class upbringing and worked part-time outside the home when her son started school. Her daughter, aged 20, had left home for university and her 17-year-old son lived at home. Denise lived with her husband, the father of her two children, and worked full-time as an ICT advisor.

Fiona (49) White British middle-class, with working-class upbringing. She commented: 'my roots are working class and my politics and my heart still are, but I am a professional so cannot now consider myself to be working-class by occupation'. Fiona worked on a part-time basis outside the home when her children were young. Her son (22) had left home for university and her 12-year-old daughter lived at home. Fiona's son was from her first marriage and she had spent eight years as a single parent before marrying for the second time. She worked full-time as a university lecturer and was undertaking a part-time PhD.

Frances (53) White British middle-class, with middle-class upbringing. She had two sons, aged 25 and 22, both of whom had left home, one into local shared accommodation and one travelling abroad. She did not engage in paid employment outside the home until her youngest son was 11. Frances lived with her husband, the father of her sons, and worked full-time as an administration controller for a local supermarket.

Gina (45) White British working-class, with working-class upbringing. Her eldest daughter (18) had left home to live locally with her partner and her youngest daughter (15) lived at home. Gina worked part-time as a bank clerk when her children were younger. She had mothered alone for 9 years. She worked full-time as a lecturer in a college of further education.

Heather (51) White British middle-class, with middle-class upbringing. She was widowed when her son was 11 months old and mothered alone for 17 years during which time she worked full-time as a teacher. Heather had remarried and was step-mother to three sons aged 24, 22 and 19. All four sons had left home for university. She worked full-time as an Education Advisor.

Helen (49) White British working-class, with working-class upbringing. She had three daughters, 15, 19 and 22. Her middle daughter had left home to live locally with her partner and baby; the other two lived at home. Helen had mothered alone for 13 years and had worked full-time when her children were young. She continued to work full-time as a teaching assistant at the time the research took place.

Ingrid (52) White British working-class, with working-class upbringing. She was in her second marriage and had one son, aged 29 and was step-mother to two other children from a previous relationship. In her second marriage she was also step-mother to a daughter aged 19 who had left home for university. Her son lived locally with his partner. Ingrid had mothered alone for 4 years before remarrying and had worked part-time during this period. At the time of the research, she worked full-time as a senior departmental secretary in a university.

Janice (50) White British working-class, with working-class upbringing. She was married to the father of her two children, a son aged 26, who had left home for university and at the time of the research had returned to live locally, and a daughter aged 24 who lived at home. Janice did not engage in paid employment outside the home until her youngest child was eight years old. She lived with her husband and worked full-time as an ICT advisor in a university.

Judith (52) White British middle-class, with working-class upbringing. Her two sons, aged 26 and 24, had both left home, the former to live locally and the latter to university. Judith had been a lone mother for five years following her divorce. At the time the research took place, she was living with her partner. She undertook paid employment when her youngest son was eight and at the time of the research, she worked full-time as a human resources manager for a local company.

Linda (52) White British working-class, with working-class upbringing. Her 18-year-old son had left home for university and her daughter, aged 14, lived at home. Linda was married to the father of her children. She had worked full-time for two years after the birth of her first child and part-time for the following nine years. At the time of the research, she worked as a full-time library assistant.

Lois (48) British with Anglo-Indian parents, middle-class with a lower-middle-class upbringing. Her eldest son (26) was from her first marriage. He had left home and lived in London but was shortly to return to live locally with his wife and child. Her 15-year-old son from her current relationship lived at home with Lois and her partner. She had worked part-time in bars when her eldest son was young and undertook a part-time undergraduate degree after the birth of her second son. Lois was employed full-time as a classroom support assistant and also worked as a musician and singer.

Maggie (48) White British/Asian Chinese, middle-class, with middle-class upbringing, commenting: 'I grew up in Hong Kong, the older of two daughters. My father was a successful businessman and became financially successful when I got to about 14'. Maggie had three daughters and one son. Her eldest daughter and her son had both left home for university. Two daughters (14 and 13) lived at home with Maggie. She had been a lone mother for 4.5 years prior to re-partnering and worked in both a full- and part-time capacity when her children were younger. At the time of the research, she worked as a part-time sixth-form teacher.

Nancy (55) White British working-class, with working-class upbringing, commented: 'depends how you define working-class, doesn't it?' Nancy worked part-time during her children's pre-school years. Her daughter, aged 25, originally left home for university and worked in Aberdeen. Her son (23) completed university and at the time of the research was travelling/working in New Zealand.

Nancy worked full-time as a primary school teacher. She lived with her husband, the father of both children.

Paula (49) White British working-class, with working-class upbringing. Her eldest son, aged 19, had left home for university. Her younger son (15) lived at home with Paula and her husband, who was the father of both children. Paula worked part-time when her children were young and continued to work in the same job as an optical receptionist at the time of the research.

Rachel (48) White British/New Zealand, working-class, with working-class upbringing, commenting: 'I have difficulty establishing myself as part of a class group – as a member of a long established New Zealand family we did not consider ourselves as part of any class'. Rachel had three daughters, aged 24, 20 and 17, all had left home. Her eldest daughter was from her first marriage, the second two from her second. She was in a non-cohabiting relationship when we met. When her children were young, Rachel owned and worked on a farm so was effectively employed full-time, but from home. At the time of the research, she worked as a higher education technician/school assistant.

Rita (47) White British working-class, with working-class upbringing. Her daughter was 21 and had left home for university. Her 18-year-old son lived at home with Rita and her husband, the father of her children. Rita worked part-time in a shop when her children were young and was employed as a full-time university administrator at the time of the research.

Sally (52) White British middle-class, with working-class upbringing. Her two sons, aged 23 and 19, both left home to join the Royal Navy. During her children's early years she worked in part-time, temporary, secretarial posts. Sally lived with her husband, the father of her children, and at the time of the research was employed part-time as a departmental secretary in a university.

Sandra (51) White British working-class, with working-class upbringing. When her son left home for university, Sandra left her husband. Her 17-year-old daughter lived with Sandra's ex-husband. Sandra commented: 'although my daughter does not actually live with me, I only moved two doors further down the same street, so I still see her as much as when we lived together'. Sandra did not work until her children were eight and ten years old. At the time the research took place, she worked part-time as a donor-carer for the National Blood Transfusion Service.

Serena (51) White British working-class, with working-class upbringing. She had a daughter aged 23 and two sons, 25 and 21. Her daughter and eldest son had left home and lived locally. Her younger son lived at home. Serena mothered alone for 4.5 years. She was re-partnered, but not co-habiting. She did not work outside the home until her youngest child went to school, she then worked part-time as a sales assistant. During and after her divorce Serena undertook her undergraduate degree full-time and later qualified as a social worker. At the time of the research, she was working full-time as a primary care mental health support worker.

Vanessa (57) White British middle-class, with middle-class upbringing. Her daughters, aged 26 and 24, both left home for university and at the time of the research were living in their own homes in different towns. Vanessa was married to the father of her children and did not work outside the home when her children were young. She undertook a part-time undergraduate degree as a mature student. At the time of the research, Vanessa worked full-time as a conference centre office manager.

Appendix 2
Interview Guide

Can you tell me what being a mother has been like for you, and about the kinds of relationships you've had with your children.

When your children were younger, did you think about them growing up and leaving home?

Did you feel s/he was ready to leave home?

Did you help her/him prepare to go? What was that like?

What was it like when s/he left? OR [if appropriate] Did you take her/him to university? What was that like?

How do you feel about her/him living somewhere else?

Tell me about how you keep in touch with each other.

Do you think where s/he lives makes a difference?

Have you talked to anyone about your daughter/son leaving?

[if appropriate] What kinds of things did you talk about?

How have things changed at home since s/he went to university? What kinds of things are different? What kinds of things are the same?

[if appropriate] How was your daughter/son affected by her/his sister/brother leaving?

[if appropriate] What are their plans?

[if appropriate] Do you think it would be different if you didn't have a daughter/son still living home?

[if appropriate] Was your partner affected by your child's leaving?

Do you think having a partner makes you feel differently about your child/ren growing up and leaving home?

How do you think you've changed since your daughter/son left?

Could you tell me about any plans you've made for the future?

Is there anything else you'd like to say, or anything you'd like to ask me?

Bibliography

Adler, P.A. and P. Adler (2003) 'The Reluctant Respondent', in J.A. Holstein and J.F. Gubrium (eds.), *Inside Interviewing: New Lenses, New Concerns*. Thousand Oaks: Sage.

Allan, G. (1996) *Kinship and Friendship in Modern Britain*. Oxford: Oxford University Press.

Allan, G. and Jones, G. (eds.) (2003) *Social Relations and the Life Course*. Basingstoke: Palgrave Macmillan.

Allatt, P. (1996) 'Children in Families: Research and Policy', in J. Brannen and M. O'Brien (eds.), *Children in Families: Research and Policy*. London: Falmer Press.

Althusser, L. (1971) *Lenin and Philosophy and Other Essays*. London: New Left Books.

Apter, T. (1990) *Altered Loves: Mothers and Daughters during Adolescence*. Hemel Hempstead: Harvester Wheatsheaf.

Arber, S., Davidson, K. and Ginn, J. (2003) 'Changing Approaches to Gender and Later Life', in S. Arber, K. Davidson and J. Ginn (eds.), *Gender and Ageing: Changing Roles and Relationships*. Maidenhead: Open University Press.

Bailey, L. (1999) 'Refracted Selves? A Study of Changes in Self-Identity in the Transition to Motherhood', *Sociology* 33(2): 335–52.

Barry, C.A. (1998) 'Choosing Qualitative Data Analysis Software: Atlas/ti and Nudist Compared', *Sociological Research Online* Vol. 3(3), http://www.socresonline.org.uk/socresonline/3/3/4.html>

Bart, P.B. (1971) 'Depression in Middle-Aged Women', in V. Gornick and B.K. Moran (eds.), *Women in Sexist Society*. New York: The New American Library.

Barthes, R. (1987) *Mythologies*. London: Paladin Grafton Books.

Batty, M. and B. Barr (1994) 'The Electronic Frontier. Exploring and Mapping Cyberspace', *Futures* 26(7): 699–712.

Bauman, Z. (2002) 'Individually, Together', in U. Beck and E. Beck Gernsheim, *Individualization*. London: Sage.

—— (2003) *Liquid Love: On the Frailty of Human Bonds*. Cambridge: Polity Press.

Beck, U. (1992) *Risk Society: Towards a New Modernity*. London: Sage.

—— (2002) 'Zombie Categories: Interview with Ulrich Beck', in U. Beck and E. Beck-Gernsheim *Individualization*. London: Sage.

Beck, U. and E. Beck-Gernsheim (1995) *The Normal Chaos of Love*. Cambridge: Polity Press.

—— (2002) *Individualization*. London: Sage.

Benson, J.E. and Johnson, M.K. (2009) 'Adolescent Family Context and Adult Identity Formation', *Journal of Family Issues*, DOI: 10.1177/0192513X093 32967.

Berger, P.L. and Luckmann, T. (1966) *The Social Construction of Reality*. New York: Doubleday.

Billington, R., Hockey, J. and Strawbridge, S. (1998) *Exploring Self and Society*. London: Macmillan.

Borell, K. and Karlsson, S.G. (2003) 'Reconceptualizing Intimacy and Ageing: Living Apart Together', in S. Arber, K. Davidson and J. Ginn (eds.), *Gender and Ageing: Changing Roles and Relationships*. Maidenhead: Open University Press.

Borland, D.C. (1982) 'A Cohort Analysis Approach to the Empty-nest Syndrome among Three Ethnic Groups of Women: A Theoretical Position', *Journal of Marriage and the Family* 44(1): 117–29.

Boulton, M.G. (1983) *On Being a Mother*. London and New York: Tavistock Publications.

Brannen, J. (1996) 'Discourses of Adolescence: Young People's Independence and Autonomy within Families', in J. Brannen and M. O'Brien (eds.), *Children in Families: Research and Policy*. London: Falmer Press.

Brannen, J., Dodd, K., Oakley, A. and Storey, P. (1994) *Young People, Health and Family Life*. Buckingham, Philadelphia: Open University Press.

Brannen, J. and O'Brien, M. (eds.) (1996) *Children in Families: Research and Policy*. London: Falmer Press.

Brown, S., Lumley, J., Small, R. and Astbury, J. (1994) *Missing Voices. The Experience of Motherhood*. Oxford and New York: Oxford University Press Australia.

Bynner, J., Ellias, P., McKnight, A., Pan, H. and Pierre, G. (2002) *Young People's Changing Routes to Independence*. York: Joseph Rowntree Foundation.

Byrne, B. (2003) 'Reciting the Self. Narrative Representations of the Self in Qualitative Interviews', *Feminist Theory* 4(1): 29–49.

Chapman, T. (1999) '"You've got him Well-Trained": The Negotiation of Roles in the Domestic Sphere' in T. Chapman and J. Hockey (eds.), *Ideal Homes? Social Change and Domestic Life*. London: Routledge.

Christensen, T.H. (2009) '"Connected Presence" in distributed family life', *New Media and Society* 11(3): 433–51.

Coffey, A. (1999) *The Ethnographic Self: Fieldwork and the Representation of Identity*. London: Sage.

Coles, B. (1995) *Youth and Social Policy*. London: University College London.

Craib, I. (1995) 'Some Comments on the Sociology of the Emotions', *Sociology* 29(1): 151–8.

Davidson, K. (2001) 'Late Life Widowhood, Selfishness and New Partnership Choices: A Gendered Perspective', *Ageing and Society* 21: 297–317.

Dey, I. (1993) *Qualitative Data Analysis: A User-friendly Guide for Social Scientists*. London: Routledge.

—— (2004) 'Grounded Theory', in C. Seale, G. Gobo, J. Gubrium and D. Silverman (eds.), *Qualitative Research Practice*. London: Sage.

Draper, J. (2000) *Fathers in the Making: Men, Bodies and Babies*. Unpublished PhD Thesis: University of Hull.

Duncombe, J. and Marsden, D. (1993) 'Love and Intimacy: The Gender Division of Emotion and "Emotion Work". A Neglected Aspect of Sociological Discussion of Heterosexual Relationships', *Sociology* 27(2): 221–41.

—— (1998) '"Stepford Wives" and "Hollow Men"? Doing emotion work, doing gender and "authenticity" in intimate heterosexual relationships', in G. Bendelow and S.J. Williams (eds.), *Emotions in Social Life: Critical Themes and Contemporary Issues*. London: Routledge.

Eco, U. (2005) *The Mysterious Flame of Queen Loana*. London: Secker and Warburg.

Edwards, R. and Ribbens, J. (eds.) (1998) *Feminist Dilemmas in Qualitative Research*. London: Sage.

—— (1998) 'Living on the Edges: Public Knowledge, Private Lives, Personal Experience' in J. Ribbens and R. Edwards (eds.), *Feminist Dilemmas in Qualitative Research*. London: Sage.

Eggebeen, D.J., Dew, J. and Knoester, C. (2009) 'Fatherhood and Men's Lives at Middle-Age', *Journal of Family Issues* 20(10):

Fairhurst, E. (2003) 'New Identities in Ageing: Perspectives on Age, Gender and Life After Work', in S. Arber, K. Davidson and J. Ginn (eds.), *Gender and Ageing: Changing Roles and Relationships*. Maidenhead: Open University Press.

Featherstone, M. and Burrows, R. (eds.) (1995) *Cyberspace, Cyberbodies, Cyberpunk: Cultures of Technological Embodiment*. London: Sage Publications.

Featherstone, M. and Hepworth, M. (1991) 'The Mask of Ageing and the Postmodern Life Course', in M. Featherstone, M. Hepworth and B.S. Turner (eds.), *The Body: Social Process and Cultural Theory*. London: Sage.

Fernback, J. and Thompson, B. (1995) 'Virtual Communities: Abort, Retry, Failure?' www.well.com/user/hlr/texts/VCcivil.html, accessed 23/05/06.

Figes, K. (2002) *The Terrible Teens: What Every Parent Needs to Know.* London: Penguin.

Finch, J. (1983) *A Labour of Love: Women, Work, and Caring*. London: Routledge & Kegan Paul.

—— (1984) '"It's Great to have Someone to Talk to": The Ethics and Politics of Interviewing Women', in C. Bell and H. Roberts (eds.), *Social Researching: Politics, Problems, Practice*. London: Routledge and Kegan Paul.

Finch, J. and Groves, D. (1989) *Family Obligations and Social Change*. Cambridge: Polity Press.

Finch, J. and Mason, J. (1993) *Negotiating Family Responsibilities.* London: Routledge.

Freed, K. (2001) 'Surviving Future Shock', www.media.visions.com/esy-fuure. html, accessed 14/08/06.

Fulton, H. (2005a) 'Introduction: The Power of Narrative', in H. Fulton with R. Huisman, J. Murphet and A. Dunn, *Narrative and the Media.* Cambridge: Cambridge University Press.

—— (2005b) 'Conclusion: Postmodern Narrative and Media' in H. Fulton with R. Huisman, J. Murphet and A. Dunn, *Narrative and the Media.* Cambridge: Cambridge University Press.

Fulton, H. with Huisman, R. Murphet, J. and A. Dunn (2005) *Narrative and the Media.* Cambridge: Cambridge University Press.

Furlong, A. and Cartmel, F. (1997) *Young People and Social Change: Individualization and Risk in Late Modernity.* Buckingham: Open University Press.

Gannon, L. (1999) *Women and Ageing: Transcending the Myths.* London: Routledge.

Gatrell, C. (2005) *Hard Labour: The Sociology of Parenthood.* Maidenhead: Open University Press.

Geertz, C. (1973) *The Interpretation of Cultures.* New York: Basic Books.

Ghuman, P.A.S. (1999) *Asian Adolescents in the West* Leicester: BPS Books.

Gibson, W. (1986) *Neuromancer.* London: Grafton.

Giddens, A. (1992) *The Transformation of Intimacy.* Cambridge: Polity Press.

Gill, T. (1999) 'Play, Child Care and the Road to Adulthood' *Children and Society* 13: 67–9.

Gillies, V. Ribbens, J. and Holland, J. (2001) *Pulling Together, Pulling Apart: The Family Lives of Young People.* London: Family Policy Studies Centre/Joseph Rowntree Foundation.

Gillies, V., Holland, J. and Ribbens McCarthy, J. (2003) 'Past/Present/Future: Time and the Meaning of Change in the "Family"' in A. Graham and G. Jones (eds.), *Social Relations and the Life Course.* Basingstoke: Palgrave Macmillan.

Glaser, B. and Strauss, A. (1967) *The Discovery of Grounded Theory: Strategies for Qualitative Research.* Chicago: Aldine.

Glucksmann, M. (1994) 'The Work of Knowledge and the Knowledge of Women's Work', in M. Maynard and J. Purvis (eds.), *Researching Women's Lives from a Feminist Perspective.* London: Taylor and Francis.

Goffman, I. (1972) *Interaction Ritual: Essays on Face-to-Face Behaviour.* London: Allen Lane/Penguin.

Goldsworthy, J. (1993) (ed.) *A Certain Age: Reflecting on the Menopause.* London: Virago.

Greer, G. (1992) *The Change: Women, Ageing and the Menopause.* London: Penguin.

Gregory, S. (1999) 'Gender Roles and Food in Families', in L. McKie, S. Bowlby and S. Gregory (eds.), *Gender, Power and the Household*. London: Macmillan Press.

Griffin, G. (2005) 'Interviewing', in G. Griffin (ed.) *Research Methods for English Studies*. Edinburgh: Edinburgh University Press.

Haraway, D. (1997) *Modest_Witness@Second_Millennium.FemaleMan©_Meets_ OncoMouse: Feminism and Techno Science*. New York: Routledge.

Harris, C., Charles, N. and Davies, C. 'Social Change and the Family' *Social Research Online* 11(2), http://www.socresonline.org.uk/11/2/harris.html, accessed 14/12/06.

Harrison, K. (1998) 'Rich Friendships, Affluent Friends: Middle-Class Practices of Friendship', in R.G. Adams and G. Allan (eds.), *Placing Friendship in Context*. Cambridge: Cambridge University Press.

Henderson, S., Holland, J., McGrellis, S., Sharpe, S., Thomson, R. with Grigoriou, T. (2007) *Inventing Adulthoods: A Biographical Approach to Youth Transitions*. London: Sage.

Hiedemann, B., Suhomlinova, O. and O'Rand, A.M. (1998) 'Economic Independence, Economic Status, and Empty Nest in Midlife Marital Disruption', *Journal of Marriage and the Family* 60 (February): 219–31.

Hockey, J. and James, A. (1993) *Growing Up and Growing Old: Ageing and Dependency in the Life Course*. London: Sage.

—— (2003) *Social Identities across the Life Course*. Basingstoke: Palgrave Macmillan.

Holdsworth, C. (2004) 'Family Support during the Transition Out of the Parental Home in Britain, Spain and Norway', *Sociology* 38(5): 909–26.

Holdsworth, C. and Morgan, D. (2005) *Transitions in Context: Leaving Home, Independence and Adulthood*. Buckingham: Open University Press.

Holland, J. and Ramazanoğlu, C. (1994) 'Situating the Production of Feminist Ethnography', in M. Maynard and J. Purvis (eds.), *Researching Women's Lives from a Feminist Perspective*. London: Taylor and Francis.

Holloway, S.L. and Valentine, G. (2000) 'Children's Geographics and the New Social Studies of Childhood', in S.L. Holloway and G. Valentine (eds.), *Children's Geographics: Playing, Living, Learning*. London: Routledge.

—— (2003) *Cyberkids: Children in the Information Age*. London: Routledge Falmer.

Hollway, W. and Jefferson, T. (2000) *Doing Qualitative Research Differently*. London: Sage.

Hornstein, F. (1994) 'Children by Donor Insemination: A New Choice for Lesbians', in A.M. Jaggar (ed.) *Living with Contradictions: Controversies in Feminist Social Ethics*. Boulder: Westview Press.

Hughes, C. (2002) *Key Concepts in Feminist Theory and Research*. London: Sage.

Huisman, M. (2005) 'Advertising Narratives', in H. Fulton with R. Huisman, J. Murphet and A. Dunn (eds.), *Narrative and the Media*. Cambridge: Cambridge University Press.

Hunter, M.S. and O'Dea, I. (1997) 'Bodily Changes and Multiple Meanings' in J. Ussher (ed.) *Body Talk: Discursive Regulation of Sexuality, Madness and Reproduction*. London: Routledge.

Irwin, S. (1995a) *Rights of Passage: Social Change and the Transition from Youth to Adulthood*. London: UCL Press.

—— (1995b) 'Social Reproduction and Change in the Transition from Youth to Adulthood', *Sociology* 29(2): 293–315.

Jackson, S. (1993) 'Even Sociologists Fall in Love: An Exploration in the Sociology of Emotions', *Sociology* 27(2): 2001–20.

Jackson, S. and Scott, S. (1997) 'Gut Reactions to Matters of the Heart: Reflections on Rationality, irrationality and sexuality', *The Sociological Review* 45(4): 551–75.

Jaggar, A.M. (1983) *Feminist Politics and Human Nature*. Lanham: Rowman and Littlefield.

—— (1989) 'Love and Knowledge: Emotion in Feminist Epistemology' in A.M. Jaggar and S. Bordo (eds.), *Gender/Body/Knowledge: Feminist Re-Constructions of Being and Knowing*. New Brunswick: Rutgers University Press.

James, A. and Prout, A. (1998) 'Re-Presenting Childhood: Time and Transition in the Study of Childhood' in A. James and A. Prout (eds.), *Constructing and Reconstructing Childhood: Contemporary Issues in the Sociological Study of Childhood*. London: Routledge Falmer.

Jamieson, L. (1998) *Intimacy: Personal Relationships in Modern Societies*. Cambridge: Polity Press.

—— (1999) 'Intimacy Transformed? A Critical Look at the "Pure Relationship"', *Sociology* 33(3): 477–94.

Jenks, C. (1995) 'The Centrality of the Eye in Western Culture: An Introduction', in C. Jenks (ed.) *Visual Culture*. London: Routledge.

—— (1996a) 'The Postmodern Child', in J. Brannen and M. O'Brien, (eds.), *Children in Families, Research and Policy*. London: Falmer Press.

—— (1996b) *Childhood*. London and New York: Routledge.

Jerrome, D. (1996) 'Ties that Bind', in A. Walker (ed.) *The New Generational Contract: Intergenerational Relations, Old Age and Welfare*. London: UCL Press.

Jolly, H. (1986) *Book of Child Care: The Complete Guide for Today's Parents*. London: Sphere.

Jones, G. (1995) *Leaving Home*. Buckingham: Open University Press.

—— (2000) 'Trail-Blazers and Path-Followers' Social Reproduction and Geographical Mobility in Youth', in S. Arber and C. Attias-Donfut (eds.), *The Myth of Generational Conflict*. London: Routledge.

—— (2002) *The Youth Divide: Diverging Paths to Adulthood*. York: Joseph Rowntree Foundation.

—— (2005) *Young Adults and the Extension of Economic Dependence*. Policy discussion paper: National Family and Parenting Institute. (www.nfpi.org/data/research/docs/YouthDept accessed 17/10/06).

Jones, G., O'Sullivan, A. and Rouse, J. (2006) 'Young Adults, Partners and Parents: Individual Agency and the Problems of Support' *Journal of Youth Studies* 9(4): 375–92.

Jones, O. Williams, M. and Fleuriot, C. (2003) '"A New Sense of Place?" Mobile "Wearable" Information and Communications Technology Devices and the Geographies of Urban Childhood', *Children's Geographies* 1(2) 165–80.

Jones, S. (ed.) (1998) *Cybersociety 2.0 Revisiting Computer-Mediated Communication and Community*. London: Sage Publications.

Jones, S. and Kucker, S. (2001) 'Computers, the Internet, and Virtual Cultures', in J. Lull (ed.) *Culture in the Communication Age*. London: Routledge.

Kaplan, E.A. (1992) *Motherhood and Representation: The Mother in Popular Culture and Melodrama*. London: Routledge.

Kenyon, D.Y.B. and Koerner, S.S. (2009) 'Examining Emerging-Adults' and Parents' Expectations about Autonomy During the Transition to College', *Journal of Adolescent Research*, 24(3): 293–320.

Kenyon, L. (1999) 'A Home from Home: Students' Transitional Experience of Home', in T. Chapman and J. Hockey (eds.), *Ideal Homes? Social Change and Domestic Life*. London: Routledge.

—— (2003) 'Young Adults' Household Formation: Individualization, Identity and Home', in G. Allan and G. Jones (eds.), *Social Relations and the Life Course*. Basingstoke: Palgrave Macmillan.

Kitchin, R.M. (1998) 'Towards Geographies of Cyberspace', *Progress in Human Geography* 22 (3): 385–406.

Klein, N. (2000) *No Logo: No Space, No Choice, No Jobs*. London: Flamingo.

Knowles, M., Nieuwenhuis, J. and Smit, B. (2009) 'A narrative analysis of educators' lived experiences of motherhood and teaching', *South African Journal of Education* 29(3): 333–43.

Kolko, B. and Reid, E. (1998) 'Dissolution and Fragmentation: Problems in On-Line Communities', in S. Jones (ed.) *Cybersociety 2.0 Revisiting Computer-Mediated Communication and Community*. London: Sage Publications.

Kramarae, C. (1998) 'Feminist Fictions of Future Technology', in S. Jones (ed.) *Cybersociety 2.0 Revisiting Computer-Mediated Communication and Community*. London: Sage Publications.

Lasch, C. (1977) *Haven in a Heartless World*. New York: Basic Books.

Lawler, S. (1999) 'Children Need but Mothers Only Want: The Power of "Needs Talk" in the Constitution of Childhood' in J. Seymour and P. Bagguley (eds.), *Relating Intimacies: Power and Resistance*. Basingstoke: Macmillan Press.

—— (2000) *Mothering the Self: Mothers, Daughters, Subjects*. London: Routledge.

—— (2002) 'Narrative in Social Research', in T. May (ed.) *Qualitative Research in Action*. London: Routledge.

Layne, L. (2000) '"He Was a Real Baby with Real Baby Things". A Material Cultural Analysis of Personhood, Parenthood and Pregnancy Loss', *Journal of Material Culture* 5(3): 321–45.

Leach, P. (1988) *Baby and Child: From Birth to Age Five*. London: Penguin.

—— (1994) *Children First: What Society Must Do – and is Not Doing – for Children Today*. London: Penguin.

Lee, L. (1969) *As I Walked Out One Midsummer Morning*. Harmondsworth: Penguin.

Letherby, G. (2003) *Feminist Research in Theory and Practice*. Buckingham: Open University.

Levin, I. (2004) 'Living Apart Together: A New Family Form', *Current Sociology* 52 (1): 223–40.

Levinson, P. (2004) *The Story of the World's Most Mobile Medium and How it Has Transformed Everything!* New York: Palgrave Macmillan.

Lull, J. (2001) 'Introduction: Why the Communication Age?' in J. Lull (ed.) *Culture in the Communication Age*. London: Routledge.

Lupton, D. (1995) 'The Embodied Computer/User', in M. Featherstone and R. Burrows (eds.), *Cyberspace, Cyberbodies, Cyberpunk: Cultures of Technological Embodiment*. London: Sage Publications.

—— (1998a) *The Emotional Self*. London: Sage.

—— (1998b) 'Going With the Flow: Some Central Discourses in Conceptualising and Articulating the Embodiment of Emotional States', in S. Nettleton and J. Watson (eds.), *The Body in Everyday Life*. London: Routledge.

Lurie, G.E. (1974) 'Sex and Stage Differences in Perceptions of Marital and Family Relationships' *Journal of Marriage and the Family*, 36: 209–69.

Markham, A. (1998) *Life Online: Researching Real Experience in Virtual Space*. New York and London: Altamira Press.

Marshall, H. (1991) 'The Social Construction of Motherhood: An Analysis of Childcare and Parenting Manuals', in A. Phoenix, A. Woollett and E. Lloyd (eds.), *Motherhood: Meanings, Practices and Ideologies*. London: Sage.

Mason, J. (1996) *Qualitative Researching*. London: Sage.

—— (2002) 'Qualitative Interviewing: Asking, Listening and Interpreting', in T. May (ed.) *Qualitative Research in Action*. London: Routledge.

Mauthner, N. and Doucet, A. (1998) 'Reflections on a Voice-Centred Relational Method: Analysing Maternal and Domestic Voices', in J. Ribbens and R. Edwards (eds.), *Feminist Dilemmas in Qualitative Research*. London: Sage.

—— (2003) 'Reflexive Accounts and Accounts of Reflexivity in Qualitative Data Analysis' *Sociology* 37(3): 413–31.

Mayall, B. (1996) *Children, Health and the Social Order*. Buckingham: Open University Press.

—— (2002) *Towards a Sociology for Childhood: Thinking from Children's Lives*. Buckingham: Open University Press.

Maynard, M. (1994) 'Methods, Practice and Epistemology: The Debate about Feminism and Research', in M. Maynard and J. Purvis (eds.), *Researching Women's Lives from a Feminist Perspective*. London: Taylor and Francis.

Maynard, M. and J. Purvis (1994) 'Doing Feminist Research', in M. Maynard and J. Purvis (eds.), *Researching Women's Lives from a Feminist Perspective*. London: Taylor and Francis.

—— (eds.) (1994) *Researching Women's Lives from a Feminist Perspective*. London: Taylor and Francis.

McNay, L. (2000) *Gender and Agency: Reconfiguring the Subject in Feminist and Social Theory*. Cambridge: Polity Press.

Miller, T. (1998) 'Shifting Layers of Professional, Lay and Personal Narratives: Longitudinal Childbirth Research', in R. Edwards and J. Ribbens (eds.), *Feminist Dilemmas in Qualitative Research*. London: Sage.

—— (2005) *Making Sense of Motherhood: A Narrative Approach*. Cambridge: Cambridge University Press.

Moi, T. (1989) (ed.) *The Kristeva Reader*. Cambridge: Blackwell.

Moores, S. (2000) *Media and Everyday Life in Modern Society*. Edinburgh: Edinburgh University Press.

Morgan, D. (1999) 'Risk and Family Practices: Accounting for Change and Fluidity in Family Life', in E.B. Silva and C. Smart (eds.), *The New Family?* London: Sage.

Morse, J.M. and Field, P.A. (1996) *Nursing Research: The Application of Qualitative Approaches* (2nd edition). London: Chapman Hall.

Niemeyer, R.A. and Anderson, J. (2002) 'Meaning Reconstruction Theory', in N. Thompson (ed.) *Loss and Grief: A Guide for Human Services Practitioners*. Basingstoke: Palgrave.

Noller, P. and Callan, V. (1991) *The Adolescent in the Family*. London: Routledge.

Oakley, A. (1976) *Housewife: High Value, Low Cost*. London: Penguin.

—— (1979) *Becoming a Mother*. Oxford: Martin Robertson.

—— (1980) *Women Confined: Towards Sociology of Childbirth*. Oxford: Martin Robertson.

—— (1981a) *From Here to Maternity: Becoming a Mother*. Harmondsworth: Penguin.

—— (1981b) 'Interviewing Women: A Contradiction in Terms', in H. Roberts (ed.) *Doing Feminist Research*. London: Routledge and Kegan Paul.

—— (2000) *Experiments in Knowing: Gender and Method in the Social Sciences*. Cambridge: Polity Press.

Oakley, A. and Rigby, A.S. (1998) 'Are men good for the welfare of women and children?', in Popay, J., Hearn, J. and J. Edwards (eds.), *Men, Gender Divisions and Welfare*. London: Routledge.

Oliker, S.J. (1998) 'The Modernisation of Friendship: Individualism, Intimacy, and Gender in the Nineteenth Century', in R.G. Adams and G. Allan (eds.), *Placing Friendship in Context*. Cambridge: Cambridge University Press.

Pahl, J. (1989) *Money and Marriage*. Basingstoke: Macmillan Education.

Parr, J. (1998) 'Theoretical Voices and Women's Own Voices: The Stories of Mature Women Students' in J. Ribbens and R. Edwards (eds.), *Feminist Dilemmas in Qualitative Research: Public Knowledge and Private Lives*. London: Sage.

Patiniotis, J. and Holdsworth, C. (2005) '"Seize That Chance!" Leaving Home and Transitions to Higher Education', *Journal of Youth Studies* 8(1): 81–95.

Phillips, J. (2000) 'Women Carers: Caring Workers' in M. Bernard, J. Phillips, L. Machin and V. Harding Davies (eds.), *Women Ageing: Changing Identities, Challenging Myths*. London: Routledge.

Phoenix, A. Woollett A. and Lloyd, E. (eds.) (1991) (*Motherhood: Meanings, Practices and Ideologies*. London: Sage.

Phoenix, A., and Woollett, A. (1991) 'Motherhood: Social Construction, Politics and Psychology', in A. Phoenix, A. Woollett and E. Lloyd, (eds.), *Motherhood: Meanings, Practices and Ideologies*. London: Sage.

Rakow, L.F. (1988) 'Women and the Telephone: The Gendering of a Communications Technology', in C. Kramarae (ed.) *Technology and Women's Voices*. London: Routledge and Kegan Paul.

Ramazanoğlu, C. with Holland, J. (2002) *Feminist Methodology: Challenges and Choices*. London: Sage.

Raup, J.L. and Myers, J.E. (1992) 'The Empty Nest Syndrome: Myth or Reality', *Journal of Counselling and Development*, 68: 180–3.

Reay, D. (2004) 'Gendering Bourdieu's Concepts of Capitals? Emotional Capital, Women and Social Class', *The Sociological Review* 52(2): 57–74.

Reinharz, S. (1992) *Feminist Methods in Social Research*. New York: Oxford University Press.

Reinharz, S. and Chase, S.E. (2003) 'Interviewing Women', in J.A. Holstein and J.F. Gubrium (eds.), *Inside Interviewing: New Lenses, New Concerns*. Thousand Oaks: Sage.

Rheingold, H. (1993) *The Virtual Community: Finding Connection in a Computerized World*, Boston, MA: Addison-Wesley Longman Publishing.

—— (2002) *Smart Mobs: The Next Social Revolution*. Cambridge, MA: Basic Books.

Ribbens, J. (1989) 'Interviewing – An Unnatural Situation?', *Women's Studies International Forum* 12(6) 579–92.

Ribbens, J. (1994) *Mothers and their Children: A Feminist Sociology of Childrearing*. London: Sage.

Ribbens, J. (1998) 'Hearing my Feeling Voice? An Autobiographical Discussion of Motherhood', in J. Ribbens and R. Edwards (eds.), *Feminist Dilemmas in Qualitative Research*. London: Sage.

Ribbens, J. and Edwards, R. (eds.) (1998) *Feminist Dilemmas in Qualitative Research*. London: Sage.

Ribbens McCarthy, J. and Edwards, R. (2001) 'Illuminating Meanings of "the Private" in Sociological Thought: A Response to Joe Bailey', *Sociology* 35(3): 767–77.

——— (2002) 'The Individual in Public and Private: The Significance of Mothers and Children', in A. Carling, S. Duncan and R. Edwards, (eds.), *Analysing Families: Morality and Rationality in Policy and Practice.* London: Routledge.

Ribbens McCarthy, J., Edwards R. and Gillies, V. (2000) 'Moral Tales of the Child and the Adult: Narratives of Contemporary Family Lives under Changing Circumstances', *Sociology* 24(4): 785–803.

Rich, A. (1977) *Of Woman Born: Motherhood as Experience and Institution.* London: Virago.

Richardson, D. (1993) *Women, Motherhood and Childrearing.* London: Macmillan.

Riessman, C.K. (1990) *Divorce Talk: Women and Men Make Sense of Personal Relationships.* New Brunswick, NJ: Rutgers University Press.

Roberts, M. (1984) *The Wild Girl.* London: Methuen.

Robins, K. (1997) 'The New Communications Geography and the Politics of Optimism', *Soundings: A Journal of Politics and Culture*, 5: 191–202.

Rogan, F., Shmied, V., Barclay, L., Everitt, L. and Wyllie, A. (1997) 'Becoming a Mother – Developing a New Theory of Early Motherhood', *Journal of Advanced Nursing* 25: 877–85.

Rose, N. (1991) *Governing the Soul: The Shaping of the Private Self.* London: Routledge.

Roseneil, S. (2006) 'On Not Living with a Partner: Unpicking Coupledom and Cohabitation', *Sociological Research Online* 3) http://www.socresonline.org.uk/11/3/roseneil.html, accessed 01/12/06.

Roseneil, S. and Mann, K. (1996) 'Unpalatable Choices and Inadequate Families: Lone Mothers and the Underclass Debate' in E.B. Silva (ed.) *Good Enough Mothering?* London: Routledge.

Sandelowski, M. (1994) 'The Use of Quotes in Qualitative Research', *Research in Nursing and Health* 17: 479–82.

Sawicki, J. (1991) *Disciplining Foucault: Feminism, Power, and the Body.* London: Routledge.

Silva, E.B. (1996) (ed.) *Good Enough Mothering? Feminist Perspectives on Lone Motherhood.* London: Routledge.

——— (1999) 'Transforming Housewifery: Dispositions, Practices and Technologies', in E.B. Silva and C. Smart (eds.), *The New Family?* London: Sage.

Silva, E.B. and Smart, C. (eds.) (1999) *The New Family?* London: Sage.

Sistare, C.T. (1994) 'Reproductive Freedom and Women's Freedom: Surrogacy and Autonomy', in A.M. Jaggar (ed.) *Living with Contradictions: Controversies in Feminist Social Ethics.* Boulder: Westview Press.

Skeggs, B. (1994) 'Situating the Production of Feminist Ethnography', in M. Maynard and J. Purvis (eds.), *Researching Women's Lives from a Feminist Perspective.* London: Taylor and Francis.

Skucha, J. and Bernard, M. (2000) 'Women's Work: The Transition to Retirement', in M. Bernard, J. Phillips, L. Machin and V. Harding Davies (eds.), *Women Ageing: Changing Identities, Challenging Myths.* London: Routledge.

Smart, C. (1996) 'Deconstructing Motherhood' in E.B. Silva (ed.) *Good Enough Mothering? Feminist Perspectives on Lone Motherhood.* London: Routledge.

Smart, C. and Neale, B. (1999) *Family Fragments?* Cambridge: Polity Press.

Spock, B. (1968) *Dr. Spock's Baby and Child Care.* New York: Pocket Books.

Stanley, L. and Wise, S. (1993) *Breaking Out Again: Feminist Ontology and Epistemology.* London: Routledge.

Stanworth, M. (1987) 'Reproductive Technologies and the Deconstruction of Motherhood' in M. Stanworth (ed.) *Reproductive Technologies: Gender, Motherhood and Medicine.* Cambridge: Polity Press.

Steedman, C. (1985) 'Listen, How the Caged Bird Sings': Amarjit's Song' in C. Steedman, C. Urwin and V. Walkerdine (eds.), *Language, Gender and Childhood.* London: Routledge & Kegan Paul.

Stoppard, M. (1983) *Dr. Miriam Stoppard's Baby Care Book.* London: Dorling Kindersley.

Summerfield, P. (2005) 'Oral History as a Research Method', in G. Griffin (ed.) *Research Methods for English Studies*. Edinburgh: Edinburgh University Press.

Sunderland, J. (2006) '"Parenting" or "Mothering?" The Case of Modern Childcare Magazines', *Discourse and Society* 17 (4): 503–27.

Teman, E. (2009) 'Embodying Surrogate Motherhood: Pregnancy as a Dyadic Body-project', *Body and Society*, DOI: 10.1177/1357034X09337780.

Thompson, N. (2002) (ed.) *Loss and Grief: A Guide for Human Services Practitioners.* Basingstoke: Palgrave.

Thomson, R. and Holland, J. (2004) *Youth Values and Transitions to Adulthood: An Empirical Investigation.* London: South Bank University Press.

Tulloch, J. and Lupton, D. (2003) *Risk and Everyday Life*. London: Sage.

Urwin, C. (1985) 'Constructing Motherhood: The Persuasion of Normal Development', in C. Steedman, C. Urwin and V. Walkerdine (eds.), *Language, Gender and Childhood.* London: Routledge & Kegan Paul.

Valentine, G. (1999) 'Imagined Geographies: Geographical Knowledges of Self and Other in Everyday Life', in D. Massey, J. Allen and P. Sarre (eds.), *Human Geography Today*. Cambridge: Polity Press.

—— (2001) *Social Geographies: Space and Society*. Harlow: Pearson Education Limited.

—— (2003) *Public Space and the Culture of Childhood.* Aldershot: Ashgate Publishing.

Wadsworth, G. and Green, E. (2003) 'Changing Women: An Analysis of Difference and Diversity in Women's Accounts of their Experiences of Menopause', in S. Earle and G. Letherby (eds.), *Gender, Identity and Reproduction*. Basingstoke: Palgrave Macmillan.

Walkerdine, V. and Lucey, H. (1989) *Democracy in the Kitchen: Regulating Mothers and Socialising Daughters.* London: Virago.

Walkerdine, V., Lucey, H. and Melody, J. (2001) *Growing up Girl: Psychosocial Explorations of Gender and Class*. Basingstoke: Palgrave.

Wallbank, J.A. (2001) *Challenging Motherhood(s)*. London: Prentice Hall.

Warner, M. (1976) *Alone of All Her Sex: They Myth and the Cult of the Virgin Mary*. London: Weidenfeld and Nicolson.

—— (1994) *Managing Monsters: Six Myths of our Time. The 1994 Reith Lectures*. London: Vintage.

Williams, S.J. (1998) 'Emotions, Cyberspace and the "Virtual" Body', in G. Bendelow and S.J. Williams (eds.), *Emotions in Social Life: Critical Themes and Contemporary Issues*. London: Routledge.

Wood, A.F. and Smith, M.J. (2001) *Online Communication: Linking Technology, Identity, and Culture*. Mahwah, NJ: Lawrence Erlbaum Associates.

Woodward, K. (1997) 'Motherhood: Identities, Meanings and Myths', in K. Woodward (ed.) *Identity and Difference* London: Sage.

—— (2002) 'Up Close and Personal: The Changing Face of Intimacy', in T. Jordan and S. Pile (eds.), *Social Change*. Oxford: Open University Press.

—— (2003) 'Representations of Motherhood' in S. Earle and G. Letherby (eds.), *Gender, Identity and Reproduction*. Basingstoke: Palgrave Macmillan.

Woollett, A. and Phoenix, A. (1991) 'Psychological Views of Mothering' in A. Phoenix, A. Woollett and E. Lloyd (eds.), *Motherhood: Meanings, Practices and Ideologies*. London: Sage.

Wyness, M. (2006) *Childhood and Society: An Introduction to the Sociology of Childhood*. Basingstoke: Palgrave Macmillan.

Index